The Action of English Comedy

The Action of English Comedy

*Studies in the Encounter of Abstraction and
Experience from Shakespeare to Shaw*

A. N. Kaul

New Haven and London, Yale University Press, 1970

71–12546

Library of Congress catalog card number: 79-104617
Standard book number: 300-01278-0
Designed by Marvin Howard Simmons,
set in IBM Press Roman type,
and printed in the United States of America by
The Carl Purington Rollins Printing-Office of the
Yale University Press, New Haven, Connecticut.
Distributed in Great Britain, Europe, Asia, and
Africa by Yale University Press Ltd., London; in
Canada by McGill-Queen's University Press, Montreal; and
in Mexico by Centro Interamericano de Libros
Académicos, Mexico City.

For Mythili

Contents

Acknowledgements

Yale University, through its generous award of a Morse Fellowship, enabled me to begin the writing of this book. I am also indebted to the following friends and colleagues at Yale: to Charles Feidelson, Martin Price, and Eugene Waith for reading portions of the manuscript and giving me the benefit of their advice; to Richard Sylvester for reading the whole manuscript in its final form and making several concrete and useful suggestions; to Wayland Schmitt of the Yale Press for his interest and confidence in the work and for suggesting its present title; and to Merle Spiegel for her thorough copyediting of the manuscript.

Abstraction and Experience

Worn-out engines become brakes. Outworn truths
become illusions.

Christopher Caudwell, *Studies in a
Dying Culture*

That books, which promise much of life to give,
Should show so little how we truly live.

George Crabbe, "Ellen Orford," *The Borough*

"Ah, they're part of the comedy. You others are spectators."
"Do you call it a comedy, Isabel Archer?" Henrietta rather
grimly asked.
"The tragedy then if you like."

Henry James, *The Portrait of a Lady*

Chapter 1

Introduction

This book has a twofold purpose. On the one hand, each of the chapters concentrates on an individual author or a small and selected group of works—or even a single text, as in the chapter on *The Portrait of a Lady*. The works discussed are sometimes plays and sometimes novels and come from various and widely separated periods of English literature. Under any rigorous standards, indeed, the book can only be looked upon as an eclectic collection of essays on a handful of works all more or less within the broad purview of comedy; and certainly I can claim for it neither the completeness of a full historical survey of the subject nor the all-comprehending validity of a theoretical "genre study." I am only too conscious of all that I have left out, both by way of what could have been accommodated within my general argument but was not and by way of what simply could not be fitted into that argument without subjecting it to severe dislocation and even disproof. To cite but one prime example, a book which has virtually nothing to say of Ben Jonson cannot be said to put itself forward as either a "history" or a "theory" of English comedy.

On the other hand, I have already indicated that the book does have an overall argument that runs through and is developed by all the individual studies. What is more, while it is not a "history" in the sense that it surveys every comic work in English literature, with respect to the works it does discuss its argument is essentially and at all points historical. Likewise, while not a "theory" that covers all English comedy, much less all comedy anywhere and at any time, it does disengage from the cases discussed a general idea of comedy—an idea that is not only common to all of them but also valid, in varying degrees, for other comparable cases not given specific or detailed consideration here in order to avoid both partial discussions and excessive repetition. The idea, it is as well to state at the outset, has to do by and large with the nature of the comic action: its characteristic conflict and resolution and the values it enforces. The action of comedy is not much discussed; indeed, criticism has mostly denied, implicitly or explicitly, that comic plays or novels can possess anything that can be called an action. I myself argue to the contrary throughout, maintaining not only that comedies, like any other works of narrative or dramatic literature, reveal recognizable actions, but also that the distinguishing attribute of comedy is to be found precisely in the distinctive nature of its action. And it is the *action* of comedy that is meant to be characterized by my subtitle as a conflict between abstraction and experience. Of course, a great deal needs to (and will) be said later in this chapter before such a rough and ready phrase can become either clear or meaningful. But it may be observed here that "abstraction" refers mainly to certain cultural ideas and ideals that survive their own time and thus provide practical living with a peculiar problem and comedy with its subject in a new age. I use the word *cultural* rather than *social* to indicate that comedy is concerned not with the structure of society so much as with what is called the social superstructure.

More specifically I am concerned with the comedies of the modern period—the period that begins with the Renaissance, when the experiences and values of the modern bourgeois society begin to emerge and take shape directly against the background of medieval culture. The process can be seen clearly in Shakespeare, and in beginning with his comedy I focus on certain historical plays, the "comic" second tetralogy, as well as the comedies written more or less at the same time. The relation between the two, which I attempt to analyze, reveals the relation between history and comedy. Chapter 3—if I may use this opportunity to provide a brief rationale of the contents—surveys some of the lines of communication, and also the discontinuities, between Shakespearean and Restoration comedy, before settling down to a full-length discussion of a few selected Restoration plays. This is followed by a short note on Sheridan (Chapter 4) which enables me to sum up for the time being one aspect, the stage comedy aspect, of the story. In Chapter 5 I go back to Fielding and focus on the comic novel. The next chapter is a still more comprehensive examination of Jane Austen. This is in a sense the climax of my study, the high-water mark of the kind of comedy that is its subject. Beyond Jane Austen, the authors who attempt this comedy face enormous, almost insoluble problems. The two writers—one a novelist (James) and the other a playwright (Shaw)—whom I discuss in the two final chapters reveal the difficulties of continuing such comedy beyond a certain point in the history of the culture which produced it.

Both James and Shaw are, however, already twentieth-century writers; and although in my discussion they figure jointly as the terminus of one line, they can also be seen as among the originators of another, different one. Indeed, a new kind of comedy may even be said to begin precisely at this juncture in literary history—a kind of comedy that has developed down to our own day and to which we give many names, including tragicomedy. One may even argue that this contemporary genre is not entirely without roots in the past and connections with the kind of comedy studied in this book. But I pursue none of these matters at any length for a specific reason—namely, the need in the criticism of comedy today to delimit specific areas with care and not reach out in all possible directions in order to arrive at single and sweeping definitions.

To the extent, then, that this book is not an eclectic collection of essays, it may be regarded as concerned mainly with presenting a general idea, and the individual studies may be seen as providing a set of successive demonstrations or examples selected not at random but with a view to revealing the historical origin, the main developments, and the decline of one recurring kind of comedy. In a word, a much abused word, my overall purpose may be described as the definition of a tradition—understood in the ordinary sense of continuous usage, of literary conceptions and principles shared as well as modified over a long span of time.

Of course, the two purposes, no matter how distinctly stated, are in practice inseparable—or at least not valuable one without the other—and normally there would be little need to offer any further preliminary explanation before proceeding to the individual studies that make up the bulk of this book. For what better way to define a tradition than by focusing on the works which embody and constitute it? But in the criticism of comedy, it is not unfair to say, such a procedure has never been sufficiently evident to become a readily acceptable norm. This method is so far from being widely recognized, in fact, that what the existing situation offers is a choice between two sharply separated approaches, two bodies of criticism apparently so alien that neither seems to have anything of importance to say to the other. Of the two, the more insistent and eye-catching approach has been that of the general discourse. Put somewhat out of countenance in other areas lately, the practitioners of this approach have tended to concentrate increasingly on comedy, so that today there are to be found more, and more fashionable, general discourses on comedy than on the lyric, the ballad, the epic, and perhaps even tragedy. Still more to the point here, these discourses on comedy are becoming more rather than less general, the scope of some of the latest and best among them assuming proportions little short of universal. The consequence is inevitably that the

individual author and the individual text come into the picture
only through an occasional passing reference or quick illustration.

Whatever else might be said of the general discourse, especially as it moves in the still more ambitious direction of the
general theory, it has not proved of any noticeable help to the
person interested in any one particular comic writer or comic
work. For witness the second of the two bodies of criticism
referred to above, the studies of individual authors, most of
which have either ignored general theories, perhaps wisely under the circumstances, or *not* ignored them but then only at
the cost of queering their own pitch. For myself I must say
that I have learned more from some of these studies of individual comic writers (such as Mary Lascelles's book on Jane Austen) about comedy in general than I have learned from general
theories of comedy about any particular comic writers.

The point, however, is that a man who recognizes, as I do,
the primary importance of detailed individual studies, but who
insists at the same time on the usefulness of viewing the individual writer as part of a group or a tradition—a man who
aims, in short, at the middle ground of a general study—is
constrained, the critical situation in comedy being what it is,
to show cause. That is, he needs to include certain preliminary
statements, explanations, and justifications of motive and
method which would otherwise be considered unnecessary. His
claims being what they are, he not only needs to delimit with
great care the boundary of the grounds on which he himself
has chosen to stand, but he must also attempt to argue in some
greater detail against the case of those who would choose a
broader or narrower ground than his own. All of which is a
roundabout way of indicating in what manner I should like to
clear the decks, as it were, in this introductory chapter. The
clearing of the decks will no doubt involve doing at certain
points some of the very things that I think should not be done.
I shall, for instance, be stepping for just this once outside the

literature, and indeed the historical period, with which I am
strictly concerned; but the step will be a brief one taken only
to arrive more speedily at my proper point of departure.

One can hardly do better than start on this preliminary discussion by citing L. C. Knights's "Notes on Comedy," a brief
and incisive essay first published as long ago as 1933.[1] I, at
least, can do no better because I simply endorse much of what
Knights has to say against the type of criticism that I have
called the general discourse or general theory: "It is almost
impossible to read a particular comedy without the interference of critical presuppositions derived from one or other of
those who have sought to define comedy in the abstract."
With this I agree, as I do with the further observation that
"Profitless generalizations are more frequent in criticism of
comedy than in criticism of other forms of literature." Regarding the most common and long-lived of these generalizations,
Knights quotes a "neglected passage of *Timber* [which] reads:
'Nor is the moving of laughter always the end of Comedy. . . .
This is truly leaping from the Stage to the Tumbrell again,
reducing all wit to the original Dungcart' "—which can hardly
be improved unless one chooses to emphasize for clarity the
words "always" and "the end." Knights's chief target, a natural one considering when he wrote, is Meredith's essay[2] which

1. First published in *Scrutiny* and collected in *Determinations,* ed.
F. R. Leavis (London, Chatto and Windus, 1934); reprinted in *The
Importance of Scrutiny,* ed. Eric Bentley (New York, New York University Press, 1964); also available in two recent anthologies of criticism
on comedy: *Theories of Comedy,* ed. Paul Lauter (New York, Anchor
Books, 1964); and *Comedy: Meaning and Form,* ed. Robert W. Corrigan (San Francisco, Chandler Publishing Company, 1965). Since the
essay can be consulted in any one of these places and since, moreover,
it is a short piece, no page references will be given for the quotations
from it which follow.
2. George Meredith, *An Essay on Comedy and the Uses of the
Comic Spirit* (New York, Charles Scribner's Sons, 1913). The essay was

he calls "a misfortune for criticism" and "a warning that essays on comedy are necessarily barren exercises." The warning, quite obviously, is still far from having been driven home, and one needs to cite a few more recent critics to update Knights's case against the generalizers. But beyond this, I propose to add one reason—and that to me the most decisive—why the time-honored "laughter theory," as it is called, needs to be finally and firmly set aside.

First, however, let us turn in the opposite direction and note what can be seen as a possible corollary of Knights's argument —namely, that each comic work must be seen strictly in its own right, and that to put so many comic works or authors together and then attempt to define their common characteristics is per se to indulge in a "barren exercise." It is not clear whether Knights would go so far, but such a critical position is not uncommon and has been taken, indeed, where the provocation for it has been not nearly as great—in tragedy, for example, and even in the relatively limited field of Shakespearean tragedy. And whether or not Knights would maintain the position in theory, his essay, with its two-part format, illustrates in practice some of the consequences that follow if we insist beyond a certain point on the phoenix-like uniqueness of a literary work. For Knights does not only argue against the various existing theories of comedy; having set them aside in the first part of the essay, he proceeds, in the second, to demonstrate how a particular comic work—Shakespeare's *Henry IV*—should properly be read and analyzed. His discussion of the play as a satire on "war and policy" is, in itself quite admirable; the more so for being free of the incubus of those presuppositions which he has already exorcized. Nevertheless, there is no sense here of the comic quality of the play, and one wonders why the discussion should figure as the sec-

delivered as a lecture in 1877 and first published in *The New Quarterly Magazine* the same year.

ond and "constructive" part of an essay entitled "Notes on Comedy." Is comedy then the same thing as social satire? If not, are the two in some way related? Furthermore, is there a connection between these two and a third and more obvious aspect of the play: its historical theme? And, above all, is it entirely futile to inquire into the relationship between, not just *Henry IV,* but the whole tetralogy of which it is a part, and the great comedies which were written at the same time and in discussing which it would not do to substitute the idea of satire for that of comedy?

These questions, some of which I attempt to answer in the following chapter, are not necessarily barren; they can be highly relevant to any discussion of English comedy in general and even to the reading of *Henry IV* in particular. However, before one jumps to the opposite conclusion, it is useful to note what happens when a critic concerned with an individual work or author does *not* reject the existing theorists of comedy but either accepts them lazily and inertly or feels compelled to square his own much sharper insights with one or the other of their hazy generalizations. Only two examples must suffice, both provided by critics of Jane Austen, and two of the best at that. I have already mentioned Mary Lascelles, and will have occasion to refer to her again. Her book *Jane Austen and Her Art,* especially the chapter on "Reading and Response," is the foundation of all modern criticism of Jane Austen; in addition, it contains hints which, if developed, would result in a theory of comedy more satisfactory than any now existing. However, while all subsequent critics of Jane Austen have drawn heavily on Miss Lascelles, no general theorists, as far as I can discover, are even remotely aware of her. But she herself—and this is the point I would make here—is not only aware of the theorists but far too accommodating toward their supposed authority. For though she realizes that "the notion of cloud-cuckoo-land . . . will not account for Jane Austen's comedy," she still believes that "it must surely be possible to discover, among definitions of comedy already current, one liberal enough to contain within its bounds the particular comic tradition to which . . . hers belongs."[3] Consequently Miss Lascelles is led to discuss such matters as Jane Austen's comic effects, good humor, and comic characters in the usual "barren" way. Her treatment of comic characters, in particular, is based on the common but silly assumption that every character in a comedy has to be "comic" in exactly the same way as every other character, and a character who fails in this must be considered either an excrescence or a special case that calls for special accounting; much as if we required every character in a tragedy—let us say Duncan and Macduff, not to mention the porter to be "tragic," and for exactly the same reasons as the tragic hero. However, when faced with such deterioration in Miss Lascelles's discussion, it is not enough to say that she should have left generalization and theory alone. Clearly for its own completeness her argument *needs* a valid and useful idea of comedy; and if her book is not finally the definitive study that it could have become, the fault lies in the fact that she is neither able to find any such serviceable idea within reach nor prepared to devise one in keeping with her own insights into the art of Jane Austen.

The second example is that of Marvin Mudrick, who, while much indebted to Miss Lascelles, fortunately does not follow her in any serious attempt to square Jane Austen with existing theories of comedy. Nevertheless, when the question of comedy comes up, as it must if one is writing of Jane Austen, he allows himself occasionally to slip into generalizations which may lose him nothing but which do not gain him much either. Thus at one point comedy becomes "the vision of a world where incongruities have no consequences except in provoking the spectator's laughter." More seriously perhaps, the argu-

3. Mary Lascelles, *Jane Austen and Her Art* (London, Oxford University Press, 1939), p. 139. See also pp. 139-46 and passim beyond p. 146.

ment of a whole chapter gets involved in the effort to show that while there are "comic scenes and comic characters in *Persuasion,*" the novel is not "comic" but "serious."[4] To this one can only reply that there is no contradiction nor any impure commingling of lightness and gravity involved—that, as Knights puts it, "Comedy is essentially a serious activity."

In summary, then, brief as the discussion so far has been, it at least indicates that while wholesale theories of comedy have proved a hindrance rather than a help, we still need a valid idea of comedy, if only for the purpose of reading a particular work as well as we can. For just as it goes without saying that what counts ultimately is the understanding we bring to individual literary texts, it also goes without saying that none can be fully grasped without a context—and contexts are made up of literary forms as much as of epochs or styles. Every work of literature straddles, as it were, several more or less continuous lines—developments of language, theme, form—and the more continuities we are able to see around it, the richer our understanding of the work. The question, then, is not whether an attempt should be made to define any of these continuities; it is, rather, which method should be followed and what delimitations are necessary if the resulting definitions are to be both true and meaningful. To revert to one of my examples above, the method to be followed is surely not the method of defining the tradition to which Jane Austen belongs by striving to fit it into one or the other of those "liberal" theories which are supposed to account for comedy universally. If it is a tradition worth talking about, Jane Austen being Jane Austen, it should arrange itself around her without too much ingenuity on our part and certainly without our having to misread her or to reduce her value in the process. Indeed, it is her works that should tell us what comedy is supposed to be and not the

4. Marvin Mudrick, *Jane Austen: Irony as Defense and Discovery* (Princeton, Princeton University Press, 1952), pp. 3, 228-39. See also passim.

other way around. Definitions of comedy, like definitions of any other literary form, become suspect only when they are treated as universal questions to be answered a priori, whereas a form, like a style or a literary epoch, is primarily a matter of certain demonstrable features common to a line or a group of individual works.

With this we can return to Knights's attack on "those who have sought to define comedy in the abstract." The attack, on the whole, is not directed against defining but rather defining in the abstract, and especially against those universal definitions which become "labour-saving devices" in "the work of detailed and particular analysis." In this respect, Meredith, Knights's chief target, cannot today be considered the worst of offenders. True, he is the first propagator of the notion of "the comic spirit" as a sort of ghost in the machine of comedy with fifth-column collaborators planted in advance among our faculties to facilitate its operations, and he thus bears the responsibility for having introduced into the criticism of comedy a monstrous abstraction which has since proved highly influential. Meredith's essay has many other faults besides, and these too have reappeared and multiplied in later criticism. Yet even in this matter of historical responsibility, one should note in all fairness that if Meredith's fallacies have proved fertile, so have his shrewd remarks on particular authors—especially what he has to say on Congreve, which is perhaps the best that has ever been said on that dramatist. As a matter of fact, the essay contains a good deal of specific and concrete discussion that is simply obscured by its insistence on the promulgation of the comic spirit. But what should be noted above all is that Meredith is by no means a universalist, that if he generalizes, he at least appreciates the necessity for some delimitation of the field that the generalization is supposed to cover. For all his trumpeting of the laughable in comedy, he knows that to insist on "idle empty laughter" is to show oneself incapable of grasping what he called "significant Comedy"—an intellectual comedy requiring an audience "wherein ideas are current and the perceptions quick." This is not altogether an unsound idea; but if we reject it along with the subsequent qualification of Shakespearean comedy as "a special study in the poetically comic"[5] (whatever that means), surely it is because we regard these as erroneous or misleading definitions and not because the process of defining by discrimination and restriction is in itself wrong.

Yet it is precisely in this respect that Meredith's followers and modern heirs have steadfastly refused to follow him. They seem to have taken their cue rather from John Palmer, an early Meredithian, who declares with metaphorical pithiness: "In the kingdom of comedy there are no papers of naturalization."[6] Other critics may discuss classical or Elizabethan or Shakespearean tragedy, primary and secondary epics, or the traditions of the English or the French novel, so that even larger generalizations in these fields, if they are to be made, can be made with the full benefit and awareness of the more elementary distinctions. But in the criticism of comedy the tendency in recent years has been in the opposite direction, with the critic of a particular comic author or tradition looking to the general theorist for guidance, and the theorists themselves obscuring all distinctions and becoming more and more general. Already the kingdom of comedy, to use Palmer's metaphor, is no longer confined even to the free and wide domains of literature; it bids fair to become an empire, one and indivisible it would seem, over all the arts and all the media of communication. Thus a recent anthologist of essays on comedy accommodates in an eleven-page introduction the following range of comic examples: that ancient standby, the absentminded professor; a newspaper story about a frustrated

5. Meredith, *Essay on Comedy,* pp. 9-10, 2, 17.
6. John Palmer, *Comedy* (New York, George H. Doran, n.d.), p. 6. The book was first published in 1915.

suicide whose cork leg saved him from drowning; *Li'l Abner;* popular Broadway hits; Chaplin's *City Lights;* along with a whole string of plays from *Lysistrata* through *The Merchant of Venice, Volpone,* and *The Cherry Orchard* to the works of Ionesco, Beckett, Pinter, and Albee.[7] Of course, this is merely the faithful editor's attempt to reflect and emulate the current fashion in his subject, as can be seen from one of the latest and most famous of the essays included in the anthology: Wylie Sypher's "The Meanings of Comedy." In this essay, which is about the size of Meredith's, Sypher displays comparable insights on an even more abundant scale. But his breadth of reference and range of interests, besides making Meredith seem little more than a provincial plodder, virtually rule out the possibility of any concrete analyses and discussions even of such limited scope as we find in Meredith's essay. Over and above the usual ancient, modern, and contemporary playwrights and the usual references to theorists like Bergson, Freud, and Meredith himself, Sypher introduces a numerous and truly motley crowd of eminent writers and artists: Benvenuto Cellini, Rabelais, Erasmus, and Swift; Cervantes, Henry James, Gide, and "Thomas Mann in his *Magic Mountain*"; Machiavelli, Kierkegaard, Nietzsche, Dostoevsky, and Kafka; Goya, Paul Klee, Rouault, and Picasso; besides uncounted others—all in one breath, as being somehow pertinent to the definition and elucidation of comedy.

I have cited these examples to make the obvious point that the longer and more ill-assorted our list of writers, the more difficult it is to find a common denominator of any substance among them; and the more universal our idea of comedy, the more likely that its definition will prove either false, or true but trite. In fact, most modern theory has not made any original contribution in this sense at all, but has been something in the nature of embroidery—new needlework of words and in-

7. Corrigan, *Comedy,* pp. 1-11.

stances around a very few set patterns of thought. For instance, Northrop Frye, whose own theory I would not include
in this category, nevertheless declares that one small ancient
work, the *Coislinian Tractate*, "sets down all the essential facts
about comedy in about a page and a half."[8] To rely on even
an unsatisfactory *critical* treatise, however, seems almost a
stroke of genius as compared with the practice of those other
modern theorists who have relied rather on the authority of
Kant, Freud, or Bergson, and thus anchored their theories in
the one idea of laughter. Whether this idea enables us to ask
any meaningful questions about comedy is a consideration
that simply disappears in the fact that laughter is, as no one
tires of reminding us, universal to all mankind. As such its
investigation belongs properly to the philosopher and the
psychologist, and all that a critic can validly do is to collect
more and more examples from more and more accessible
fields. The result has been that even Meredith's "significant"
comedy has yielded to mere comedy, and his "thoughtful"
laughter has become mere laughter. As William K. Wimsatt
observed, surveying the field a few years ago: "Here, at this
terminus of sheerly affective theory about laughter, we are a
long way from being able to frame any critical discourse about
works of comic literary art."[9]

Yet something still further needs to be said about this
theory. It is to begin with a fallacious theory inasmuch as its
self-evident truth is in reality based on the dubious converse of
a proposition which in itself is open to question. For even
granting that *all* comedy makes one laugh, which is by no
means certain, it still does not follow that all that makes one
laugh is comedy. The point is worth making since it is on the
strength of the converse rather than the original proposition

8. Northrop Frye, *Anatomy of Criticism* (Princeton, Princeton University Press, 1957), p. 166.
9. William K. Wimsatt, Jr., ed., *English Stage Comedy*, English Institute Essays (New York, Columbia University Press, 1955), p. 8.

that theorists have promulgated the most irrelevant extensions of "the kingdom of comedy." The laughter theory seems in fact fitted with a built-in tendency toward not only irrelevance but also vulgarity, and a vulgarity not of the common and coarse kind at all, but something peculiarly precious and pedantic—a sort of "philosophical" vulgarity. Critics who do not emphasize the role of laughter are often accused of making heavy weather of what is after all only comedy. In truth the charge should be made against those who no doubt see comedy as only a laughing matter, and yet are never prepared to let the matter go at that, but train their heaviest artillery on the subject of laughter itself. Kant, in paragraph 54 of Book II of *Critique of Judgment*—the ultimate source of the philosophy of laughter—may be ponderous; the literary critics who have followed him are only pompous, with a sense of being at one and the same time both low and lofty, philosophical and popular. L. C. Knights excoriates the "idle pose" of Meredith's essay, the pose of "an inaugural lecture in a school of *belles-lettres.*" What, then, is to be said of Meredith's successors? Consider the opening and closing sentences of Palmer's book on comedy: "The curse of Babel only fell among men when they learned to laugh. . . . Let us insist that reason has no seat in this distracted island; that an Englishman is either a genius or a fool; that, even when an Englishman is a fool, he usually fits the celebrated definition of a good Tory: He is one of those d-d fools who are usually right in the end."[10] Or the words of Wylie Sypher: "Or comedy can be a mechanism of language, the repartee that sharply levels drama and life to a sheen of verbal wit." Or Christopher Fry (himself a comic writer like Meredith): "In tragedy every moment is eternity; in comedy eternity is a moment. . . . Laughter may seem to be only like an exhalation of air, but out of that air we came; in

10. Palmer, *Comedy,* pp. 5, 64.

the beginning we inhaled it; it is a truth, not a fantasy, a truth voluble of good which comedy stoutly maintains."[11] It is a perverse irony that comedy, which is so consistently the enemy of pompousness and pedantry, should have received more abundantly than any other form of literature the attentions of such criticism.

The sins of undue generalization and philosophical vulgarity must, however, be accounted venial when set beside what remains for any critical purpose the cardinal objection to the laughter theory—namely, that this theory does not merely disregard but practically invalidates the whole idea of comic *action*. In tragedy, when we speak of tragic moments, it is with a full though often only implicit awareness of continuity. We know that the heightened moment, no matter how intense and concentrated in itself, depends for its effect on the action that has gone before, even as it prepares us for the action that is to come. Thus every moment is implicated in every other moment, and none would be what it is except through its place in the whole. This at least is true in the best examples. Indeed, there is nothing tragic even about the death of tragic heroes except the drama that leads up to it. And as most tragic moments do not end in death or any immediate catastrophe, they cannot on their own strength be called tragic even in the ordinary journalistic sense. Some in fact have a happy outcome, like the moment that culminates in Gloucester's plunge from the cliff at Dover. Detached from the rest of the action, if we can ever think of it as so detached, this incident would be purely farcical, as indeed certain recent critics have shown it to be by simply superimposing on it another context—the context of modern tragicomedy. Thus no single moment or incident in *King Lear*—neither Lear's and Cordelia's death nor Lear's ranting passion on the heath, and least of all such incidents as the arraignment of the daughters or Gloucestor's

11. Corrigan, *Comedy*, pp. 29, 15, 17.

plunge—can be called tragic except within the development of the action of which it is a part. But laughter, as we are told by authorities from Kant to Freud, depends on no such sustained action or preparation. Elaboration of any kind is, in fact, notoriously its enemy; by its very nature it is incidental, spontaneous, and momentary. The result is that all criticism of comedy on the basis of the laughter theory becomes a matter of pointing up fragments such as laughter-raising moments, single incidents, or idiosyncratic characters—anything that reveals its meaning and impact, its "comedy," instantaneously. Hence, not merely the unembarrassed equation of literary comedy with jokes but, more important, the easy relegation of the plot or action of comedy to the superficialities of literature.

Not many critics have examined closely the possibility that comedy, too, might involve an action that is continuous, developed, and complete. Fewer still have conceded that, at least in the best examples, such an action might be important in itself rather than as a makeshift vehicle for comic effects. Even L. J. Potts, who does not hold with the laughter theory and whose book is distinguished in many other ways as well, recommends that in dealing with comedies the word *plot* as it is commonly understood should be put "out of commission" since "the only kind of plot we are accustomed to recognize is a pattern in time." There is, however, Potts goes on to argue, "no justification for this narrow view. There are at least two kinds of plot: the tragic plot, in *time,* and the comic plot, in *space.*" "The pattern we want in comedy is . . . a grouping of characters rather than a march of events."[12] It is not necessary to distinguish spatial from temporal patterns in order to salvage and justify some use of the word *plot* for comedy, and to assign only spatial patterns to comedy is itself as narrow a

12. L. J. Potts, *Comedy* (London, Hutchinson's University Library, n.d.), pp. 128, 140, 130. (The book was published ca. 1949.)

view as that which it seeks to rectify. For, as I shall attempt to
show, insofar as Potts's distinction is a valid one, it has nothing
to do with the question of tragedy and comedy but can be
applied to works within each form, not to mention works
which clearly belong to neither category. However, whether or
not one agrees with Potts, at least his statement is not unan-
swerably philosophical. It is rather calculated to promote, not
hinder or sidetrack, the business of framing a "critical discourse about works of comic literary art." Of course, in this
effort Potts by no means stands alone. Aside from the critics
who have written on individual comic artists, others, besides
Potts, have defined comedy in a general way and still proved
useful. I will refer to them more fully when, with their help, I
develop my own definition of comic action.

We can start with Northrop Frye's two essays, or rather two
versions of the same essay.[13] Frye is, of course, a general
theorist, indeed an Einstein of literary and critical theory.
Nevertheless, he is primarily concerned with literary comedy,
and with only one kind of comedy at that. For although he
claims, with the characteristic sweep of a theorist, that "New
Comedy is . . . contained, so to speak, within the symbolic
structure of Old Comedy, which in its turn is contained within
the Christian conception of *commedia,"*[14] his subject is mainly the tradition of classical New Comedy as transmitted from
Menander through Plautus and Terence to the Renaissance,
and from there down to our own day. Today, as Frye observes, "when we speak of comedy, we normally think of

13. "The Argument of Comedy," *English Institute Essays: 1948,* ed.
D. A. Robertson, Jr. (New York, Columbia University Press, 1949), pp.
58-73; and "The Mythos of Spring: Comedy," *Anatomy of Criticism,*
pp. 163-86. In references that follow, the two essays are cited as "Argument" and "Mythos."
14. "Argument," p. 66.

something that derives from the Menandrine tradition."[15] No doubt in these terms, especially with everything that we normally think of as comedy today thrown in, New Comedy assumes the proportions of a vast and somewhat amorphous body of writing. Nevertheless, set beside some of the imperial claims we have seen staked out in the name of comedy, it remains a compact province with boundaries well defined. The more so, since—and herein lies the most helpful aspect of his account—Frye, guided by the *Tractatus Coislinianus* rather than by Kant, defines this comedy in terms of its plot or, in his own phrase, its "argument." Here is the later of the two versions:

> What normally happens is that a young man wants a young woman, that his desire is resisted by some opposition, usually paternal, and that near the end of the play some twist in the plot enables the hero to have his will. . . . At the beginning of the play the obstructing characters are in charge of the play's society, and the audience recognizes that they are usurpers. At the end of the play the device in the plot that brings hero and heroine together causes a new society to crystallize around the hero.[16]

In the earlier version the emphasis falls more on the implications of paternal opposition than on the crystallization of a new society:

> New Comedy unfolds from what may be described as a comic Oedipus situation. Its main theme is the successful effort of a young man to outwit an opponent and possess the girl of his choice. The opponent is usually the father . . . [who] frequently wants the same girl. . . . The girl is usually a slave or courtesan, and the plot turns on a

15. Ibid., p. 58.
16. "Mythos," p. 163.

cognito or discovery of birth which makes her marriage-able.[17]

The "comic Oedipus situation" and the "movement from one kind of society to another" would, according to Frye, be the two main "complex elements" in what he otherwise considers a "simple pattern," a plot structure "in itself less a form than a formula."[18] The extent to which this can be called a just account of New Comedy is difficult to ascertain dogmatically, considering all that we are asked to think of as New Comedy. But, on the whole, while Frye's analysis of plot structure is accurate enough under the circumstances, not everyone will accept without question his interpretation of the complex elements it contains. The interests of this comedy are not nearly as psychological and as social as he suggests; its characters are most often idiosyncratic or moral types rather than psychological or social types; and not merely its plot structure but its whole argument is so simple, so much on the surface, that any attempt at profound analysis can only exaggerate its implications. Whether or not this is true must be left to the reader's own judgment, for it is impossible to cite examples to cover all the cases that fall within the long and teeming tradition of New Comedy Frye defines. But one may briefly cite a case or two if only to make one's meaning clear. A good or at least logical example would be *The Grouch,* the recently discovered and only complete play of Menander's that we have. Of the two fathers in this play, one readily consents to both his son's and his daughter's marriage. The other, the grouch of the title—for whose benefit the first father might be regarded as something of a foil—can certainly be called an obstructionist. But before we read any deep psychological implications into his opposition to his daughter's love affair, we must remember that this old skinflint is an obstructionist on

17. "Argument," p. 58.
18. "Mythos," p. 163.

general principle—"anti-men," as he is called in the prologue, hostile to all men and women, old and young alike. He is, in short, a misanthrope, and the play gives us no warrant to proceed with him beyond the simple moral implications of this type—unless, of course, we are prepared to consider the incident of his falling into the well a piece of elaborate psychological symbolism or at the very least as having given him more than a knock on the head. If a reader does wish to interpret the fall in this way, as is not inconceivable at the present time, he would have to remember that the incident is not merely the clue but the sole evidence for such a reading. At any rate, it is worth pointing out that when the time for his daughter's marriage finally comes around, the old grouch actually speaks for her before he knows that she is spoken for.

This is not to suggest that all fathers in New Comedy welcome their children's amours or marriages; they respond as variously as fathers do in actual life, and for equally varied reasons. Most frequently parental opposition has less to do with psychological motivation than with such questions as family standing, due form and observance, and above all—as in Terence's *Phormio*—with the simple question of dowry. Indeed, the term "comic Oedipus situation" can in itself mean something far less portentous and even different from what it may at first suggest, and since Frye himself has dropped it in revision, there is no need to labor it any further. The possible meaning and implications of this situation will be discussed later, not in connection with classical New Comedy but with more recent works which offer the possibility of incest openly as a part of the concrete comic love situation rather than a hidden parallel theme.

Here we turn to Frye's other, more persistent theme. The mention of dowry and family standing above would suggest that New Comedy is capable of involving itself, if not with the problems of deeper psychology, at least with current social and cultural problems. And so it is. To think otherwise, to call this comedy pure romance, would be a mistake, for it is based on reality. But to consider it as depicting the crystallization of a *new* society is something else again. For the coming together of young lovers at the end signalizes the formation of a new society as little as the opposition of old men reveals per se the workings of unconscious psychology. In fact the moment we ask *new* in what sense, it becomes obvious that the two themes are not separable but absolutely though vaguely inter-dependent, and that what Frye means by new is some sort of a free and easy spiritual condition. If so, the whole procedure of apparently sharp psychological and social analysis becomes ir-relevant, and we are back to the old idea of the comic "spirit," universal and indefinable. In any more specific sense there is simply no question of a "movement from one kind of society to another." For, considering just the concrete social questions introduced into the plays, at the last curtain the idea of dowry is not abolished, slave girls have not received a general license to marry patrician grooms, and penniless women have not sud-denly been elevated to the same social standing as scions of great merchant houses. The end of the play, as Frye himself observes, assures us rather that the girls in question are neither penniless nor ignobly born; they can therefore be awarded the full measure of success and happiness precisely, and only, on the basis of the established social patterns. The discovery at the end, which leads to the happy outcome and which consti-tutes the most constant feature of New Comedy, is thus not merely a twist in the plot but equally a twist in the meaning. And this meaning has no public, let alone social, significance worth talking about. New Comedy is not interested in social conflict, in the necessity or even the possibility of social change. It takes the existing world for granted and addresses itself to the unusual private case: the case of the lucky individ-ual, the favorite of the gods or the circumstances, the happy man whose difficulties turn out to be thinly-disguised bless-ings.

In fact no comedy, at least none with which I am primarily concerned in this study, deals with social conflict in any fundamental way. Much of it takes happily for granted the basic social and economic structure of the existing world. Nevertheless, in it there is a larger significance that New Comedy typically lacks—a sense that the private case, the private individual even in his most private concerns, is still somehow implicated in a public cause. We can see exactly what this means by turning first to Aristophanic or Old Comedy—a comedy which was becoming outmoded in Aristophanes' own lifetime and which yielded the stage entirely to New Comedy within sixty or seventy years of his death. In comparing these two kinds of comedy, one could reverse Frye's phrase and distinguish Old Comedy as "less a formula than a form." To do so, however, would not necessarily mean to assign all artistic merit to the earlier form and leave none to the later one; it would still less be to assert an absolute contrast between the two, with nothing shared in common. Nor would the word *form* as applied to Old Comedy refer primarily to its well-known and elaborate technical features, the more important of which were in fact already on the point of disappearance in Aristophanes' own later work. (For instance, in the two fourth-century plays, *Plutus* and *The Ecclesiazusae*, the parabasis has been omitted and the role of the chorus considerably reduced.)

What we do mean by saying that New Comedy reduced the form of Old Comedy to a formula is, first of all, that in place of the variety of comic possibilities that we get in Aristophanes, Menander and his Roman followers substituted a uniform and predictable sameness. Of course, a formula has its own advantages, such as neatness, tightness, and a suave surface logic. In comparison with the more polished works of the Menandrine tradition straight through some of the latest Hollywood comedies, Old Comedy seems not only uncouth and disorderly but also shapeless. Aristophanes, like many other great and popular dramatists after him, was conscious of providing within the format of one catch-all performance different fare for different tastes. As he has the chorus say to the audience at the end of *The Ecclesiazusae:* "I have but a few words to say: let the wise judge me because of whatever is wise in this piece, and those who like a laugh by whatever has made them laugh." Nor is there any evidence in the plays to suggest that he sought to please the lovers of laughter any less energetically than he did to please "the wise." On the contrary, Aristophanes' comic energy is nowhere more visible than in his constant exploitation of anything and everything that will raise a laugh: not merely all manner of buffoonery and horseplay but also caricature, personal invective, topical lampoon, and, of course, endless jests based on the coarsest details of physical living. Indeed Terence's claim, "Nothing human is alien to me," is more literally true of Aristophanes than of Terence himself. Scholars have had difficulty determining whether Aristophanic drama can rightly be called comedy or whether it is more properly burlesque, farce, comic opera, or a sort of pantomime takeoff on the fashions and follies of the hour. It certainly combines elements of all these and at the same time adds to them the arts of literary review and public debate, thus exhibiting a range of interests stretching all the way from the most trivial facts of commonplace life to ideas and public policies of the most far-reaching significance.

Clearly, then, if we are to speak of the form of Old Comedy, it is going to be a form that is not as neatly related to the plot as it is in New Comedy. The plot of Old Comedy does not in fact depend so much on a nice combination of intrigue, stratagem, and discovery as it does on a broadly conceived central conflict to which the many diverse incidents are more or less vitally connected. This central conflict, though exemplified through its bearing on individual lives, is primarily concerned not with a private case but with a general issue of public importance. Indeed, of all comic writers, Aristophanes is the most public in his interests, the most directly political. This is true because of the obviously political character of his main themes and also in many other unnoticed ways. It has been said, for instance, that there is much sex but little love in Aristophanes; and insofar as sex is the public name for love and love the personal or accidental name for sex, this in itself suggests the difference between the interests of Aristophanes and those of the Menandrine comedy down to our own day.

Among the central conflicts which often function as the backbone of Aristophanes' comedies, there is one that needs to be underlined in the present context—the kind of dramatic conflict in which ideas are represented on the stage and play a major role *as* ideas. In saying this I am not preparing to invoke the so-called theater of ideas—a concept bristling with all sorts of unsettled questions and, as it turns out, proving itself each day more and more hospitable to the claims of an increasing number of dramatists, both old and new. Aristophanes certainly is not the playwright as thinker, not even by the side of his own contemporary and *bete noir,* Euripides. It is in fact embarrassing to speak of ideas in connection with a dramatist who puts himself forward time and again, as Aristophanes does, as the sworn enemy of all ideas, especially all new ideas. His heroes are often those coarse earthy fellows who torment literary geniuses and wage war against all but the most rudimentary form of thinking; one of his plays ends with the "Thinkery" of Socrates going up in flames, and much of the substance of another play consists of indignities heaped upon an extraordinarily silly-looking and witless Euripides. It is true that Aristophanes' targets, as he represents or misrepresents them, deserve little better than what they get; we can only reflect that in his blind conservatism, his rooted opposition to innovation in art, philosophy, and education, this is all he saw in two of the finest spirits of the age. In a very real sense Aristophanes can be called a proponent of crude and even deadly anti-intellectualism. Socrates found his accusations fatal,[19] and it is not impossible even today to revive the danger along with the dramatist. And yet, as is equally clear, Aristophanes did not ignore ideas; he realized the extent to which they mattered in the business of living, even and perhaps especially in the business of ordinary everyday living. He assigned a definite role to ideas within the structure of his comedies, often grossly distorting the ideas in order to fit them to that role; and it is the nature of this role rather than the specific character of Aristophanes' ideas that is useful for understanding the type of comedy with which I am concerned.

To generalize on the basis of Aristophanes' conservatism and call all comedy "probable, normal, and conservative"[20] is to oversimplify matters and also lose sight of a formal principle in Old Comedy that is considerably more important and representative than its particular political or philosophical standpoint. There is, of course, a connection between Aristophanes' defense of traditional patterns of government, art, and thought and the widespread crisis of the time, the crisis which, accompanied by an expansionist war lasting through most of his lifetime, resulted in the transformation of Athenian society from an agricultural to an artisan and mercantile society. But not all comic writers even in periods of comparable crisis and

19. See Socrates' defense at his trial:

I do not know and cannot tell the names of my accusers; unless in the chance case of a Comic poet. . . . Well, what do the slanderers say? They shall be my prosecutors, and I will sum up their words in an affidavit: "Socrates is an evil-doer, and a curious person, who searches into things under the earth and in heaven, and he makes the worse appear the better cause; and he teaches the aforesaid doctrines to others." Such is the nature of the accusation: it is just what you have yourselves seen in the comedy of Aristophanes.

[*The Dialogues of Plato,* trans. B. Jowett, 2 vols. (New York, Random House, 1937), *1,* 402.]

20. Albert Cook, *The Dark Voyage and the Golden Mean: A Philosophy* (Cambridge, Harvard University Press, 1949), p. 62.

change can be said to have followed Aristophanes' wholesale advocacy of the declining age and ethos. Consider, for example, one striking and, for our purposes, extraordinarily revealing aspect of the issue—the aspect that can be termed the battle of the books. Here, as against Aristophanes' defense of old literary masters threatened by new concepts in poetry, we have in later years the more frequent spectacle of comedy attacking rather than defending the literary conventions of the previous age. This later practice is certainly true of Cervantes, for example, whose *Don Quixote* was born, as we are informed, out of its author's quarrel with the two dominant European literary traditions of his youth: the pastoral romance and the tale of knightly adventure and courtly love. In fact, Cervantes would claim little credit for the book beyond its success in administering a coup de grâce to these moribund conventions. Many subsequent comic writers have kept up this pose, proclaiming the attack on past literature as their sole inspiration if not their only purpose. And yet this is not altogether an idle pose The battle of the books is not only something of a constant feature in comic literature, but it is also of the utmost relevance in understanding both the form and the meaning of much literary comedy. And it is this feature in Aristophanes' writing rather than his conservative handling of it that later writers share. More generally, then, not in his specific ideas, but only in his manner of dealing with them can Aristophanes be called a broadly representative writer of comedy.

The question is essentially one of method, a method in the use of which Cervantes and Aristophanes—two writers otherwise separated by more than just the centuries—may be said to stand allied in the common kinship of comedy. The matter can be put simply by saying that both these writers represent certain ideas as abstractions, though the term *abstraction* is not in itself simple and will need constant annotation. We can begin here by saying that it means knowledge that is divorced from

reality or unrelated to the situation to which it is applied—
logos (theory) without *ergon* (fact). There is no need to labor
the point with regard to *Don Quixote,* a work whose narrative
consists of numerous episodes organized to show fact breaking
in upon theory. More important, the highly theoretical hero,
the well- but not wisely-read Don, is himself made conscious
of the point behind his story. This does not just come suddenly at the end, at the moment of his final self-realization and
death, but earlier as well, in such episodes as the one concerning the cave of Montesinos, where Lady Dulcinea's request for
a loan against the surety of a cotton skirt surprises the Don
into asking his host aloud: "Is it possible, Sir Montesinos, for
people of quality when enchanted to be in want?" Don Quixote is thus not merely a spectacle to the other characters and
the reader; he is to some extent a deliberate spectacle to himself, in the end more fully conscious of what the spectacle
means than any other character. This is not to suggest that the
action of *Don Quixote* is simple or that the outcome of its
central conflict is uncomplicated and one-sided. But whether
we think of the novel in terms of the juxtaposed characters of
Quixote and Sancho Panza or in terms of their interlocking
fortunes and respective metamorphoses, and however complex
the division of sympathies in the novel—indeed, however questionable finally the very act of dividing appearance or willed
perception from reality—the confrontation between what I
have called theory and fact, between ideal imaginings and intractable situations, is the one ever-present principle of the
novel's structure and significance. It constitutes the vital and
astonishingly simple comic base of the novel, and while there
are readers who proceed no further from this unifying base, no
reader should proceed so far as to leave it out of account
altogether.

There is no comparable unity or consistency to be found in
Aristophanes' work. The confrontation of *logos* and *ergon* is
not the one principle of form and meaning behind all the

eleven extant plays. Even where it is that, or comes close to being that, it cannot be said to unify every part of the action. Most frequently the principle appears fitfully in the guise of heroes whose affairs have become snarled with the political policies, legal sanctions, legislative procedures, and bureaucratic regulations of an imperial metropolis—all of which they regard as unnecessarily complicated and often fraudulent arrangements without any relation to the real problems of the citizen's life. Thus Dicaepolis (Honest Citizen) of *The Acharnians,* after being prevented by the war party from getting so much as a hearing in the public assembly, literally concludes a separate peace and resumes forthwith a brisk trade with impoverished individual farmers like himself from enemy states. The ribald central conceit of *Lysistrata,* another "peace" play, depends for its effect on the battle of the sexes as much as on the contrast between the political issue of war and the most private of all possible strategies employed to settle it—the point again being to show up by means of a real necessity the false necessity of war and of the arguments advanced in favor of it. In *The Birds* Eulpides (Hopeful) and his companions are driven by their troubles with the law courts to dream of a city where "the most important business transacted" would consist of mutual invitations to nuptial feasts, though Aristophanes knows that such a city would be so far from the groundwork of reality that it could exist only on "the plains of the air."

Thus abstractions in the sense of abstruse complications of living and false theories of what is possible or necessary in life play their part, be it large or small, in much of what Aristophanes wrote. But his best symbol of pure abstraction is Socrates in *The Clouds,* the man who lives suspended in a basket so that he can "traverse the air and contemplate the sun" and "mingle the subtle essence of my mind with this air." The play's chorus of clouds reinforces this symbol because, just as in *The Frogs* the chorus of frogs suggests the cacophany of the new poetry that the play attacks, clouds are what Socrates lives in and, like him, stand for abstract knowledge. The effect is achieved, of course, at the expense of subjecting Socrates to severe comic metamorphosis, or plain distortion. For, if we are to believe Plato, Socrates never practiced the two modes of thought attributed to him in *The Clouds:* fruitless scientific investigation and unprincipled sophism. Nor can Plato's picture be dismissed as equally poetic and therefore unreliable; Xenophon's more authentic historical account confirms Plato rather than Aristophanes. There is a possibility, of course, that both accounts are accurate—Aristophanes presenting the young and sophistic Socrates, and Plato and Xenophon drawing on the mature philosopher of later years. But whether Aristophanes' representation of Socrates is historically true or false, the important question with regard to the play is this: to what purpose are ideas reduced to abstractions and in the name of what principle are they discredited and overthrown? This other purpose is simply the exigencies of the practical situation that the play centers on—the demands of experience, if we may with some courtesy use that term here. For the prime cause of the action is not a search for knowledge but Strepsiades' problems with his debts and with the scapegrace son who incurred those debts. Thus though Strepsiades searches out the schoolhouse of wisdom, it is not because he desires to "know the truth of celestial matters" or to "converse with the clouds," as Socrates at first supposes. All other expedients having failed, he has turned to the philosophers because he believes that they are conversant with the art of winning "lawsuits, whether they be just or not." The clouds, "venerable goddesses" to Socrates, are to him mere "fog" and "vapor." And when at the end his scheme boomerangs upon himself, it is the clouds he clamors against—the learning he had sought as practical knowledge but that turned out to be anything but a dependable guide to action. "Oh! Clouds! all our troubles emanate from you, from you, to whom I entrusted myself, body and soul."

As in *The Clouds* so in *The Ecclesiazusae* there is a historical question concerning the abstraction—in this case, the theory of a utopian state—that the play is built to test. But again there is no need for us to determine whether Aristophanes was drawing on Plato's *Republic,* whether Plato's treatise followed the play, or whether both derive from a common source in current speculation. Nor is it as certain as most people seem to believe that the play unambiguously discredits the idea of community of property and women. It is not only that the play can be read as a satire against the conditions that inspire the communistic scheme in the first place, although such a reading is possible. Also, unlike Socrates and his schoolhouse in *The Clouds,* Praxagora and her system emerge victorious. But beyond this is the more important fact that whenever Praxagora gives her spirited exposition of the new dispensation, which happens during a considerable part of the play, the dramatist raises no serious objections. "There will be no more thieves, nor envious people, no more rags nor misery, no more abuse and no more prosecutions and law-suits. . . . I want all to have a share of everything and all property to be in common; there will no longer be either rich or poor. . . . The life in common. Athens will become nothing more than a single house." To all this her listeners assent with an enthusiasm that is as much a part of the play as are its objections to the utopian theory.

What it has to say against the theory, however, it says with decisive finality. In this connection it is worth noting that the test at the end of the play, while typical of Aristophanes and also illustrative of the method of comedy more generally, is not altogether relevant to the theory outlined in *The Republic.* Aristophanes, in fact, prepares for his most telling blow by having his heroine add a further clause to Plato's system of community marriage—a clause that decrees priority in courtship to the old and the unattractive. Insofar as this is a distortion of the Platonic scheme, it is as revealing as the distortion of Socratic thought in *The Clouds.* For to whatever extent it improves upon Plato's idea in the direction of logic and justice, to that same extent it makes the idea more ludicrously unpractical and unworkable. "By Poseidon! 'tis grand if true," says Praxagora's husband of her entire system, but, he adds, he fears this final clause is going to prove the least true. It is indeed this clause that Aristophanes exploits most tellingly as he arranges the comic confrontation between theory and truth, or abstraction and experience, in the last two scenes before the finale of the banquet. In the earlier of the two—the scene devoted to the practical testing of the idea of community of property—while the first citizen's packing his belongings shows acceptance of the new law, the second citizen's doubts suggest more a wait-and-see policy than outright rejection. But it is the bizarre contest between the two old hags and the disappointed young lovers in the second scene that provides the final proof—or rather disproof, for now the theory stands judged unambiguously as just not answering to the realities of the case.

The traditions of classical Old and New Comedy lie behind modern English comedy as it begins its long career at the height of the Renaissance. True, so far as the question of influence is concerned, by and large only the Roman models were consciously and repeatedly imitated by the Elizabethan dramatists. Nevertheless there are some comedies, some of Elizabethan times and certainly many more thereafter, which are not simply imitations of Plautus and Terence. My argument, however, has little to do with questions of influence and conscious imitation. I have discussed and contrasted Old and New Comedy as exemplifying two kinds of comic action, with the suggestion in mind that, regarded in this formal aspect, certain features of each will prove helpful in understanding and defining the action of later English comedy. In expanding this suggestion we can begin by observing that most English comedies deal primarily—as do the comedies of Plautus and

Terence—with matters of private life, mainly indeed with the single problem of love, courtship, and marriage. Another question raised frequently is that of honor, but it is a question of reduced meanings to begin with and soon becomes identified with the theme of love as domestic honor. Political or philosophical comedy is a rarity; indeed the moment such large issues as matters of public or national policy or questions bearing upon the fundamental nature of man enter into comedy, during the entire modern period, it tends to become something other than comedy. Thus, to cite a few examples, the comedy of Gulliver is satire, the stage pieces that Fielding wrote before turning novelist are farces, and Gay's *Beggar's Opera* is something of both but essentially *sui generis.* Even Molière, the most satirical of all purely comic writers, realized that in order to be itself comedy had to center on private life—its subject could only be the family and not the state.

In English comedy, as in classical New Comedy, the plot complications that accompany the domestic adventure or the adventure of love, although apparently formidable when they arise, are in the end quite easily resolved. Most often, in fact, they are resolved by the same simple device of discovering that they never really existed. In a play like *Much Ado About Nothing,* where the title itself makes the point clear, the audience does not even have to wait to the end to have its happy expectations fulfilled. The plot that threatens and very nearly destroys the nuptials of Hero and Claudio is brought to light on stage at the very moment of its execution, and, however humbling the ways of the Watch who apprehend the villains, we are assured that the discovery has virtually canceled the threat even before it has become a threat. Or consider a more serious kind of threat, the threat of incest such as that arising in the course of Tom Jones's amorous adventures. True to type, it too arises only to cancel itself as Tom first suspects Mrs. Waters of being his unknown mother and then is made to discover that she is not. And in *Joseph Andrews* we have those

sudden twists and turns of the story in the final chapters
where Fanny is discovered to be the long-lost Andrews girl and
therefore Joseph's sister until Joseph himself turns out to be
not an Andrews but a Wilson, all these last-minute alarms and
revelations undoing the original mischief of a remote and
rather hypothetical band of child-lifting gypsies.

Now if these incestuous situations are comic, this results not
so much from their happy resolution as from the fact that the
supposed difficulty is only a chimera and there is therefore no
need to resolve anything. Which is to say that these are situations that change without anything really changing in them,
least of all the characters most vitally concerned. The case of
Tom Jones may perhaps be an exception, but even if he can be
said to have changed on account of the temporary but terrible
fear of having committed incest, the connection would still be
slight and purely incidental. By and large it is the plot that
does all the changing that is called for, leaving the heroes and
the heroines little by way of a moral task, an effort of self-
examination or choice or moral adjustment. But, and this is
where we must go beyond the formulas of New Comedy, these
intrigues, conspiracies, stillborn threats, baseless appearances,
unnecessary trepidations—in a word, these much ados about
nothings—though they are to be found in the plots of most
comedies, do not in every case constitute the entire comic
plot. In the most interesting cases their introduction and can-
cellation is a preparation for, or is accompanied and paralleled
by, a radically different type of ado, one that possesses essentially the nature and possibilities of a moral action. Once this
action is recognized, the false complications become subsidiary
and peripheral, like so many diversionary engagements
launched sporadically in support of the main action. Not that
instances are wanting in the history of comedy, as in military
history, where the supporting operations so confuse and over-
whelm the major campaign that it never gets off the ground
and is before long discarded and forgotten. But even in the

cases where there is no such miscarriage, even in the comedies whose main action stands out in clear distinction, one may often fail to recognize it for the truly dramatic action that it is. The reason for this is not hard to find, particularly with the examples of Aristophanes and Cervantes before us. In a very important sense comic heroes are pitted against relative intangibilities, invisible foes outside and unrecognizable spies within. They are pitted against abstractions, as in Old Comedy, but often without the benefit of Aristophanic allegory that gives a human name and shape to abstractions on the stage.

What the abstractions that figure in modern comedy are specifically, and how they are diagnosed and combatted in the various comedies of the period, will become apparent in the chapters that follow. Here it is instructive to enlarge a little on the comparison with Aristophanes. Nothing will point to the validity of this comparison as readily as the battle-of-the-books aspect of Aristophanes' comedy, since it is the aspect most widely shared by later writers. Thus where Aristophanes found his targets in Euripides and Socrates, Shakespeare more or less begins the period with constant skirmishes with the pastoral and other "artificial" literary traditions and styles of his time, *The Rehearsal* fires the opening salvoes for Restoration comedy by attacking Dryden and the fashion for heroic drama, Fielding trains his guns on Richardson and Cibber, and Jane Austen starts out with a burlesque of the literature of sensibility and the Gothic novel. Examples can be multiplied at will, but the important thing is to point out that, for these writers, attacking literature is not a matter of reaching for the scalps of enemies and rivals but rather of engaging certain theories of conduct, certain false attitudes and values, which have inspired various books and are in turn further propagated and sustained by these new books. The kind of book that is attacked, or the kind it is made out to be in the process of that attack, is the best clue to the purpose of the attack. It is never an evil book or an immoral book or a badly-written book, even though the book concerned may indeed be all these things, and the comic writer himself may recognize this fact. But the attack is almost always mounted because the book is judged to be pure romance, promoting ideas and theories that have no relevance to life and are yet capable of complicating, obstructing, and even frustrating the real business of living.

Of course, there are obvious differences on this score between Aristophanes and the modern writers, not to mention the differences among modern writers themselves. The main difference that must be noted here, however, is that quite consistently modern English comedy views and condemns the role of abstract ideas and theories in the sphere where its condemnation rightly belongs. Aristophanes often finds theory offensive precisely where it has a valid part to play: on the subject of organizing a state, for example, where there is no way of rational discourse or action except through reliance on conceptual abstraction. One cannot attack mathematics for being mathematical or economics for speaking in terms of economic categories. To suggest that because politics, economics, or sociology rely on large-scale ideas and concepts, they can have no relevance to the ordinary concerns of individual human beings, is to display a simple-mindedness that can only confuse the issues; and it is for some such display of deliberate confusion rather than for any crudities of taste that Aristophanes tends to become shallow and unsatisfactory. Of course, with the true method of comedy, Aristophanes demolishes philosophical and political theories by bringing them to the test of private and indeed intimate experience, as in the courtship scene at the end of *The Ecclesiazusae*. But this nevertheless remains sleight of hand, something that gives us the sense of true means employed for dubious ends.

To avoid possible misunderstanding, it should be made clear that if there is this sense of trickery in Aristophanes' drama, it does not arise from the attempt to relate the political with the private too closely, but rather from the failure to relate the two closely and convincingly enough. In fact, there is often only a startling juxtaposition, and we are aware that all the play's real problems belong to one sphere and all its proofs to the other. Aristophanes could do this with some measure of credibility in his own day because imperial Athens still retained more than a touch of city-state homeliness. Thus Praxagora's absurd claim that women will make better stewards of political economy because of their experience in domestic economics is not quite as absurd as it would be today, or at least not absurd in quite the same way. (The meaning of the root Greek words *oikos* and *nomos* is itself evidence of this.) Aristophanes is above all a political dramatist; the domestic instance is for him just that, an instance or illustration of the real theme. On the other hand, modern comedy is concerned primarily with the private case. In this respect the sexual aspect of Praxagora's scheme provides a better basis for comparison, for she suggests, however distantly, the situation of many a heroine of later comedy—Beatrice's anti-romantic pose in *Much Ado,* for example, or one aspect of Elizabeth Bennet's matrimonial problem in *Pride and Prejudice.* The situation of the three heroines is comparable in that it involves in each case a dissatisfaction with the existing arrangements of courtship and marriage. But while Aristophanes' play is a debate of which the very stuff and substance is a public issue, the English comedies are stories of love and marriage, of personal experience complicated by but not directly addressed to social sanctions and attitudes. The difference may seem only one of emphasis, but it is nevertheless crucial and, in fact, enables us to sum up the relation of modern comedy not only to Old Comedy but to New Comedy as well. For if modern comedy is not political in the way in which Aristophanes is political, neither does it confine itself wholly to the private case. Unlike New Comedy, it recognizes that in the real world there are no adventures worth the name which are exclusively private. Indeed, at its best, modern comedy takes for its subject the confrontation between modes of public thought and the modes of moral and emotional intelligence necessary for the fulfillment of personal life. To this extent, it may be said to combine or synthesize the two forms of classical comedy.

We may now proceed to define in a general way the nature of comic action as a clash between abstraction and experience. The term *abstraction,* as already noted, is not simple. Nor, for that matter, is the term *experience.* Their varied meanings and also the meaning of their clash will become clear in and through the later concrete analyses of this study; here we can only lay down preliminary working definitions. Thus abstraction, in keeping with its dictionary meanings, includes the following shades and extensions of a purely theoretical way of regarding things: a romantic or ideal as opposed to a real or practical view, a habit of deducing from general principles and disregarding concrete situations, the wisdom of maxims disengaged from particular examples, didacticism without moral consciousness, a partial truth standing for the whole, a truth assumed without the backing of the sort of experience that alone can reveal why it is a truth and what its being true means. Above all, and especially at the beginning of the period, abstraction denotes a traditional abridgment of conduct into rules and conventions which are no longer valid and which have not only lost their point but—in surviving one historical age and passing into another—have changed their character and become obstructions rather than aids to conduct. For, in Christopher Caudwell's words: "Worn-out engines become brakes. Outworn truths become illusions."[21] As for the term *experience,* we cannot do better than reproduce here the definition given by Henry James in the preface to *The*

21. Christopher Caudwell, *Studies in a Dying Culture* (London, The Bodley Head, 1938), p. xx.

Princess Casamassima: "Experience, as I see it, is our apprehension and our measure of what happens to us as social creatures—any intelligent report of which," as James goes on to add, "has to be based on that apprehension."

The best philosophical analysis of the clash between abstraction and experience, in terms of the effect of incongruity and laughter, is to be found not in Kant but in Schopenhauer.[22] The important thing is not Schopenhauer's location of the source of laughter in the "incongruity of sensuous and abstract knowledge," nor his explanation of why such an incongruity should arise in the first place—"although abstract rational knowledge is the reflex of ideas of perception, and is founded on them, it is by no means in such entire congruity with them that it could everywhere take their place: indeed it never corresponds to them accurately"[23]—but the application of this idea to the analysis of such minor devices associated with the art of comedy as verbal wit and the pun and such common comic subjects as foolishness and pedantry. Thus Schopenhauer sees wit as a matter of taking two or more very different real objects and intentionally identifying them through the unity of an abstract concept which comprehends both. On the other hand, the pun or double entendre "brings two different concepts, by the assistance of accident, under one word. . . . In the case of the witticism the identity is in the concept, the difference in the reality, but in the case of the pun the difference is in the concepts and the identity in the reality, for the terminology is here the reality."[24] Folly arises from the incongruity of concept and reality when, neglecting the difference between the two, we proceed by means of action directly from

22. Arthur Schopenhauer, *The World as Will and Idea*, trans. R. B. Haldane and J. Kemp, vol. 1 (Boston, J. R. Osgood, 1883), pp. 76-80; vol. 2 (Boston, Ticknor, 1886), pp. 270-84.
23. Ibid., *1*, 76.
24. Ibid., *1*, 79.

one to the other. Pedantry is a species of folly in which a person, lacking confidence in his own understanding and not trusting it to recognize the particular case, confines himself to general concepts, rules, and maxims, in all questions of thought and conduct.

Suggestive and helpful as these notes are, they leave us a long way from formulating the full possibilities of comic action. For, where Schopenhauer is not analyzing the mere ornaments and local strategies of the comic art, he too thinks of comedy as either an assemblage of laughter-raising devices or, at best, a static form incapable of projecting a dramatic or developing action. Here in fact we can return to Potts's view of the comic plot as a spatial arrangement of characters rather than a sequence of events. The essence of this idea was expressed even more sharply and succinctly by Maynard Mack in his introduction to *Joseph Andrews,* published a year before Potts's book. Reflecting on the contrast between Fielding and Richardson, Mack too refers to the distinction between comedy and tragedy or, in his own words, between "the comic mode in fiction and what, for want of a better name, may be called the tragic one":

> Character in the tragic mode, though it need not end in death, always inhabits, like Richardson's Clarissa, a world of choices followed by consequences. . . . The curve of tragic action, in other words, is a curve of self-discovery. On the other hand, the comic curve is one of self-exposure. . . . the great comic characters of literature, whether Shakespeare's, Fielding's, or Dickens's, do not *essentially* change. They are enveloped by events without being involved by them . . . Thus at the close of *Joseph Andrews,* Lady Booby, on the one hand, and Parson Adams, on the other, are as self-deceived as they were at the start; they have uncovered others, but they have not discovered themselves. . . . comedy presents us with life

apprehended in the form of a spectacle rather than in the form of experience.[25]

Susanne Langer likewise finds absence of character development "essentially a comedy trait." Comic characters, she observes, "are good or evil, as the case may be, in the last act as they were in the first. . . . the protagonists do not change in the course of the play, as they normally do in tragedy."[26]

Now while these are accurate observations concerning two literary possibilities, they provide little basis for distinguishing comedy from tragedy. The confusion arises from the fact that, in thinking of tragedy, we always think of the best examples known to us—of *King Lear* rather than *Gorboduc,* of *Hamlet* rather than *The Spanish Tragedy*—while in comedy our attention is somehow drawn invariably to the less rather than the more estimable specimens. For no self-discovery worth the name is involved in the career of Gorboduc or of Kyd's tragic hero; Tamburlaine is not really different in Marlowe's last act from what he was in the first; and Vittoria Corombona and Flamineo do not essentially change in the course of *The White Devil.* On the other hand, while we can grant critics such as Maynard Mack and Susanne Langer their observations on comedy with regard to a work like *Joseph Andrews*—which indeed is Mack's specific subject—it cannot be maintained that life in Jane Austen's novels is apprehended in the form of a spectacle and not in the form of experience.

To the extent, then, to which these are criteria that cut across the lines of tragedy and comedy, they become properly the criteria of excellence applicable to both forms or modes. This was realized by E. M. Forster, whose definition of flat

25. Maynard Mack, ed., *Joseph Andrews,* by Henry Fielding (New York, Rinehart, 1948), pp. xiii-xv.

26. Susanne Langer, "The Comic Rhythm," in Corrigan, *Comedy,* p. 127. The essay reprinted in Corrigan's anthology is a part of Miss Langer's *Feeling and Form,* 1953.

and round characters is perhaps the common source of the above critics but who was careful not to make his distinction a distinction between comedy and tragedy. The important point in Forster's discussion is to be found, not in the adjectival and metaphorical description of what is meant by flat and round, but in a characteristically offhand statement that he adds almost as an afterthought. Speaking of the few small advantages that flat characters may be said to enjoy over their superiors, Forster observes that for one thing "they are easily remembered by the reader afterwards. They remain in his mind as unalterable for the reason that they were not changed by circumstances."[27] Such characters, however, may appear in any kind of literary work. As Forster points out, there are tragedies—boring ones no doubt—whose characters cry for Revenge or identify themselves with some other equally hair-raising and unvaried formula every time they enter. On the other hand, among the round personalities of literature Forster includes not only all the characters of Jane Austen—even Miss Bates and Elizabeth Elliot—but also Fielding's Parson Adams and Tom Jones.

It is possible to disagree with Forster's specific examples and judgments but not, I think, with the basic point that comedy, as much as tragedy, is capable of both types or levels of literary performance. What distinguishes one type from the other is not any difference in subject matter but rather a difference in treatment and thereby in the character and quality of experience that the subject treated in one or the other way provides. Put simply, whatever the subject of a work, is there or is there not a relation established between the external events or happenings of the story and the moral consciousness of the character concerned? Indeed, according to James's definition, it is only through some such relation between the inner and

27. E. M. Forster, *Aspects of the Novel* (New York, Harcourt, Brace, 1927), pp. 105-06.

the outer that experience really becomes experience. The key question, as Mack points out, is whether the action involves mere discovery or also in some sense self-discovery. Aristotelean critics in the Renaissance used to speak of two kinds of comic plot: simple or complex, depending on whether the events leading to discovery proceed in an expected or unexpected sequence. But the discovery itself was always a matter of external knowledge, of recognizing the true state of affairs. The truly complex examples of comedy, however, are precisely those in which, as in comparable tragic examples, discovery and self-discovery are inseparable. In *Philebus* Socrates goes so far as to make lack of self-knowledge the special province of the comic or the ridiculous: "The ridiculous is in short the specific name which is used to describe the vicious form of a certain habit; and of vice in general it is that kind which is most at variance with the inscription at Delphi—'Know thyself.' "[28] The author of *Joseph Andrews* would agree with this as much as would the author of *Pride and Prejudice* and *Emma.* But if Jane Austen's comedies are better or more complex than *Joseph Andrews*—*Tom Jones* is perhaps not as simple a case—part of their complexity lies in the fact that "know thyself" does not serve only as their general moral inscription but constitutes a complex process in them—a process involving initial blindness followed by the achievement of self-recognition and eventually some sort of moral adjustment and growth. In this sense the actions of the best of Jane Austen's comedies belong less in the class of *Joseph Andrews* and more in that of *King Lear.* A heroine like Elizabeth Bennet does not only help to uncover pride and blindness in others but must, like Lear, discover them in herself. Her story, as much as Lear's, is a story of experience.

The point of all this is to suggest that, just as we must reject the meaningless definitions of comedy in terms of trite univer-

28. *The Dialogues of Plato, 2,* 383.

sals, we should stop defining the form on the basis entirely of
its lesser examples. Surely it is better to define the best there
is, and apply the definition mutatis mutandis to the inferior
achievements. But here we are faced at once with a question
that is unavoidable though less profitable than other such
questions when discussed in general terms. For, if comedy at
its best also deals with experience, wherein lies its difference
from tragedy? To answer this question it is well to begin with
the answer that is most often given: comedy differs from tragedy in the areas of life to which it addresses itself and, more
important, in the mood with which it approaches and apprehends those areas. In *The Quintessence of Ibsenism,* comparing
Shakespeare with Ibsen (and, more generally, conventional
theater with the "natural" new drama), Shaw writes:

> Now the natural is mainly the everyday; and its climaxes
> must be, if not everyday, at least everylife, if they are to
> have any importance for the spectator. Crimes, fights, big
> legacies, fires, shipwrecks, battles, and thunderbolts are
> mistakes in a play, even when they can be effectively simu-
> lated. . . . Shakespear had put ourselves on the stage but
> not our situations. Our uncles seldom murder our fathers,
> and cannot legally marry our mothers; we do not meet
> witches; our kings are not as a rule stabbed and succeeded
> by their stabbers; and when we raise money by bills we do
> not promise to pay pounds of our flesh. Ibsen supplies the
> want left by Shakespear. He gives us not only ourselves,
> but ourselves in our own situations.[29]

We are not concerned here with the merits and demerits of
these observations other than to point out that what Shaw
calls the natural should more properly be called the comic: the
comic as it defines itself both in opposition to the false situa-

29. Bernard Shaw, *The Quintessence of Ibsenism* (New York, Hill
and Wang, 1961), pp. 176-77, 182.

tions of romance (legacies, shipwrecks, etc.) and in distinction to the exceptional situations of tragedy (fratricide, incest, etc.). Shaw no doubt gives the impression of equating these two kinds of situations as almost equally unnatural. Furthermore, this passage was written in 1913; today, a half century later, the extent to which playwrights or other writers would grant the distinction between the everyday quality of life and the terror of the exceptional tragic situation is in question. The most striking contemporary writers have in fact tended to identify the two so increasingly that the most dominant literary form today is neither tragedy nor comedy, but tragicomedy. Even Ibsen, according to Shaw himself in a later essay (to which I refer more fully in my last chapter), wrote tragicomedy in this modern sense, and this fact as much as anything else was responsible for the quality of newness in his drama and for its enormous influence.

This tendency in contemporary literature to erase the line between tragedy and comedy is, however, no reason for supposing that such a line never existed or that it never had any meaning. And in explaining the distinctions represented by this line, we should at least begin with Shaw's distinction between the everylife comic situation and the exceptional situations of tragedy. Life in the tragic mode, to use a fine phrase of Nathan Scott's, is always "lived at the difficult and perilous limits of the human condition."[30] The word that needs to be emphasized here is neither *difficult* nor even *perilous*, but *limits*. For life, in becoming the subject of comedy, does not necessarily lose all its dangers and perils. Comic situations are everyday or everylife situations only in the sense that they deal with the common ground of man's social experience rather than those limits of it where most men are neither called upon nor able to follow the exceptional tragic hero.

30. Nathan A. Scott, Jr., "The Bias of Comedy and the Narrow Escape into Faith," in Corrigan, *Comedy*, p. 91.

Often, indeed, comic situations are simply the commonplace situations of love and marriage. The popular notion that a story is a comedy if it ends in marriage is erroneous only because marriage is not just the end but the subject of comic stories. It is, in fact, a test of everyday life, just as love is the highest attainable form of everyday social experience.

Since, however, there are also tragedies of love and marriage, we need to add that comedy addresses itself to this large area of common experience in a mood that insists on prosperity, success, and fulfillment. A description of the comic mood does not by itself take us very far, for the question remains of how this mood is made possible and acceptable in terms of the comic action. Why, since comedy also deals with conflict and contradiction, is it able to ensure the happy outcome that it insists upon? Here again we must note the nature of the comic conflict rather than merely the mood and subjects of comedy. As most people would agree, conflict in tragedy involves a conflict of two realities which are not only opposed but irreconcilable. Even when one side appears more in the shape of an ideal of which the hero is possessed than as a reality, it still remains an ideal irreconcilable with reality—one of those ideals which, "like the gods of old," to quote Shaw again, "are constantly demanding human sacrifices."[31] Thus tragedy leads us to the ramparts and barriers beyond which man's will can find no satisfactory expression, let alone success. It shows the limits of human freedom in the given situation. When the tragic hero reaches out for what he takes to be his freedom, it turns out to be an illusory freedom, one that is lost in the past or asserted before its time or unreal because of some still more fixed and unalterable law or reality. It is in this sense that we often think of the ideals of tragic heroes as illusions. Now comedy also deals with the question of illusion and reality—indeed this is its one constant conflict—but it does so in a very

31. Shaw, *Quintessence of Ibsenism,* p. 154.

different way. For in comic actions it is the heroes' ideals which are real, and it is the power of the opposing forces that turns out to be illusory. What the comic hero seeks is not only reconcilable with reality but perfectly attainable without any serious dislocation of the existing situation; what he must battle is not the basic law or structure of his society but some parts of the cultural superstructure which do not accurately or fully reflect the possibilities of that society itself. His enemy is the power of abstraction as it exerts itself both in the social situation and in his own consciousness. The laws that obstruct his path, although they retain a ghostly power, are nevertheless laws that no longer exist on the statute book. Comedy, in a word, is the revelation of existing freedom.

However, just because such comic ideals as love are attainable, it should not be imagined that they are for that reason represented as easy or automatic. Indeed, by the time we come to Jane Austen, these ideals seem so imperilled that the achievement of them is already precarious though still possible for the exceptional character. In this respect there is a mistake that is made as often as the one about emotion being alien and repugnant to the spirit of comedy. For it is widely assumed that since comedy deals with the commonplace areas of life, the comic hero must therefore be in every respect a commonplace man. But in truth the comic hero shares only his situation with other men, not the outcome of his story or the excellence of his character. In the last two respects he is a model figure rather than an average representative, and a model in nothing so much as in his readiness to struggle for the highest possible good rather than accept easily the lower and easily attainable one. Although it is an everyday or everylife battle, he is its hero because he alone understands its nature and the stakes involved and is prepared not only to fight but to use and acquire the qualities needed to win. Nor is it surprising, remembering the nature as well as the prize of the comic battle, that the qualities emphasized should be those of

vitality and intelligence—not as two separate qualities in the
end, but rather as the one supreme quality of vital intelligence.
For in this sense intelligence is specifically the enemy of the
sort of detached thinking that Schopenhauer calls pedantry. It
responds to the living moment, and in it thinking and feeling
are not two separate considerations. It is a capacity for modification of total behavior through experience, and its growth is
accompanied by a growing complexity of both moral and emotional living. Thus the more mature the theme of love in comedy, the higher its valuation of this quality of vital intelligence.

A word about the historical period with which I am concerned will conclude this chapter. While such areas of experience as love, courtship, and marriage are the constant subjects
of comedy, they are also the areas in which past ages and
conventions tend to survive most tenaciously. We are accustomed to thinking of the Renaissance as the point of origin of
an altogether new phase of Western culture, and so in fact it is.
But the many radical changes for which it is a collective and
convenient name did not all take effect at once in every sphere
of life. As Huizinga puts it: "The transition from the spirit of
the declining Middle Ages to humanism was far less simple
than we are inclined to imagine it. . . . the characteristic modes
of thought of the Middle Ages did not die out till long after
the Renaissance."[32] What concerns us directly here is one
aspect of the late medieval code of chivalry—a code which
combined the idea of love and heroism in an elaborate and
intricate pattern and which not only survived into the new age
but was even revived on the literary side in such romances as
the cycle of Amadis of Gaul. Even in its heyday, however, the
chivalric code was an ideal pastime or ritual rather than a true
reflection of a reality that was barbarous and violent. "The life

32. J. Huizinga, *The Waning of the Middle Ages* (London, Edward
Arnold, 1948), p. 297.

of aristocracies," to quote Huizinga further on the subject, "when they are still strong, though of small utility, tends to become an all-round game. In order to forget the painful imperfection of reality, the nobles turn to the continual illusion of a high and heroic life." Nevertheless, though it was "a cloak for a whole world of violence and self-interest," the chivalric ideal remained "a source of energy" as well. But even this could not be said of it when it survived in an age "of new forms of political and economic life (absolutism, capitalism), and new modes of expression (Renaissance)."[33] All its motive power gone, it then became one of those ideas which, like worn-out engines, can only act as brakes.

Thus modern comedy may be said to begin with the task of demolishing the medieval mode of thought wherever it obstructs the proper business of the new way of life. But it chiefly concentrates on the idea of love which it sees as not only a new or different but also a real value—not a ritual pastime confined to a limited circle but that necessary emotional quality of sexual relations and domestic life to which the ordinary man can and must aspire. Concentration on this new value of love is in fact intimately connected with an increasing confidence in the new individual. The process begins in literary history in the late sixteenth century and goes on beyond the middle of the nineteenth, as we observe comic heroes moving down the social scale from aristocratic or semi-aristocratic stations, through the condition of mere courtiers and gentlemen, down to footmen and foundlings, and then up again with the buoyant fortunes of the middle class to increasingly numerous and diversified positions of importance. And in the midst of all their prosperity comedy considers them fortunate in no greater respect than that of having discovered and realized the good fortune of love.

To summarize in this way is necessarily to oversimplify and

33. Ibid., pp. 69, 66, 46.

perhaps also to convey the suggestion that the theme of English comedy remains unchanged over a period of three centuries. Nothing can be farther from my intention, as I hope to make clear in the following chapters in which I trace the development of a tradition and not the rigid outlines of an unchanging formula. Here I can only say that the antagonists of the new freedom and the new love are not always the ghosts of medieval thought. Even at the outset they are the chief but not the only adversaries, and before long we find comic writers questioning, in their defense of love, that very modern culture which had first brought it forth. And at the end of the period, in a writer like Henry James, love again becomes an idea that may well recall Huizinga's picture of medieval chivalry: an elaborate ritual among choice spirits, a heroic but empty form that is no longer a motive power and a real value but itself now a great and dying illusion.

Chapter 2

Shakespeare's Comedy of
Love and Honor

The idea that "the play is the thing" needs more qualification
or clarification in comedy than in other kinds of drama. A
comic play reveals its importance and even its true nature only
in terms of what it is played against. Often in fact there is no
play, no agon, except what might be called the play of the
foreground against the background. The background may be
bodily incorporated into the action or it may be assumed and
hinted at in less overt ways. But without this explicit or implicit opposition, comedies remain stories without dramatic
conflict and hence without any interest except the superficial
one of surprise and suspense at the level of events and happenings.

As I suggested at the end of the last chapter, the ideas and
value systems—"the characteristic modes of thought"—of the
Middle Ages lie behind Shakespeare. In the foreground are the
many complicated realities of contemporary life and experience. John F. Danby, in *Shakespeare's Doctrine of Nature*,[1]
has demonstrated with great insight in what manner the clash
between the two enters into the actions of some of Shakespeare's tragedies. In the history plays the nature and importance of this clash is or at least should be almost self-evident.
But in some of the comedies the same sort of clash, though

1. John F. Danby, *Shakespeare's Doctrine of Nature: A Study of
King Lear* (London, Faber and Faber, 1949).

not equally evident, is in reality still more important. What Viola says in *Twelfth Night* of the clown and his art—the "wise man's art," as she calls it—may well be said of Shakespeare's own comic art:

> He must observe their mood on whom he jests,
> The quality of persons, and the time.

Viola's lines are, of course, meant to refer to ordinary tact and propriety, to the sort of judgment the clown must exercise in order to make his general license suit the specific occasion. But, in Shakespeare's case, to observe the "quality of persons, and the time" would mean something more important, something more like the art of which Hamlet speaks to the players. It would mean the art that shows "the very age and body of the time his form and pressure."

It is, indeed, the argument of this essay that if certain history plays (the second tetralogy) come to grips with one aspect of the new age in which Shakespeare wrote, certain comedies (*Much Ado* in particular) come to grips with another aspect of the same age—another aspect of the "form and pressure" of the same "body of the time"—and, furthermore, that the two achievements proceed from one and the same effort of the historical imagination. These plays, it is worth remembering at the outset, were written within a short space of each other in the closing years of the century, with *Much Ado* following immediately after the two parts of *Henry IV* and in turn followed just as quickly by *Henry V*. But the connection between them is not only one of proximate composition. Beneath the simple fact of chronology, the two works—one a historical drama and the other a "pure" comedy—reveal a relation that is far more interesting. It is a relation that stems from a specific stage of Shakespeare's development: his acquisition and exercise of an understanding that functions as a common insight into the nature of contemporary reality on the one hand and the possibilities of a truly contemporary comedy on the other. In discovering the quality of his time, Shakespeare, one can say, also discovered the comedy of the time.

Considered together, the two works do not merely reveal the relation between the historical and comic imaginations of the Renaissance, they seem almost to obliterate the line between Shakespeare's histories and comedies. *Henry IV,* at least, has always figured in both columns, regarded by all as a history play which is at the same time as comic as any comedy. This mixture of comic and serious parts has created a problem for Shakespearean critics, a problem pertaining equally to *Much Ado.* Having discussed this difficulty in general terms in the preceding chapter, I need not labor the present instance in order to show how it rests on a fanciful assumption concerning the nature of the comic and, in particular, its supposed incompatibility with anything serious. This further resemblance between the history play and the comedy can be used instead to make a more interesting point. For though both plays have their serious parts (to preserve the terminology for the moment), the nature of these parts—the nature of the seriousness —is not the same. This difference between them will become clear and meaningful, as will other differences to be discussed later, if we remember that the realities of the new age with which the two plays deal are not the same but that each is concerned with a different aspect of the new reality. Thus both plays can be seen as comedies, not primarily because of any similarities in the interests that occupy the foreground of their respective actions, but rather because they play these interests against a certain kind of common background, because in fact to a large extent this play or interplay *is* their action, and because it is thus and in no other way that they seek to grasp and define the form and pressure of the age.

The background or the aspect of the medieval "modes of thought" most directly relevant here is simply the code or convention of love and honor. But before discussing how this background enters into the actions of the mature histories and

comedies and the role it plays, it is useful to first turn briefly
to some of the earlier comedies as well as the first historical
tetralogy. The earliest comedies of Shakespeare, like the later
ones, are comedies of love. But they are immature—a combination, as most readers would judge, of pastiche and prentice
work. A reader might in fact go so far as to regard them as a
rather pointless mélange of "tiresome jokes about horns, obscure topical allusions, a far-fetched plot, incredibly credulous
characters, [and] careless finishing off."[2] Yet, given a reader
who is unsympathetic enough, precisely the same phrases can
be applied to some of the later comedies as well. Which is to
say that if plays like *Love's Labour's Lost, The Two Gentlemen of Verona,* and *The Taming of the Shrew* are to be considered immature, we must have some better idea of what
comprises their immaturity. To begin with, these plays share
with the later comedies not only the general theme of love but
also certain more specific situations and character types—the
situation, for instance, in which the claims of love conflict
with those of friendship; the mutually combative situation of a
pair of witty lovers; or the character of the shrew, the girl who
is unmarriageable because she is notoriously set against all
ideas of love and marriage. More important, however, is what
can be called the element of parody or burlesque, the attack
on conventions of both love and literature, which these plays
share with the later comedies as well.

It is in fact in this element of parody that we can see most
clearly the weaknesses of the early comedies as well as their
great interest for us regarding what was to come later. The
interest is essentially of the sort we find in the earliest writings
of subsequent comic writers—the interest of Jane Austen's
"Love and Freindship," for instance, or Fielding's *Shamela.*
All these are works which, whatever their relative merit and

2. *The Observer,* 24 July 1955, quoted in John Russell Brown,
Shakespeare and His Comedies (London, Methuen, 1957), p. 12.

mutual distinctions, strike us as being alike in that they are not works of comedy so much as works of necessary comic apprenticeship. Their interest is in the critical testing of certain conventions of love which seem ridiculous and false to the writer concerned and which he also finds readily available in the shape of equally false literary works and conventions. In these early works we see a new intelligence at work—but only negatively, only for the joy and pleasure of its own first exercise, only to demolish the false, but not as yet to substitute the true in its place.

Thus if we say that the early comedies are immature, we do not mean this in any narrowly technical sense, as if to say that Shakespeare had not yet learned to draw character, to write dialogue, or to manage a scene or a plot. No doubt this sort of immaturity exists in his early work, but we find a more basic or at least more important type as well. For it is not as though Shakespeare aims too high and falls too short, laboring after a conception too difficult for him to realize at this stage. It is rather the comic conception itself that is slight and insufficient. This can be seen in many ways, suggested of course by our knowledge of Shakespeare's own fuller conception in some of the later comedies. Thus, for example, although other literary styles are parodied effectively enough even at this early stage, they are not only parodied but also to some extent imitated. Or consider the motif of the shrew, the girl whose humor is to awe and scatter instead of attracting suitors. In *The Taming of the Shrew* Shakespeare is content to leave the shrew as much a personal idiosyncratic type as she was in his source. Or again, if Biron and Rosaline, the famous early avatars of Benedick and Beatrice, seem to us dabs of comic characterization rather than the comic characters they were to become later, at least part of the reason lies in the fact that Shakespeare uses them negatively, for purposes of parody, but does not at the same time develop their motivation in an equally novel but positive direction. Indeed, the inadequacy of the comic idea becomes most apparent in precisely these places where the various styles of love and modes of marrying or not marrying—of winning or losing the labor of love—are seen as somehow false and therefore as fit materials for parody, but where there is no corresponding conception of any alternative styles, modes, or motivations: the places where cultural and literary conventions are tested and judged but not supplanted.

The one thing most obviously missing here is a firm idea of the reality as opposed to the mere convention of love—the sort of idea that Shakespeare was to introduce into his later comedy, *Much Ado* in particular. And it is the absence of this idea that leaves the insights and materials of the early comedies fragmented, unable to be galvanized into a comic action. It is in fact interesting to consider Shakespeare's attempts at this stage to unify his comedies, for he did make at least two marked and distinct ones: he attempted to adapt the plot of romance to comedy, and he imitated the plots of Latin comedy. The curious thing about these two attempts is that they point in opposite directions. For while romance brought Shakespeare the burden of the medieval world, putting him in touch with its forms and value systems, the recourse to Latin comedy represented a way of breaking out of this same world of the immediate past. Of course, Shakespeare was not alone in seeking fresh perspectives in the classics; the whole world of Renaissance thought was turning to them in an effort to free itself from the dead hand of medievalism. But though classicism could help in breaking the intellectual grip of the immediate past, it could not by itself ensure an understanding of the present. As Huizinga puts it, though classical forms were "an indispensable support in the process of cultural renovation" that we call the Renaissance, they "never were its moving power. The soul of Western Christendom itself was outgrowing medieval forms and modes of thought that had become shackles."[3]

Shakespeare's comedies are deeply implicated in this "process of cultural renovation," a process involving not only the testing or discarding of the historically obsolete but also the grasping of that which has newly come into being. And this in its turn involves some understanding of the fundamental "moving power" of the new culture, the secret of its energy. It is this fullness of insight, indispensable to the historical and the comic imaginations alike, that Shakespeare displays increasingly through the course of the second historical tetralogy. The early histories contain fragmentary intuitions in this direction but remain, by and large, chronicle plays, narratives of royal succession and of the rights and wrongs of kings judged according to either the superficial demands of the Tudor propaganda line or a universalized form of feudal political morality. The second cycle reveals by comparison an altogether different order of the historical imagination: though set in a remoter period, these plays are addressed directly to contemporary political and social realities. In them Shakespeare comes to grips with his time and discovers its "form and pressure." He apprehends at one stroke, as it were, both the common (and comic) ground swell of modern history and the historical basis of modern comedy.

There is a passage in *2 Henry IV,* III.i, that speaks of

> . . . the nature of the times deceased;
> The which observed, a man may prophesy,
> With a near aim, of the main chance of things
> As yet not come to life, which in their seeds
> And weak beginnings lie intreasured.
> Such things become the hatch and brood of time.

Like the other speeches about time and necessity in the second

3. Huizinga, *Waning of the Middle Ages,* p. 307.

tetralogy, this one has both the character of a general statement and a specific, highly limited reference within its strict
dramatic context. It is made by the Earl of Warwick in answer
to a question raised by Henry IV as to how Richard, Henry's
predecessor, could predict so accurately at the moment of his
downfall the troubles that now beset Henry himself. Shaken as
always by the merest suspicion of rebellion—something his
own conscience is burdened with—the sleepless King finds himself in a troubled and indecisive mood, reminiscing and mar-
veling about the events of the recent past: the time "not ten
years gone" when Richard was king and the powerful Northumberland was his great friend, and then two years later when
Northumberland joined hands with Henry to overthrow Richard and "toil'd in my affairs / And laid his love and life under
my foot." But the wheel at last has come full circle, and what
Richard foretold has come to pass—Northumberland, once
false to Richard, is now up in arms against Henry himself.

Henry's speech itself is not, of course, a mere review of a
decade's events; it too is in the nature of a general comment
on the way in which things work out in life. With its heavy
accent on "the book of fate" and "the revolution of the
times"—on "how chances mock, / And changes fill the cup of
alteration"—it is a reflection on the fickleness of fortune and
the many ironies of the wheel that proverbially turns but does
not move. Warwick's answering speech likewise contains a
meaning that goes well beyond the immediate situation. Both
are in a sense statements of inevitability, but Henry's sense of
historical inevitability is not so much historical as personal,
moral, and superstitious. To this extent it may in itself be seen
as a throwback to the dominant view of "the times deceased"
rather than a sign of those coming to life. It regards history as
full of changes but capable of no change, as essentially static
underneath its repetitive cyclical movements. According to
this view, action and ambition can only be evaluated ultimately as varieties of vanity and delusion.

The Warwick speech counters this wheel-of-fortune view of history, emphasizing not inevitability but necessity, including the necessity of action, voluntary or otherwise. In the midst of his reflections on fate and futility, the King himself has acknowledged how, though he had no conscious intention of usurping the throne, "necessity so bow'd the state / That I and greatness were compell'd to kiss." Roused from his temporary mood of indecisiveness and foreboding, he now meets the present emergency in the same spirit:

> Are these things then necessities?
> Then let us meet them like necessities.

The difference between the two views, however, does not lie primarily in the degree to which they promote or hinder activism in a moment of crisis. Nor is it entirely a question of considering or refusing to consider the morality of individual acts, including the acts dictated by personal interest and ambition. There is a more basic difference which concerns the meaning of historical change itself, a difference most clearly revealed by the two contrasted metaphors. For Warwick, as revealed by the lines quoted above, does not see history as only possessing the impersonality and amorality of a natural process; he sees it as a real process, a process of real change. Historical time should not be likened to a wheel showing either the deceptive contrast of the half circle or the true and complete likeness of the full. The connections and changes of history are far more real and complicated: old times do die, but then their death becomes the seed of the succeeding age. This new age is thus both related to and yet different from the old one; it is an age whose main features, though new and alive, must yet be defined by some reference to those of "the times deceased."

This view, struggling here to extricate itself from older concepts and become independently articulate, governs the historical imagination that we find at work in the second tetralogy. As fused into the whole dramatic body of the work, it is of course nothing so detached and self-conscious as a "view." It functions rather as an insight and an energy, playing its special part in the perception, invention, and ordering of the materials—creating this very sense of historical necessity as a process that involves numerous diverse persons and personages and yet is larger and more impersonal than all of them; constantly projecting the political, social, and cultural realities of the new age against the background of the more or less immediate past; accenting everywhere and in many ways not what is right or wrong but what is of the past (and therefore illusory) or of the present (and therefore real); holding the deed up against the accompanying rhetoric or incongruous habit of thought; and at times, especially in moments of crisis such as the one in *2 Henry IV* discussed above, revealing with some subtlety the confusion of action and belief confronting actors in a period of historical change.

Before turning to the sort of drama implied by such an imagination—or at least that part of the drama which concerns us specifically in this study—it would be useful to support my general preface with a few concrete points. To begin with, while the work as a whole is concerned more with the present than the past—perhaps not directly with the past at all—the movement of the plays from *Richard II* to *Henry V* nevertheless seeks to convey the sense of a movement from the past to the present. Indeed, what we have to notice is the particular sort of emphasis given to this overall sense of movement—a movement that takes us from the elaborate ritual of the lists at Coventry, through various interlocking feudal uprisings and internecine conflicts, to the great war against a foreign power at Agincourt; from a king presiding over a tournament to another moving through the camp of war, checking on the morale of common soldiers; or, to take another point of view, from Richard's opening line: "Old John of Gaunt, time-honour'd Lancaster," with its stilted backward-looking piety, to the natural and breezy freedom of the youthful King's address to his newly-won bride in the last scene of *Henry V:* "O Kate, nice customs curtsy to great kings. Dear Kate, you and I cannot be confined within the weak list of a country's fashion: we are the makers of manners, Kate."

What all this gives us, however, is not so much the contention between the old and the new as the emergence or definition of the new against the background of the old. Richard himself, with whom the cycle begins, is in no complete sense a figure of the past, a paradigmatic medieval king. Far from it. In his actions, in what he does and is responsible for, and in what is done to him—in his historical role—he represents the present only a little less fully than Bolingbroke or even Henry V. Most characters in these plays are in fact contemporary figures, although most of them are also compromised, in varying degrees and ways, by the surviving ethos of the past. None quite merge with the background of medievalism; all stand at some distance from it and are measured and placed in terms of this distance. Thus the background itself is created less through action than through the ceremonial and spiritual accompaniments of action and, of course, through the rhetoric of some of the key figures. For instance, in *Richard II* the dying Gaunt, a "prophet new inspired," is moved by the signs he detects of shame and dishonor in store for the country to make his famous speech. Yet the speech is not remembered for its denunciation of present events nor for its prophecy of a worse future—its main purpose as well as half its substance— but rather for the contrasting picture it draws of a garden-like England of the past; and it is rightly remembered as such, for that is where its power lies. The "time-honour'd" Gaunt's rhetoric is in fact particularly appropriate for evoking this image of a picturesque medieval England—the "scepter'd isle," the "womb of royal kings" renowned for "Christian service and true chivalry."

In this respect, as the plays move forward there is a steady

diminution of emphasis in one direction and a steady increase
in the other. As the substance of the times takes greater shape,
the shadows of the past recede. Consider Richard's own famous speech at the time of his return from Ireland to face the
Bolingbroke-Northumberland uprising. In the greatest crisis of
his reign, he is content to do nothing more than invoke super-
natural agencies and earth's mystical powers to come to his
aid. When his counselors' urge for more practical measures, he
only replies: "God for his Richard hath in heavenly pay / A
glorious angel: then, if angels fight, / Weak men must fall, for
heaven still guards the right." This reliance on divine sanctions
to the point of total paralysis of the will can be contrasted
with Henry IV's quick recovery of a sense of reality and practical urgency in the similar situation already discussed. But the
real contrast comes later, in Act IV of *2 Henry IV,* where
Prince John first makes the defeat of the rebels doubly sure—
relying not only on the strength of his arms but even more on
a highly politic and plainly treacherous maneuver—and only
afterwards finds time to declare: "God, and not we, hath safely fought to-day." Or consider the many cases of single combat mooted through the succeeding plays. None actually takes
place, but in *Richard II,* though policy prevents the fight itself
at the last minute, a whole scene is devoted to the preceding
ceremonies, which are gone through to the last detail of prescribed form and solemnity. Compare this with Hal's challenge
to Hotspur—the challenge from a man who has "a truant been
to chivalry" to one most notable "now alive / To grace this
latter age with noble deeds." Although Hal's challenge has a
solemnity and even a seriousness of its own and is, like the
earlier meeting between Bolingbroke and Mowbray in *Richard
II,* foiled only through politic intervention, it is an impromptu
affair, relegated to the corner of a scene and on the whole
submerged in the more pressing business of war at Shrewsbury.
By the time we come to the end of *Henry V,* to Fluellen's
baiting of the boastful but wholly discreet Pistol and to the

King's challenge to a common soldier (with its inevitably complicated and "comic" aftermath), the whole idea of chivalric combat, of fighting for honor, has been reduced to a deliberate farce.

As the old forms lose their dignity and the erstwhile modes of thought their relevance, the shape and pressure of the new reality become all the more recognizable. No quick paraphrase of these, or of their emergence and consolidation through the tetralogy, is possible or necessary here. It will suffice to note a few points of obvious contrast. The present, as seen against the background of the past, is a time of self-service rather than "Christian service," of policy rather than chivalry—a time not for the observance of traditional forms but for the exercise of a new will, a new energy, and a new sense of freedom from precisely these same concepts and restraints of the past. Together with all this there goes also, of course, increased rapacity and even lawlessness. For all his weakness and pious backward-looking rhetoric, Richard himself reveals the workings of this new spirit; he is, as Gaunt knows and tells him, the "landlord" of England, not its king. His crusades lie toward Ireland. The brusque comment with which he dismisses Gaunt's death is apt enough: "His time is spent, our pilgrimage must be. / So much for that. Now for our Irish wars." Using the occasion to seize Gaunt's estate on the spot, he dismisses equally unceremoniously the protesting York (Gaunt's brother and another shadow from the past), who argues that by usurping Bolingbroke's inheritance Richard is taking away "from Time / His charters and his customary rights" and thereby undoing the very laws upon which his own title to kingship is based. Richard replies, "Think what you will, we seize into our hands / His plate, his goods, his money and his lands." Nor is the king alone in this; he is surrounded by lords and minions whom Bolingbroke describes as "caterpillars of the commonwealth." The concept of the caterpillar, as has often been noted, recurs in one way or the other throughout the tetral-

ogy. As the plays move forward in time, the caterpillar operations extend downward into the social fabric, until the whole
kingdom stands exposed to rapacity at the hands of not just
kings and counselors but many other sorts and conditions of
men, all of whom, as Gadshill puts it, "pray continually to
their saint, the commonwealth; or rather, not pray to her, but
prey on her, for they ride up and down on her and make her
their boots."

Just as the attitude expressed in the tetralogy toward this
great historical movement, its subject, is not simple but complex—ranging from satire at one end to something like a dis-
criminating but nevertheless glad acceptance at the other—so,
within its overall context, the possibilities for *drama* are many.
For such a presentation of history need not be merely panoramic: the past and present—background and foreground—
need not merely distance each other mutually. They can also
meet and contend with each other in an action or series of
actions which then become both historical and dramatic and
which, needless to add, can be invested with varying degrees of
moral and psychological interest. We are concerned here only
with the main comic action, but the conflict between the pressures of present reality and the assumptions still surviving from
"the times deceased" can create divisions and dramatic tensions which are other than comic. Consider, for instance,
Henry IV—the murderer of Richard II on the one hand and the
begetter of Henry V on the other—who provides, as it were,
the narrative link in the transition from the old to the new.
The drama of the change, however, is not reflected so much in
the facts of his career as it is in his divided consciousness (if
not divided conscience). Of the three kings he is in a sense the
least assured and self-confident, the least free of moral doubts
and scruples concerning his role. Even Richard can proclaim
confidently: "they well deserve to have, / That know the
strong'st and surest way to get"; and if he agonizes, it is not

over the validity of this principle but over his own weakness and failure when the principle goes against him. The same tenet is affirmed by the infinitely stronger, shrewder, and more successful Henry V. His reply to his father's "How I came by the crown, O God forgive" is wholly untroubled: "You won it, wore it, kept it, gave it me; / Then plain and right must my possession be." By contrast, Henry IV, while acting on this general principle, is at the same time constantly plagued by the hold of another, more moral consciousness. Hence his inner doubts and vacillations as he wavers between a sense of guilt and an assertion of righteousness, shifts from policy to conscience and back again, and is obsessed with the idea of the Holy Land which recommends itself to his conscience as a way of absolution and to his policy as a way of busying "giddy minds" with "foreign quarrels." He too is a weak character, but his weakness is a matter of this divided consciousness. His doubts are not all hypocrisy. A true instrument of the times, he is also a man stricken with a sense of the past.

Clearly this particular sense of the past is shown as independent of the past or present to the extent to which it involves a moral sense that the present actions and realities may contravene but which they do not for that reason invalidate. To this extent, then, the drama of historical change is judged in terms of a morality which is more or less absolute. This sort of attitude appears not only in the case of Henry IV's conscience but elsewhere too—as one possible aspect of an overall judgment. However, there are parts of the total work where the drama is seen in cultural rather than absolute moral terms, and these are the parts which, insofar as we can separate them, constitute the main comic action. In them we see a specific side of what Huizinga calls "the process of cultural renovation"—a process involving, among other things, the final overthrow of obsolete "modes of thought." "But thought's the slave of life, and life time's fool." These dying words of Hot-

spur, like the Warwick speech discussed earlier, have the character of a general statement; they can serve as a motto for the
comic action of these historical plays if we interpret
"thought" to mean the thought or concept most closely associated with the character of Hotspur—honor. This cultural concept, through the workings of time and of historical change,
has lost not only its supremacy but also its validity; its status is
now that of an irrelevant abstraction. Although, as the character of Hotspur shows, honor can still function as a conscious
value and even a conscious motive, its relation to culture can
never be what it was in the past. Once it served to order
cultural realities in the manner of a paradigm or ideal configuration; now *they* serve to mock it.

The comedy of *1* and *2 Henry IV* is built around this abstraction, and its chief actors are Falstaff, Hal, and Hotspur,
not just Falstaff alone. By the time we come to *Henry V,* the
comedy of honor is more or less played out. The new reality
has so completely established itself that the troublesome ghost
has rejoined the shadowy past that first produced it. Honor
may still be a common word, but it is now universally recognized as just a word. "What is honour? a word. What is in that
word honour? what is that honour? air." So Falstaff had to
catechize and prove the point earlier; now the point is so well
accepted that honor, meaningless even as a word, can be
claimed or disclaimed indiscriminately. Thus the Chorus introduces Act II of *Henry V* by blandly informing us:

> Now all the youth of England are on fire,
> And silken dalliance in the wardrobe lies:
> Now thrive the armourers, and honour's thought
> Reigns solely in the breast of every man:
> They sell the pasture now to buy the horse,
> Following the mirror of all Christian kings.

Not only does this speech recall some of the earlier tensions,
but its tongue-in-cheek tone makes clear how completely the

tensions have been resolved, how completely the concepts of self-service and Christian service, of foreign wars and crusades, are now identified. Likewise, it is not only the armorers who thrive; "honour's thought" is itself now indistinguishable from such thriving. For, as we learn from the Boy's straightforward commentary on the field of battle—a commentary anticipated by the above speech—it is the thought of freebooty that fires the zeal of the youth of England. Only a rare man and honest soldier like Williams would hesitate to call this "honour." When "the mirror of all Christian kings" himself observes that one could not "die any where so contented as in the king's company; his cause being just and his quarrel honourable," Williams replies curtly: "That's more than we know."

This and other instances in the same vein are simply the aftermath of the comedy that has gone before. The comic issue has already been resolved in the two preceding plays. At the end of *1 Henry IV* the issue, which is triangular, is more or less decisively settled at two of its three points. Hotspur is dead, Hal and Falstaff having each in turn "killed" him. With Hotspur out of the way at last, comedy turns in *2 Henry IV* to decide the remaining question between Hal and Falstaff.

The two farthest poles of the comedy of honor are, of course, Hotspur and Falstaff, one representing the principle of abstraction and the other the principle of reality; Hal stands halfway between the two. The representative qualities of Hotspur and Falstaff as well as their mutual opposition are fairly obvious and would call for little further discussion were it not for an objection that is often raised—an objection to the equation of the character of Hotspur with the idea of honor. It is true that Hotspur is described at various points in the play as "the king of honour" and "the theme of honour's tongue." But, so goes the argument, these descriptions cannot be taken at their face value; it is a mistake to see Hotspur as a knight of medieval gallantry if only because his motives are mixed, to say the least. In fact, the clue to his character lies less in his vaunted sense of honor than in his own words: "But in the way of bargain, mark ye me, / I'll cavil on the ninth part of a hair."

Yet if there is an objection to be raised on this score, if the analysis of the Hotspur-Falstaff conflict does require qualification, it seems to lie in the opposite direction. For while critics have questioned the equation of Hotspur with honor, it is the other equation—the total equation of Falstaff with the new cultural reality—that really raises questions. As for Hotspur, the objections are mistaken, and the mistake stems primarily from seeing the issue too much in terms of absolute morality and too little in terms of history. Thus, contrary to supposition, to say that Hotspur represents honor is not to regard him as the embodiment of an absolute value, uncompromised and uncompromising, but as the representative of a specific historical concept—a figure attempting to assert in "this latter age" one of the cardinal principles of an older and obsolete code. Even in its own time and proper setting, that code did not have the relation to reality that is assumed in the judgment disqualifying Hotspur from being its representative. Indeed, those who concede the historicity of Hotspur's character but still feel impelled to point to "the ninth part of a hair" inaccuracy in the portrait can only be said to labor under a Sir Galahad notion of medieval chivalry.

> This illusion of society based on chivalry curiously clashed with the reality of things. The chroniclers themselves, in describing the history of their times, tell us far more of covetousness, of cruelty, of cool calculation, of well-understood self-interest, and of diplomatic subtlety, than of chivalry. None the less, all, as a rule, profess to write in honour of chivalry, which is the stay of the world.[4]

4. Ibid., p. 56.

This hits the mark of Hotspur's private world almost as precisely as it does that of the late medieval world at large. Hotspur not only manifests this same combination of covetousness and calculation on the one hand and apparent dedication to a sense of chivalric honor on the other, but, like the medieval chroniclers and eulogists of chivalry themselves, he is not in the least troubled by the incongruity. Indeed he is hardly conscious of it. Of course, the incongruity or the contradiction is obvious to us, but then that is the main dramatic or comic point of the portrait. Not only we, but Hotspur's own contemporaries notice in him as a peculiarity, a personal idiosyncrasy, something that would have gone unnoticed in the past and blended harmoniously with the culture's idea of itself. When this happens, when an ideal is seen not as "the stay of the world" but as an aberration and a hindrance, then that ideal ceases to be an ideal and becomes a comic idea. Thus it is not surprising that Hotspur's famous speech about plucking up "drowned honour by the locks" should provoke the comment: "He apprehends a world of figures here, / But not the form of what he should attend." Hotspur is lost here, however temporarily, in a world of abstract figures or images, doubly so since that world itself is quite lost and irrecoverable even as an abstract configuration. This sense of abstraction twice removed from reality is in fact both the cause and the effect of Hotspur's exaggerated stance, his loud and extravagant rhetoric. What his wife says of him is right:

> . . . by his light
> Did all the chivalry of England move
> To do brave acts: he was indeed the glass
> Wherein the noble youth did dress themselves:
> . . . .
> He was the mark and glass, copy and book,
> That fashion'd others.

But it is right only because it comes after Hotspur's death and is cast in the past tense. It is a funeral oration for a fashion which has disappeared even as a fashion. In fact, postmortem sentiments aside, the very scene of Hotspur's death has made the fashion seem even more ridiculous than had the manner of his life and rhetoric.

The character chiefly responsible for showing up the absurdity of the ideal of honor—for showing up its irrelevance—is, of course, Falstaff. He does this through many well-known speeches on the subject and also through actions which deliberately parody honor and heroism. But the antithesis between Hotspur and Falstaff is expressed most profoundly through their antithetical imaginations: one rigid, stilted, and given to abstraction; the other flexible, vital, and constantly fastening upon the figures of this world rather than "a world of figures." Above all, Falstaff exercises his imagination to humor or deceive others, never himself. It is a practical and productive imagination. Hotspur when most fanciful is also the most isolated. Falstaff's fancy is the instrument whereby he lives in and off his society. His consciousness has little to do with the past and everything to do with the present and the future. This is the truth behind his fantastic insistence on his personal youthfulness and his instinct for always counting himself among the young. The "noble youth" who fashioned themselves after Hotspur, according to the funeral eulogy above, exist in the play only as an idea in the background. But the "youth" whom Falstaff inspires—and leads as well as misleads and bullies and cozens—are to be found everywhere. For all his false pretensions, the wilder his plans and stratagems, the more recognizable he becomes as a child of his age, unusual but authentic, his mind in closer touch with reality than even his huge commoner's body.

It is as easy for this commoner to "kill" the formidable Hotspur as it is necessary that he do so. Falstaff's "killing" of Hotspur in the penultimate scene of *1 Henry IV* is in fact a great piece of comic symbolism—an act that captures the es-

sence of comic action, of what comedy does and what it is
about. For while history may already have accounted for an
age, comedy must still grapple with its survivals. After the
great drama and the rousing encounter, the stage still remains
to be cleared finally and decisively. " 'Zounds, I am afraid of
this gunpowder Percy, though he be dead," Falstaff says before stabbing and carrying off the dead body. "Therefore I'll
make him sure." Even Hal's earlier, "real" killing of Hotspur
is, in a sense, part of the same process of "making sure." For
the emblem of honor that Hotspur wears when alive, the emblem of his identity, itself signifies that he is not one of the
living. As pointed out in Falstaff's catechism long before the
final battle, "But will it [Honour] not live with the living?
no. . . . Honour is a mere scutcheon."

Having jointly overthrown Hotspur, Hal and Falstaff must
face each other to settle the remaining question. Seen in one
way, since the old values have lost their pertinence, this is the
question of discovering new ones to be applied to the new
situation. Mature comedy always includes some such positive
effort, and indeed it is one of the attributes that distinguishes
comedy from the neighboring genres of burlesque, parody, and
satire. In the present case the question is decisively settled by
Hal's public rejection of Falstaff in the last scene of *2 Henry
IV*. Again, however, neither the question nor its resolution can
be understood clearly if we insist on values in any absolute
sense. The resolution in particular, to the extent to which it
strikes us as both right and inevitable, is right and inevitable
only in limited historical terms. For Falstaff, although an unmistakable representative of the new reality, is not that master
of it which he imagines himself to be. The mythical aspect of
his character, noted and written about in various ways by
many readers, derives from the sense he conveys of power to
bring about virtual impossibilities with little exertion and none
of the needed equipment. But since he functions in a land of

hard reality rather than one of myth and miracle, the impossibilities remain impossibilities, and we are led instead to note the incongruity between the scope of the man's imagination and the limits of his practical abilities and predilections—the incongruity between what he would grasp and what he is actually capable of grasping. On the one hand, there is the imagination of a master spirit of the age: daring and recklessly corrupt, prompting visions of an expansive destiny; on the other hand, the incorrigible pettiness, the total contentment with "small beer," the little thievings and cozenings, and above all the grossness—that open dedication to the flesh which Hal, in the pious language of the time, calls vanity. Falstaff's pettiness and grossness are so overwhelming that they make his daring and his ambition not just incongruous but almost unrecognizable. In the prodigal prince we can always see the future king, but not in the companion of his riot the future king's minister, military commander, or even chamberlain. Falstaff himself seldom distinguishes his ambition from his pursuits; but Hal, who does, snubs neither the one nor the other for itself, but the one because of the other. While the rejection speech reads like a sermon and a statement of conversion combined, what it does coolly underneath is to reject Falstaff's ambition, as unsupported so far by required and proven abilities.

It is not that Falstaff lacks virtue, for who in these plays really has that? What he lacks are the virtues—the virtues of success. Hal, who knows him better than anyone else and is the one person who berates him mercilessly, seldom even refers to his dishonesty, his unscrupulousness, his parasitism, or any other aspect of his true viciousness. Most of the famous speeches and epithets excoriate the man's grossness, and this grossness is repulsive to Hal because it sums up all that is contrary to the successful spirit of the age. It denotes not merely the absence of such minimal virtues as industry, sobriety, and a public front of honest respectability—of "conversations" that appear "wise and modest to the world," as John of Lancaster puts it in summing up the cause of Falstaff's banishment—but, more important, the absence of all equipment for true ambition such as stamina, self-discipline, and a sustained will. Falstaff himself seems to recognize this meaning of grossness when, after Shrewsbury, he appears to himself well-launched on the road to success and is moved to declare: "If I do grow great, I'll grow less; for I'll purge, and leave sack, and live cleanly as a nobleman should do." But of course the recognition is momentary, and if there is a change in Falstaff, it is certainly not a change in this direction. On the contrary, while the grossness remains and even increases, the only thing that grows less is the old appealing human quality of it. "If sack and sugar be a fault, God help the wicked! if to be old and merry be a sin, then many an old host that I know is damned." The early and most winning Falstaff may well have the right of weak human nature on his side and perhaps also the right of an older, less strenuous culture; he does not have the right of his own age. "Now, Hal, what time of day is it, lad?" are the very first words that he speaks, and indeed we realize in the end that he both knows and does not know the time of day. "What a devil hast thou to do with the time of the day?" as Hal replies, adding the particular article.

If anyone knows the time of day in its totality, it is Hal, the all-around hero of the histories. He combines Falstaff's instinctive sense of reality with Hotspur's conscious will to dominate it, and he can both act in accordance with its forces and give them the larger direction that they demand. Once Hal becomes king he even shows a Hotspur-like urge to gild reality, but, unlike Hotspur, he does so knowingly and purposefully, and not so much as to lose sight at any time of the substance underneath. Hotspur's picturesque values all lay on one side and his practical interests on the other: he lived in the past and functioned in the present. Henry V, on the other hand, attempts to draw from the present itself the sense of values to

heighten his present interests and experiences. He even seeks
to press the idea of honor itself into the service of such new
political values as patriotism and national unity. This attempt
to transfer usable emotions and sanctions of the past to the
present is one that every historical and comic hero makes. But
in the present case, the attempt is not sustained by the play
and is neither successfully nor perhaps sincerely made by the
hero.

The result in *Henry V* is a panoramic or epic drama accompanied by a small but constant strain of satire. On the main
subject of patriotism and national unity, for instance, the foreign campaign draws together representatives of all the prov-
inces of the realm as well as all sorts and conditions of men,
but the union remains superficial, limited, and negative. It is
the sort of unity, the unity of a modern bourgeois state, that
Melville describes by means of an extended metaphor in Chapter 163 of his allegorical novel *Mardi:* a mollusk-like confed-
eracy of individual self-sufficient units, each unconcerned with
the rest, with the whole body politic showing no common
purpose except when at war against a foreign body. Thus, as
though by logical development, Falstaff's spirit, now freed
from the burden of the comic battle against false heroism,
becomes in his survivors a spirit of unqualified practical cynicism. Pistol in particular appears as a well-accommodated and
wholly degraded reincarnation of the dead knight. In place of
Falstaff's fighting wit and leaping imagination he substitutes
the gibberish of his far-fetched rhetoric, but this has nothing
to do with his aims and ambitions, which are altogether as
petty and cynical as he himself. He not merely carries on some
of Falstaff's activities but improves on them in this sense. For
instance, Falstaff had his own parasitic relations with Hostess
Quickly; Pistol, who marries her, turns the relationship into a
shrewd and stable arrangement in other ways as well. "Look to
my chattels and my movables: / Let senses rule; the word is
'Pitch and Pay:' / Trust none." It is the same with the profit to

be reaped from the wars, both while they last and afterward. Falstaff's " 'Tis no matter if I do halt; I have the wars for my colour . . . I will turn diseases to commodity" is echoed by his practical heir as he exits finally toward the end of *Henry V:*

> Old I do wax; and from my weary limbs
> Honour is cudgelled. Well, bawd I'll turn,
> And something lean to cutpurse of quick hand.
> To England will I steal, and there I'll steal:
> And patches will I get unto these cudgell'd scars,
> And swear I got them in the Gallia wars.

In Falstaff these are aspects of a larger character and dramatic function; in Pistol, the whole man. It is to be accounted to Shakespeare's sense of the full significance of Falstaff's character as well as the true issues of comedy that, against his announced intention, he kept the old hero personally out of the historically stabilized and dramatically issueless world of *Henry V.*

Commenting on Pistol's exit at the end of the penultimate scene of *Henry V,* Dr. Johnson wrote: "The comic scenes of *The History of Henry the Fourth* and *Fifth* are now at an end, and all the comic personages are now dismissed. Falstaff and Mrs. Quickly are dead; Nym and Bardolph are hanged; Gadshill was lost immediately after the robbery; Poins and Peto have vanished since, one knows not how; and Pistol is now beaten into obscurity."[5] Pistol's being "beaten into obscurity" is, indeed, as good a sign as any of the stabilization of the new social order. The obscurity is proof that, while Pistol and those like him will continue to play their part in the world, the part will no longer have the interest or the importance of a comic role. In the absence of any opposing fictions, the facts can

5. *Samuel Johnson on Shakespeare,* ed. W. K. Wimsatt, Jr. (New York, Hill and Wang, 1960), p. 91.

only be themselves: normal, accepted, undramatic. Dr. Johnson's description, however, conveys the impression of a gradual thinning out of the comedy until the very end of *Henry V*.
This is not so. The break, and it is a sharp one, comes with
Hal's dismissal of Falstaff at the end of *2 Henry IV*. After this
there is no comedy, only its aftermath. Few of the comic
personages except Pistol have anything to do or say in the last
play of the tetralogy. Pistol, who is given a bigger part, is also
presented in a different light; by the end of the play he is
almost a different character. If he reminds us of the old comedy, it is only as something that has had its day.

A new comedy, however, begins immediately after Pistol's
exit and continues through the final scene of *Henry V*—the
more promising comedy of love. Here the results of historical
change can be exploited apart from the accompanying political
cynicisms and pieties we confront in historical drama proper.
Here in fact we see comedy moving into its proper realm—the
realm of cultural rather than political values. In this play, of
course, such comedy makes an abrupt and short-lived appearance, as Shakespeare allows his hero, newly triumphant in war,
only one scene in which to make both peace and love. The
young king has literally no time, even if he has the inclination,
to stand on ceremony. He speaks prose:

> I know no ways to mince it in love, but directly to say "I
> love you:" then if you urge me farther than to say "do
> you in faith?" I wear out my suit. . . . Marry, if you would
> put me to verses or to dance for your sake, Kate, why you
> undid me: for the one, I have neither words nor measure,
> and for the other, I have no strength in measure, yet a
> reasonable measure in strength. . . . I speak to thee plain
> soldier: if thou canst love me for this, take me; if not, to
> say to thee that I shall die, is true; but for thy love, by the
> Lord, no; yet I love thee too. And while thou livest, dear
> Kate, take a fellow of plain and uncoined constancy . . .

for these fellows of infinite tongue, that can rhyme themselves into ladies' favours, they do always reason themselves out again. . . . I know, Kate, you will . . . dispraise
those parts in me that you love with your heart: but, good
Kate, mock me mercifully . . . By mine honour, in true
English, I love thee, Kate: by which honour I dare not
swear thou lovest me; yet my blood begins to flatter me
that thou dost, notwithstanding the poor and untempering
effect of my visage. . . . O Kate, nice customs curtsy to
great kings. Dear Kate, you and I cannot be confined within the weak list of a country's fashion: we are the makers
of manners, Kate.

Thus concludes the final campaign of Henry V. In a discur-
sive and largely monological form, the speech gives us a résumé
of some of the motifs, even the very words, of Shakespeare's
three main love comedies. It recalls, for instance, Rosalind's
famous line: "men have died from time to time and worms
have eaten them, but not for love"; Beatrice's mockery and
"dispraise" of her lover even after he has won her; or Benedick's soldierly visage and much vaunted plainness of speech as
well as his attempt at sonneteering which he abandons with
the words: "Marry, I cannot show it in rhyme . . . I was not
born under a rhyming planet, nor I cannot woo in festival
terms."

The three comedies not only share but develop and dramatize the opposition between the new manners, the manners
that are in the making, and the "weak list" of outmoded fashion. They too regard fashion as false, as a matter of literary
convention, a poetical abstraction, and see the new manners as
somehow reflecting the true, unadorned, but nevertheless
strong fact of love—a fact at once less exalted and more important than its ceremonial alibi. Being love (rather than, say, the
matter of royal succession or courtly honor), it naturally
comes closer to the business and bosoms of ordinary men;

indeed, Shakespeare's comic heroes are already less than royalty. (Soon they will be only gentlemen and eventually just men.) The opposing fashion, however, is still a recognizably medieval fashion—be it expressed in the courtly love of an Orsino, the pastoral love of an Orlando, or even, ironically, the love of a real rustic like Sylvius. True, pastoralism itself began as a reaction against the fashion of courtly love, reflecting this same sense of dissatisfaction with its formalism and its complicated ritual. But far from becoming simple and natural, it merely continued the fashion of courtliness under the disguise (and added complication) of simple rusticity. An imitation of an imitation, it was in the end twice as poetical and therefore twice as removed from reality, from truth. The following piece of dialogue between Touchstone and the rustic Audrey states the case:

> *Aud.* I do not know what "poetical" is: is it honest in deed and word? is it a true thing?
> *Touch.* No, truly; for the truest poetry is the most feigning; and lovers are given to poetry, and what they swear in poetry may be said as lovers they do feign.

Of course, Touchstone himself speaks prose, as do for the most part the other opponents of feigning in love. Their prosaicness is comedy's answer to poetical love, just as the wit and intelligence of that prose are the weapons used to set aside the long-established abstractions of such love. Over sixty years later, in *The Rehearsal,* George Villiers was still making a dramatic manifesto of sorts out of a similar impulse, using almost the same words:

> Let's have, at least, once in our lives, a time
> When we may hear some reason, not all rhyme:
> We have these ten years felt its influence;
> Pray let this prove a year of prose and sense.

The "prose and sense" of modern love is what Shakespeare's

mature comedies are about. They are the first rehearsal of a theme that English comedy was to rehearse again and again for three centuries on a shifting historical and cultural stage.

Much Ado in particular can be regarded as the prototype of modern English love comedy. While its comic treatment of false love is as sharp and significant as that of the other two plays with which it is usually grouped—*As You Like It* and *Twelfth Night*—it alone provides a clear definition of the experience and value of real love, and provides this definition not only against the background of outmoded convention but also through an evaluation of opposed tendencies in the present reality itself. Consider, for instance, the heroines of the other two plays, Rosalind and Viola, who along with Beatrice of *Much Ado* partly represent and partly foreshadow some of the main qualities of almost all the subsequent heroines of English comedy. Included among these qualities is the sort of emotional intelligence that makes each heroine see through the effusions and sanctioned forms of poetical or otherwise unreal conventions of love. And yet, in the case of both Viola and Rosalind, there is a noticeable uncertainty right here, at the very center of their comic function. They are almost required to indulge the very forms that they parody. Thus within a single scene of *Twelfth Night* (I,v) Viola, representing her master's suit to Olivia, seems both to mock the convention of the languishing lover enslaved to a cruel mistress and to affirm it as an ideal of fidelity and perseverance that cannot fail of eventual success. Indeed, given her being in love with the same Orsino whose love for Olivia she must mock, this sort of uncertainty is inherent in Viola's role and makes her own love itself somewhat poetical in the end.

Rosalind's case is even more pointed. She too, while making the clearest case against the falsities of poetic pastoralism in love, nevertheless goes through the play wrapt in the conventions of the pastoral form. She herself realizes this when, upon hearing the lamentations of Sylvius, she rhymes: "Jove, Jove! this shepherd's passion / Is much upon my fashion," to which Touchstone adds: "And mine; but it grows something stale with me." While there is much sense in Rosalind's rebukes to the deluded Phebe, there is at least some in Jacques's comment upon Rosalind herself: "Nay, then, God be wi' you, an you talk in blank verse." Nor is there any difference between Phebe's "Who ever loved that loved not at first sight" and Rosalind's and Viola's equally instantaneous passions—to which they adhere not only faithfully but also somewhat uncritically—except, of course, that poor Phebe's first glance happens to fall on a disguised woman. Indeed, the heavy reliance on superficial disguise in the plot-machinery of these two comedies is itself a sign of the relative lack of sustained significance beneath the surface of their plots.

The clearest sign of this lack is seen, however, neither in the heroines nor in the plots but rather in the heroes with whom Rosalind and Viola are matched—Orlando and Orsino. By being as lifeless as the literary conventions they embody, they prevent the heroines' positive intuitions from crystallizing dramatically into a firm sense of new values. Of course, there are down-to-earth characters like Touchstone and Toby Belch, but they are in the comedies what Falstaff (not Hal) is in the histories; their down-to-earth business is simply not the whole business of comedy. Their marriage decisions, which is virtually all we see of their love, are in the nature of negative comments on the proceedings of the official lovers, and as such are valuable. But beyond this their love has no meaning. In fact, these short-circuit matrimonial arrangements have the effect of shutting out the positive side of the subject altogether. They do not represent the prose and sense of love, as we may be tempted to think, but a denial of love's existence as either an emotional experience or a cultural value. By contrast, in *Much Ado* the two main critics of love are themselves the two main lovers; therefore what we get in the total action of that play is not only ridicule of the old conventions but also simultaneously something of the new reality of love—something, indeed, that itself marks the beginning of a new and triumphant convention.

The relative inadequacy of *As You Like It* and *Twelfth Night* in this respect can also be approached in terms of the relation between these plays and their literary sources. The love stories of both depend heavily—a little too heavily in the end—on borrowed material. In *As You Like It,* while Shakespeare discarded the euphuism of the original and emphasized its pastoralism, he nevertheless followed Lodge's story with great fidelity, limiting his inventions to a few characters of little consequence aside from Jacques, Touchstone, and Audrey. In *Twelfth Night* he likewise took over the basic situation intact from his sources which, in this case, also supplied suggestions for such subsidiary characters as Toby, Maria, Feste, and Malvolio. But in *Much Ado* Shakespeare invented not only the two major characters of love, Beatrice and Benedick, but with them also their own appropriate love story. This stroke of invention enabled him to exploit as well as dominate his sources; it gave him the viewpoint and the dramatic footing needed for not merely testing but also supplanting the old conventions.

Thus it is not surprising that Charles T. Prouty, who has studied in great detail the relation of *Much Ado* to its sources, should have given us at the same time the most satisfactory analysis of the play as a love comedy—an analysis to which my own is indebted. To quote Prouty's conclusion briefly, Benedick and Beatrice "are not really enemies of love; they are enemies of the dreary conventions." Benedick "is not so much a scorner of women ('my custom, as being a professed tyrant to their sex') as he is a scorner of false emotion. When Pedro prophesies that one day Benedick will 'look pale with love,' it is not love but the conventional pallor of the lover which Benedick denies. . . . Benedick and Beatrice are interested in an emotion which is real and a relationship based on reality instead of convention. In other words," as Prouty sums up the argument, "Shakespeare's reinterpretation is basically a reaction to the ideas and characters of his sources."[6]

Yet it perhaps needs to be emphasized that this literary battle is not purely literary; it includes the question of history as well. Shakespeare's reaction to his sources is at the same time a reaction to the sort of culture represented in those sources, and his reinterpretation involves likewise a sense of the altered cultural reality—the new "quality of persons, and the time," the new manners shaking themselves loose from the weak list of fashion. We have already noted the summary dismissal of the conventional fashion of love in the last scene of *Henry V. Much Ado* gives us the comic process that lies behind that dismissal. Here too the wars are over and the gallants can turn at last to the business of love and marriage. Benedick, like Henry V, will have nothing to do with the prescribed forms. Yet, curiously enough, the very staunchness of his attitude becomes one of the means of dramatizing those forms within the play. His rhetoric is the rhetoric of convention turned against itself. "Will your grace command me any service to the world's end?" says Benedick, but *not* to his mistress; for it is not in love's service but to escape love that Benedick is willing and ready to undertake the most hazardous and wildly improbable missions:

I will go on the slightest errand now to the Antipodes that

6. Charles T. Prouty, *The Sources of Much Ado About Nothing* (New Haven, Yale University Press, 1950), p. 63. Even readers professedly unsympathetic to source approaches will no doubt find pp. 39-64 of the book richly rewarding. These pages constitute a more or less independent critical essay on the play. As the passage cited above shows, it is also one of those essays which, while concerned strictly with a single comic work or author, nevertheless carry implications relevant to any general discussion of comedy. In this it is comparable to Mary Lascelles's study of Jane Austen referred to in Chapter 1 above.

you can devise to send me on; I will fetch you a tooth-picker now from the furthest inch of Asia, bring you the length of Prester John's foot, fetch you a hair off the great Cham's beard, do you any embassage to the Pigmies, rather than hold three words' conference with this harpy.

This anti-fashion is a fashion too—a defense through total parody that must itself be discarded eventually. But in the meantime it brings to life within the Benedick-Beatrice story the sort of background against which that story is enacted.

The conventional forms and rhetoric put to an inverted use by Benedick are, of course, used "straight" by some of the other characters. In the very first scene, for example, Don Pedro, having first reassured Claudio on the matter-of-fact question of Hero's financial expectations, puts this practical aspect to one side and goes on to apostrophize Claudio as one who will be "like a lover presently / And tire the hearer with a book of words." In Claudio's case the incongruity is not merely rhetorical; it extends to the very role he plays. Unlike Benedick, whose attitude toward the conventions is never in any doubt, Claudio is something of a dramatic shuttlecock. His motivation is fixed and simple, in fact quite crude. But his attitudes are mixed and apt to change direction, swinging quite freely between the most down-to-earth realities on the one hand and the most irrelevant abstractions of convention on the other. For one thing, he consciously plays the role of lover as a *role.* As Benedick points out: "He was wont to speak plain and to the purpose, like an honest man and a soldier; and now is he turned orthography; his words are a very fantastical banquet, just so many strange dishes." This role is obviously one that takes Claudio right back into the weak list of outmoded fashion. Insofar as he attempts to formalize love, to give it at least for a time the status of a detached ritual, he becomes identified with the past.

As for Claudio's motivation, it has more to do with the

present (and even the future) than with the past. Saying this might seem to be a mistake about Claudio's love comparable to the one noted earlier concerning Hotspur's honor, for by itself the businesslike aspect of Claudio's marriage disqualifies him as little from being the representative of conventional love as "the ninth part of a hair" bargaining disqualifies Hotspur from representing conventional honor. The incongruity is in each case the incongruity of convention itself. In "the actual practice of feudal society," to quote C. S. Lewis on the subject, "Marriages had nothing to do with love, and no 'nonsense' about marriage was tolerated. All matches were matches of interest."[7] This, however, is not Claudio's position. If it were, Claudio would hardly strike us as the unpleasant, almost deliberately hypocritical character that most readers have felt him to be. Marriage and love are not for him two separate issues—marriage for the sake of interest and love for its own sake. Rather, he determines to love what he is to marry and marry only that which is to his interest. Thus for all its surviving ceremonial and rhetorical trappings, love itself becomes as prudential as only marriage had been in the past. In this Claudio represents a marked tendency of the new bourgeois culture. While marriages "had been arranged for financial reasons in the Middle Ages," as L. C. Knights points out in *Drama and Society in the Age of Jonson*, "the proportion of economic marriages increased in the sixteenth century." The ancient system of dowry became one of the widely recognized and practiced means of enrichment in an age constantly devising new ways of getting rich quickly. One of the results was a cultural situation in which love and passion became increasingly identified with the new lust for wealth—a situation commented upon, as Knights points out, by a variety of contemporary men of letters, and perhaps best summed up by Ben

7. C. S. Lewis, *The Allegory of Love: A Study in Medieval Tradition* (Oxford, Clarendon Press, 1936), p. 13.

Jonson's designation of Lady Pecunia in *The Staple of News* as "the Venus of the time and state."[8] To the extent, then, to which Claudio's motivation stems not from the separation of love and interest as in the medieval code, but from the commercialization of love implied by their equation, he reflects his own times and also foreshadows the broad theme of prudential love in a wide range of future writers from the sentimental dramatists through Fielding and Jane Austen to Henry James.

Thus each of the two love plots of *Much Ado* can be seen as providing an independent variation on the same comic theme: the interplay between the background of old abstractions and the foreground of new realities. But the two plots are not at all independent, for, like the comedy in the historical tetralogy, the comedy of *Much Ado* also involves a triangular issue. Jointly posed against past convention, the two love stories are posed against each other over the question of present reality itself, and the third point of the action is again concerned with the definition of a new sense of values. This sense, uncertain in the political world of the histories, is both strong and convincing here. To make the experience of love plausible is by no means as easy a literary task as we are apt to imagine; English literature in particular can boast of only a handful of truly successful love stories. For all its limitations, the story of Beatrice and Benedick must be counted as one of that handful. In the face of long accustomed abstraction or mere trifling sentimentalities on the one hand and crude realities on the other, to forge with a light but sure touch the expression of a love that makes itself felt both as real in substance and superior in value—this is what Shakespeare achieves through Beatrice and Benedick. This is his pioneering contribution to the literature of modern love.

True, this love has none of the intensity or anguish or time-

8. L. C. Knights, *Drama and Society in the Age of Jonson* (London, Chatto and Windus, 1937), pp. 125-26, 122; also Chapter 3, "New Elements in the National Life," pp. 96-139.

less quality of high passion. But this is the definition, almost
the condition, of its being; it is in no sense the mark of a
special destiny, a rare experience in a world where all men
marry but only a happy or unhappy few can love. It is something possible in its world and time, not in spite of them. To
recognize this, however, is one thing; to deny all quality of
emotion to the sort of love represented by Beatrice and Benedick is quite another. Interestingly, a comparable charge is
made against Jane Austen's heroes and heroines, and for some
of the same reasons—among them the fact that the true emotional quality of their relationship also involves, as does the
case of Beatrice and Benedick, the exercise of an intelligence
that is generally assumed to betoken the absence of all true
emotion. Yet it is plain that, given the comic situation, none
but false emotion could exist without the accompanying intelligence, so that the exercise of intelligence takes nothing
away from but rather authenticates the emotional quality of
the relationship.

While this subject will be pursued somewhat further in the
chapter on Jane Austen, it is interesting here to suggest a more
concrete comparison—a comparison between the story of Beatrice and Benedick and that of Elizabeth and Darcy in Jane
Austen's *Pride and Prejudice.* Each story, to begin with, is
supported by a subsidiary love story that concerns two highly
eligible but obviously limited and rather superficial persons.
These two fall in love so quickly, in such a predictable and
straightforward manner, that they act as a foil to the main
characters—suggesting by contrast the difficulty as well as the
deeper character of *that* love, throwing into relief the process
of development and discovery involved in it, highlighting, in a
word, its quality as an experience. At the outset, Beatrice and
Benedick, like Elizabeth and Darcy, are rated highly as characters of wit and intelligence but poorly in terms of their emotional possibilities. And in this estimate they themselves
happily concur. They are drawn to each other without being

conscious of the fact and long before they can bring themselves to acknowledge it. Thus Beatrice's first words, which are an inquiry after Benedick and a revelation of her interest in him, are also sincere in their mockery of the gentleman. Equally sincere is the fun she makes of the messenger's reply reporting the high esteem Benedick has earned for himself. She herself cannot at this stage distinguish her interest in Benedick from her almost professional sportiveness, but we already suspect what she will openly acknowledge much later in the play: "others say thou dost deserve, and I / Believe it better than reportingly"—which is to say in her heart. Likewise Benedick, having first dismissed Beatrice as "Lady Disdain" in the opening scene, can answer Claudio's praise of Hero soon after with the half-sporting, half-serious words: "there's her cousin, an she were not possessed with a fury, exceeds her as much in beauty as the first of May doth the last of December."

However, what one might call the pride or prejudice theme of *Much Ado* finds full expression only later in the play through the inner discovery and development of the protagonists. Of course, the pride and prejudice or disdain that keeps the lovers from attaining self-knowledge and knowledge of their love is not mutually induced; it is more a consequence of their common reaction to convention, to what the world expects them to do. But this reaction of mutual disdain affected by Beatrice and Benedick is itself comic. Indeed, as already suggested, it is an inverted form of the same fashion which it seeks to oppose. It too shows the workings of that ultimate villain who is identified, mainly by virtue of garbled conversation, in that uproarious scene where the Watch are led to believe that they have run him to earth at last through the happy chance of overhearing Borachio and Conrade: "this fashion," the "deformed thief," who soon becomes personified as "one Deformed," the wearer of a lock and the well-known offender of long standing. But though the Watch succeed eminently in capturing the two flesh-and-blood villains, the elusive offender escapes their grasp. He is in fact beyond apprehension, except by the best intelligence of his intended victims.

And yet even the intelligence of Beatrice and Benedick has to be aided and abetted. *Much Ado* is a play of many happy ironies, of things coming to light through the least expected means. The example of the Watch clearing up the muddle their betters have made is well known: "what your wisdoms could not discover, these shallow fools have brought to light." In the same spirit, it takes a sportive plot to make Beatrice and Benedick see through the blind wall of their own sportiveness, a deliberate deception to undo their unconscious self-deception, and a false report to reveal the true state of affairs. What the plotters achieve is not the inducement of love, as they imagine, but only its discovery by the lovers. Thus the common theme of the two soliloquies in which the lovers modestly examine themselves is pride—or that same anti-fashion which has so far obscured their mutual love. In Beatrice's words:

> What fire is in mine ears? Can this be true?
> Stand I condemn'd for pride and scorn so much?
> Contempt, farewell . . .
> . . . .
> And, Benedick, love on; I will requite thee,
> Taming my wild heart to thy loving hand.

And Benedick echoes: "Love me! why, it must be requited. I hear how I am censured: they say I will bear myself proudly."

Nothing would be more false than to suggest that Beatrice's and Benedick's self-discoveries have the effect of transforming them out of recognition. In a sense they never stop being their old selves. But in Benedick in particular, we notice a new seriousness following his soliloquy which is gradually harmonized with the rest of his personality. It is this inner development rather than any mechanical sense of loyalty to Beatrice that sets him apart from his two erstwhile companions after the denunciation of Hero. Consider the following piece of dialogue in V, i:

> *Claud.* We had like to have had our two noses snapped off with two old men without teeth.
> *D. Pedro.* Leonato and his brother. What thinkest thou? Had we fought, I doubt we should have been too young for them.
> *Bene.* In a false quarrel there is no true valour.

Claudio and Pedro are still jesting, twitting two bereaved old men at their back for the feebleness of their age. In spite of all that has happened, they continue to be what Antonio has just called them: "fashion-monging boys."

Not so Benedick. There is much truth in his simple declaration after his self-examination: "Gallants, I am not as I have been." Although Leonato, who "knows" what the change signifies, responds in the true spirit of convention: "methinks you are sadder," the Benedick we now see is not a sadder but a *happier* and a wiser man. A true comic hero, he has realized, despite the promptings of fashion and anti-fashion, a relationship and a value which, unlike conventional love, are proof against all "quips and sentences and . . . paper bullets of the brain." As he declares in the very last scene of the play: "In brief, since I do purpose to marry, I will think nothing to any purpose that the world can say against it; and therefore never flout at me for what I have said against it; for man is a giddy thing, and this is my conclusion."

Chapter 3

The Inverted Abstractions of
Restoration Comedy

The trouble with the immoral drama of the Restoration period is not its immorality but rather its lack of dramatic quality. The bulk of Restoration comedy involves little beyond a flat exemplification of a value system or a philosophy which, in its turn, rests on a set of remarkably uncomplicated and unexamined assumptions. No values or attitudes can be said to emerge from it since the condition for such emergence—the condition of enquiry, of conflict, of dramatic testing and endorsement—forms no part of its design. Of all British drama, Restoration comedy is the least tendentious. Unlike sentimental comedy, which succeeded it in popular favor, it does not even resort to the crude device of special pleading; it takes its case for granted and engages for the most part in an undramatic illustration of that case.

This, of course, is not strictly true of every play written from the time of Etherege to that of Farquhar. The relation to sentimental comedy just alluded to provides one significant criterion of distinction. It is a relation with which the present essay will be extensively concerned, both implicitly and explicitly. It also happens to be a relation which, I think, is often misunderstood. A common view maintains, for instance, that Restoration comedy begins with a deliberate and total exclusion of anything remotely resembling sentimentality and yields the stage to sentimental comedy so gradually that no characteristic attitudes of the latter are visible before Farquhar (or perhaps, as some would suggest, Congreve). This can be both true and misleading—misleading, as I shall attempt to show, mainly because of the relation that is supposed to exist between the underlying values and attitudes of these two kinds of comedy. Here it is enough to point out that the sentimental strain of Restoration comedy exists, inevitably, from the outset; it can be seen not only in Congreve but also in Etherege, and in Wycherley more than in Farquhar. More to the point, it is only in an exceptional play (chiefly in Vanbrugh's *The Relapse*) that the sentimental attitude is properly brought into play—that is, brought into some sort of conflict with the more characteristic Restoration attitudes and values—and thereby utilized to create the kind of dramatic interest which, however limited in significance, nevertheless represents a quality all too often lacking in the comedies of the period. Likewise, other plays bring another kind of conflicting perspective to the usual materials of Restoration comedy, the most notable example of which is Wycherley's *The Country Wife*. These, one can say, work entirely within and even uphold the assumptions of Restoration comedy. But they also introduce into this world of uniformly accepted and ratified convention some element of an alien nature—perhaps nothing more important than a small but intractable fact or some thought or act of natural emotion. The fact may finally be brushed aside as irrelevant and the emotion judged and stamped as naive; but to the extent to which they are brought into play against the governing attitudes and assumptions, we find contrived again situations of limited but genuine dramatic interest.

Eventually we must turn to these qualified and qualifying examples of Restoration comedy, but first it is necessary to clarify some of the above generalizations. Thus, even at the risk of some repetitiousness, this essay will have to be written in two parts: first a general discussion and then, from that vantage point, a detailed analysis of a few distinguished plays.

One might as well begin with a reference to Charles Lamb's well-known Elia essay, "On the Artificial Comedy of the Last Century." Lamb's view of the world of Restoration comedy as a "Utopia of gallantry," a "fairy land"—a place of "escape from the pressures of reality"—is no doubt highly fanciful. Yet the view, or at least the argument used to support it, can by no means be dismissed as wholly erroneous. It rests in fact on two more or less distinct observations, and in advancing it Lamb seems to me both right and wrong at the same time. On the one hand, Lamb insists on the sameness of these plays—not just the family likeness between one play and the next, but the essential identity of the actions, motives, and attitudes of the characters within each play. With "few exceptions," as he puts it, the characters of Restoration comedy, "male or female . . . are alike. . . . Judged morally, every character in these plays—the few exceptions only are *mistakes*—is alike essentially vain and worthless." In this sense Congreve alone, according to Lamb, made no mistakes; the greatness of his art lies precisely in the fact that, whether instinctively or through conscious design, he scrupulously excluded from his plays characters with the slightest "pretensions to goodness or good feelings." He spread over his scenes so uniform "a privation of moral light" that his creatures (his "shadows") "flit" before us "without distinction or preference."

To cite all this is not necessarily to agree with every detail, but the overall idea of sameness or flatness nevertheless represents a valid and valuable observation which could well be disengaged from Lamb's whimsicality and developed in some more appropriate terms. One cannot, however, pursue the idea too far without coming up against Lamb's second observation: that the world of Restoration comedy presents us with "altogether a speculative scene of things, which has no reference whatever to the world that is." In a sense, of course, if one accepts the first observation, one can also accept the second. For it can be argued that a picture of the world that excludes all sense of conflict and contradiction, a picture that is dominated by sameness, can certainly bear little reference to "the world that is." To this extent one can even accept Lamb's main descriptive terms such as "artificiality," "Utopia," "fairy land." And yet it is much more forcefully clear to us that the world of Restoration comedy, for all its undramatic flatness, represents no "speculative scene of things"; it is, if anything, only too brutally realistic.

This seeming paradox is in reality no paradox at all; it only clarifies the relation between the "realism" of Restoration comedy and its undramatic quality. The two are in fact so closely connected that it is impossible to separate them. For it is not by being speculative but by determining to be nothing but realistic that this comedy becomes both flat and, in the end, not realistic at all. And here we must first see this realism in its true proportions. To begin with, we know very well what Lamb seems to have completely overlooked—that the Restoration dramatists, far from being unconcerned with the real world, sought to reflect accurately the contemporary court culture, the highly self-conscious attitudes of the fashionable society in and around the court after the restoration of the monarchy. To leave it at that, however, is to belittle the underlying grasp of cultural realities in Restoration comedy. It is possible that the dramatists were conscious only of being faithful to what they regarded as the exclusive life-style of their courtly patrons. The patrons themselves no doubt believed that their style and attitudes were exclusively their own, something that set them apart from the surrounding bourgeois world and even stamped their uncompromising hostility to the values and mentality of that world. The cultivation of wit or reckless pleasure-seeking or the attitude of bored cynicism were the answers of courtiers or gentlemen to the citizen's or the cit's materialistic zeal and moral fanaticism.

Without question such a contrast or opposition potentially constitutes a sufficiently dramatic argument, but it is rarely, except in the most superficial sense, the argument of Restoration comedy. Consider, for instance, the pleasure-seeking, the "vice" that is the commonest feature of Restoration comedy and through which it opposes the cit's doctrine or ideology of "virtue." That this opposition, whatever its theoretical merits, has no standing within the plays—that as a rule this sort of conflict forms no part of their action—is an argument to which I shall return repeatedly. Here one need only point out the extent to which pleasure and vice are the motivations, not just of courtiers or gentlemen, but of almost everyone in these plays. Alderman Gripe of Wycherley's *Love in a Wood* provides an obvious illustration: a "commonwealth's-man, an implacable magistrate, a sturdy pillar of his cause," he comes close to being a perfect cit. Yet these descriptions and his sanctimonious religious phraseology are all that we see of the cit in him; the motives and objectives that go with these are simply left out of the picture, which is as completely and exclusively one of amorous intrigue and vice in Gripe's case as in the case of his gentlemanly antagonist and rival, Dapperwit. Thus what we get in Gripe is a man older and less successful than, but not essentially different from, the rakish gentleman. However much the manner might differ superficially, the purposes and the pursuits are identical.

One might pursue this idea of sameness further by asking what exactly is the nature of the pleasure that everyone seeks in Restoration comedy—the answer of course being that it is the pleasure of love, of vice, of unfettered sexual activity. Yet there is something in this vice, as it is practiced, which can be said to underline its affinity with one of the signal virtues of the age. For the pleasure that everyone seeks in Restoration comedy is above all the pleasure of competition, of besting everyone else in the field. Hardly anyone seems to enjoy, in and of itself, the sexual activity that goes on everywhere; it is chiefly desired as a means of building up formidable reputations. The heroes are not even men of unprincipled passion, but rather men who are able to chalk up the highest gains through intrigue and ingenuity. Horner's ingenious device in *The Country Wife* to corner the sex market is too well known to need comment—upon it rests his position as the beau ideal of Restoration comedy. But even lesser men, though not as successful as Horner, are nevertheless similarly motivated: their drive, like his, is more competitive than sexual. For instance, if Alderman Gripe seeks what he calls communion with the common prostitute Lucy Crossbite, it is more for the sake of getting the better of Dapperwit than for the sake of the communion itself. As he declares in the very first scene: "If Dapperwit should contaminate her!—I cannot rest till I have redeemed her from the jaws of that lion." The same is true, though in a far more complicated way, of Etherege's hero in *The Man of Mode.* In many respects there simply could be no comparison between Gripe and Dorimant: one an authentic gull and the other not only a representative hero of Restoration comedy, like Horner, but also one of its truly insidious figures. Yet, in being driven by the demon of almost purposeless competition, the gull and the hero are alike. As Bellinda, the object of his current pursuit, observes of Dorimant: "He is never well but when he triumphs—nay, glories to a woman's face in his villainies." He himself acknowledges quite openly and sincerely that "there is no charm so infallibly makes me fall in love with a woman as my knowing a friend loves her." The friend in question may only be Sir Fopling Flutter, whose rakish aspirations no one takes seriously; the love a hoax of Dorimant's own devising; and the woman none other than his old and discarded mistress, Mrs. Loveit—yet the charm of this totally fabricated situation is sufficient to rouse Dorimant afresh to the pleasure of humiliating Mrs. Loveit. Here, indeed, we have a case of morbid sexual psychology by comparison with which Horner's stratagems seem precisely that—stratagems to spice what remains a cultural rather than a sexual insight.

The so-called licentiousness of Restoration comedy has been so much taken for granted at its face value that few people have enquired what makes it peculiarly repulsive even as licentiousness. Only recently have critics pointed out the extent to which its lewdness is couched in terms of gross appetite often involving a perversion of religious values and terminology. Thus Alderman Gripe's declaration about "communion" already cited reads in full: "There can be no entertainment to me more luscious and savoury than communion with that little gentlewoman. . . . I fast till I see her." But much more often the language of love is the language of money and commerce; and what needs to be emphasized is that in thus combining the languages of love, commerce, and religion, the gentlemen again reveal something of the spirit of the "commonwealth's-man" Gripe though, of course, without Gripe's occasional sanctimony. Thus we have the following exchange in *The Man of Mode* (III, iii):

> *Dor.* I have been used to deep play, but I can make one at small game when I like my gamester well.
> *Har.* And be so unconcerned you'll ha' no pleasure in't.
> *Dor.* Where there is a considerable sum to be won, the hope of drawing people in makes every trifle considerable.
>
> . . . .
> *Har.* . . . Could you keep a Lent for a mistress?
> *Dor.* In expectation of a happy Easter.

Of course, Harriet being marked out for a wife rather than a mistress, there is no "taking up" there (as Bellair soon reminds Dorimant) "without church security."

While Restoration comedy carefully designates women as whores, mistresses, or wives, it characteristically treats all without distinction as commodities—some to be paid for by one party and some by another, but none acceptable or available without a price. In this respect there is no need to look beneath the surface to see how the philosophy of the marketplace gets modulated into the philosophy of the boudoir. "Marriage is rather a sign of interest than love," as Harcourt puts it in *The Country Wife,* "and he that marries a fortune covets a mistress, not loves her." Or, as we see in the following piece of dialogue from the same play:

> *Horn.* But prithee, was not the way you were in better? is not keeping better than marriage?
> *Pinch.* A pox on't! the jades would jilt me, I could never keep a whore to myself.
> *Horn.* So, then you married to keep a whore to yourself. Well, but let me tell you, women, as you say, are like soldiers, made constant and loyal by good pay, rather than by oaths and covenants. Therefore I'd advise my friends to keep rather than marry.

The subject of marriage, indeed, shows us most clearly how far the way of the world with which Restoration comedy deals is not the way of this or that isolated coterie but of a far more unified and representative world. On this subject the gentlemen are neither bored nor cynically indifferent but as alert and calculating as any citizen. With a few exceptions, there is hardly a comedy of the Restoration period that involves a matrimonial intrigue which is not primarily an intrigue for money. Critics often discuss these comedies as though they were all pleasure and no business; however, in reality the stories of Restoration lovers are concerned not only with the fortunes of their sexual ambitions and exploits but with the fortunes of their fortunes as well. Wycherley, who recognized this fact most clearly, put it in sharp focus in all his plays except the wholly farcical *Gentleman Dancing-Master.* His very first play opens with the widow Flippant exclaiming: "Not a husband to be had for money!" and closes with an equally astonished Dapperwit declaring, upon finding himself married to Gripe's daughter but without Gripe's money: "I am undone then! ruined, let me perish!" In *The Plain Dealer,* when Fidelia asks Olivia what made her "dissemble love" to a hated man, the answer is: "That which makes all the world flatter and dissemble, 'twas his money: I had a real passion for that." Pinchwife in *The Country Wife* has the true philosophy of the age when he observes that "our sisters and daughters, like usurers' money, are safest when put out; but our wives, like their writings, never safe but in our closets under lock and key." And if he declares brutally in the first act: "I must give Sparkish to-morrow five thousand pound to lie with my sister," Sparkish himself proves him right in the last when he renounces the sister, Alithea, with the words: "I never had any passion for you till now, for now I hate you. 'Tis true, I might have married your portion." Money is likewise the only question involved in the subplot of Vanbrugh's *The Relapse,* where the rivalry between Lord Foppington and his brother is the rivalry for the £1500 a year that goes with the unseen and otherwise unknown country maiden, Hoyden.

While any number of further examples to the same effect can be cited, I should like to concentrate instead on Congreve's *The Way of the World,* the double intrigue of which tangles the matrimonial with the financial interests of the parties concerned so completely that it is impossible to tell where the various characters' plotting for love ends and their plotting for money begins. My reason for choosing this play is that not only is it reputed to be the crowning achievement of Restoration comedy but it is also defended as a piece of genuine drama, a play whose action involves a meaningful conflict. Two sorts of arguments are and always have been advanced in support of this view. One of these, in a recent restatement, claims that Congreve is "not an apologist for, but rather a satirist of the way of the world," contrasts Fainall with Mirabell by emphasizing "Mirabell's humane use of power," and concludes that in this play "behavior is based on and judged by principles . . . hence the morality reflects those permanent and universal values which civilized man . . . has

promulgated and cherished."[1] The other argument maintains
that it is precisely because of this sort of moral interpretation
that we misunderstand not just *The Way of the World* but
most of Restoration comedy; while we insist on a moral
drama, on heroes and villains, this comedy proposes an interest
of an altogether different order. The real drama, so the argument runs, is a drama of wit, and by wit is meant a completely
disengaged intellectual activity.

The latter argument was indicated by Congreve himself in his
famous dedication to *The Way of the World,* where he expressed doubt that "hasty judges could find the leisure to
distinguish betwixt the character of a Witwoud and a Truewit"
and sought therefore to emphasize and explain the distinction
himself. In *The Restoration Comedy of Wit* Thomas Fujimura
has recently both developed the argument and extended its
scope to cover other important Restoration dramatists as well.
He shows very plausibly how some of the characteristic attitudes of Restoration comedy reflect not a coterie culture but a
much wider intellectual background—mainly the Hobbesian
principles of empiricism, relativism, and hedonism which
everyone accepted. The task that the playwrights undertook
was to offer, without stepping outside of these principles, the
drama that could still result from the collision between superior and inferior minds. Therefore it is not to be expected
that the dramatic conflict in these plays will be between better
and worse people in any traditional sense; it will rather be a
conflict between those who, because of their mental agility
and innate good taste, can exploit the situation ruthlessly yet
gracefully and those who, though they pretend to have the
same mental qualities, are in reality neither nimble and ruthless nor graceful enough to succeed.

Particularly valuable here, I think, is the redefinition of wit

1. Paul and Miriam Mueschke, *A New View of Congreve's Way of
the World,* University of Michigan Contributions in Modern Philology,
23 (Ann Arbor, University of Michigan Press, 1958). pp. 13. 39, 66.

as something other than what is commonly understood by the term—not liveliness nor intelligence so much as the sort of sharpness that is quick to take advantage, bent on winning, artful, and unscrupulous. An emphasis on the relation between the drama of wit in this sense and the general mentality of the age in which it was written is also valuable. Nevertheless, as an overall interpretation of Restoration comedy and particularly as a defense of its dramatic quality, the argument presents difficulties. We can leave for the moment the question of whether there can be an intellectual attitude in a play which does not also include, at least implicitly, a moral attitude. But even at face value the Truewit-Witwoud distinction turns out to be either a distinction without a difference or a distinction based essentially on a criterion other than wit. It is true, for instance, that Dorimant, the Truewit of *The Man of Mode,* is superior in the sense here understood to the play's Witwoud, Sir Fopling Flutter; thus Dorimant succeeds where Sir Fopling fails. But if we turn to a play like *The Relapse,* we find in its Lord Foppington a character who defies and even overturns the formula. Although he is immeasurably superior to all the other characters in the play—a truly witty man as well as a Truewit—he is nevertheless cast in the standard Witwoud role. Foppington is, in fact, a lineal descendent of Etherege's Sir Fopling and is left in the end with neither mistress nor legal wife. What this means is that he is represented as a Witwoud not because of his mental inferiority but because he happens to be the play's least rewarded character. Thus, while some characters in Restoration comedy are no doubt palpably superior to others, the correlation between such superiority and success is not what it seems in theory. If a general principle were to be asserted, it would not be that Restoration comedy awards success to those who are witty but that it attributes wit, plausibly or implausibly, to those who are successful. The question of success and failure is itself primary, and the question of wit follows it by a sort of inverted logic. Where there are many contending for the same prize, some will succeed while others fail; successes are Truewits, would-be successes Witwouds; Truewits succeed because of true wit, Witwouds fail for want of it—thus, rather than the other way round, runs the logic of these plays. And in this paradox of ex post facto justification we again see a peculiar extrapolation of contemporary values. The post-Puritan bourgeois mentality had solved the paradox for its own purposes by associating worldly success with the old Calvinist idea of grace and by justifying that success itself in terms of the virtues; in Restoration comedy the idea of innate grace degenerates into the idea of innate gracefulness, and the justification by superior virtue becomes justification by superior wit.

In any event, what we get in the Truewit-Witwoud collision is not really a collision and certainly not a dramatic conflict in any sense. It is rather a competition—a sort of race run by similarly motivated people for the same goals. We can see this by returning to *The Way of the World.* Congreve had good reason to fear that the distinction between Truewits and Witwouds would go unrecognized: it hardly exists in the play. One of the reasons that this is an insufferably dull play is that, except for the most trivial of variations, most of its principal characters—particularly the "villain" Fainall and the "hero" Mirabell—speak, think, and act alike. Nor can the thinking and the acting—the intellectual and the moral attitudes—be in any way separated. For the thoughts of these characters are not just their thoughts but also their values, their motives, the springs of their conduct; no matter where we start, we are in the end forced to return inevitably to the moral argument. Is there then any discoverable justification why Mirabell should succeed and Fainall fail, other than the justification of success itself? Can one call the motives and mental capabilities of the one superior and the other inferior? To begin with, what exactly is the object of their rivalry? It is not love. Even if that name be given (as some people do give it in all earnestness) to the few brief exchanges of modish sentimentalities between Mirabell and Millamant, we still have to realize how very little this has to do with the action of the play. The rivalry of the two men—and with it the play itself—centers on Millamant's fortune. Her hand is an accessory for which one of the two rivals is automatically disqualified through prior marriage. Fainall is in fact eager to promote the match between Mirabell and Millamant in the expectation that such a step will lead to Millamant's disinheritance and the furtherance of his own hopes for her fortune. To this end he employs the services of his mistress, Mrs. Marwood. This, however, is exactly what Mirabell does too—using his mistress, in this case Mrs. Fainall, to further his own intrigue and frustrate that of his rival. The intrigues and counter-intrigues for the control of Millamant's and other subsidiary fortunes involved in the situation engross as much the energy of one man as of the other.

The extent to which the hero Mirabell and the villain Fainall are alike becomes clear in the last act, when both men are forced to come out into the open. It then turns out that while the villain was scheming to deprive the hero of his marriage portion, the hero had already schemed to the same purpose against the villain—and succeeded. For not only had Mirabell palmed off his mistress on Fainall, he had first made her sign away her estate in trust to himself. Fainall, his own intrigue exposed, declares: "If it must all come out, why let 'em know it; 'tis but the *way of the world,*" to which Mirabell, producing Mrs. Fainall's deed of conveyance, rejoins triumphantly: "Even so, Sir; 'tis the *way of the world,* Sir." Clearly this is his way as much as that of the world or of Fainall. One final touch might, however, be added. To his mistress's question as to why he had made her marry Fainall—a particularly valid one since he himself was equally available, though neither Mrs. Fainall nor Congreve raises this point—Mirabell replies with the utmost complacency: "Why do we daily commit disagreeable and dangerous actions? To save that idol, reputation. If the familiarities of our loves had produced that consequence of which you were apprehensive, where could you have fixed a father's name with credit, but on a husband," ending with a judicial note unsurpassed in its priggishness and gratuitous cruelty: "A better man ought not to have been sacrificed to the occasion; a worse had not answered to the purpose." To take this sort of self-righteousness for "permanent and universal values" of civilized man or to make it a basis for distinguishing Mirabell's "use of power" as "humane" is absurd. Lamb was right in maintaining that all the characters of Restoration comedy are "alike essentially vain and worthless," that especially in Congreve no distinctions could be made between one character and another, and that of all Restoration dramatists Congreve had spread the most uniform "privation of moral light" over all his creatures.

This is not to deny that there is an occasional attempt on Congreve's part to sentimentalize Mirabell, but then what he sentimentalizes is exactly what he occasionally satirizes—with the result that both attempts remain half-hearted gestures without direction or meaning. In this, too, Congreve represents a general dilemma experienced by many Restoration dramatists—by any writer, in fact, who would rise above the accepted values of his age but has no grasp of any alternative values; a writer who would assert a moral perspective without possessing one. It is indeed futile to inquire whether Congreve is an apologist for or a satirist of the way of the world; no other "way" was available to his imagination. He, like most other Restoration dramatists, simply lacked the perspective to question it, let alone approve or disapprove of it. To them it was *the* way of the world—something settled, something that was not to be judged and tested but only exemplified.

The peculiar moral and philosophical position of Restoration comedy may finally be summed up by pointing to the connection that exists between this position and the facts of the contemporary historical situation. Literary historians tend to overemphasize the relation between the motivating spirit of this drama on the one hand and, on the other, the violent animosities generated by the many economic, political, and social dislocations that culminated in the Civil War. Restoration comedy is thus seen as continuing in literature the battle that was lost in history. The product of a restored court, it is supposed to assert the values of a courtly and, at least relatively, humane tradition against an increasingly business-minded and acquisitive world. This view, however, simply overlooks the important fact that the seventeenth-century war had already yielded to the seventeenth-century compromise, a compromise of which the restoration of monarchy was itself the most manifest symbol. It is this practical compromise more than any continued sense of hostility or crisis that lies behind Restoration comedy, accounting for both its superficial confusions and its basic lack of drama. The culture it reflects is in no vital sense a divided culture; it is, as I have pointed out, universally a commodity culture, utilitarian, mercenary, and competitive—a culture of unprincipled acquisition, of joyless but unappeasable appetite. With these attitudes accepted by courtier and citizen alike, and that too as the basis for the most intimate of human relations, Restoration dramatists are left with no real case for the superiority of court culture. They are left with only the superficial sense of a case—that is, with various trivial dilemmas which they set out to solve in various trivial ways. The idea of hostility gets reduced to the idea of snobbery, for it is snobbery when a superior style is asserted without any discernible superiority of substance. On the one hand, the basic philosophy of bourgeois culture is adopted but under the guise of opposition to that philosophy: competition in virtue becomes competition in vice. On the other hand, the old courtly concepts of love and honor are systematically invoked but again only to be translated into their polar opposites.

In this cynical rendering of their age lie both the interest and the weakness of Restoration dramatists. The weakness is primarily dramatic. What, one may ask, could the dramatists do to avoid the flatness of the picture, to dramatize rather than merely exemplify the "way of the world"? Here there is no need to speculate: we will soon see what was actually done by some of them. But it may be useful to first look at the example of a few writers outside of the Restoration period, Shakespeare in particular. The comparison with Shakespeare has been attempted before, if only to draw a parallel between his pair of lovers, Benedick and Beatrice, and Congreve's Mirabell and Millamant. The comparison, however, becomes less fanciful if we think of it in terms of a general and continuing problem. For we have seen how Shakespearean comedy too dealt with the problem of the new reality; how it played this reality against the old concepts of love and honor, and thereby explored both the sordidness and the possible values of the new age; and, above all, how the Benedick-Beatrice story dramatized a love-relationship that was new and real without being cynical.

It is true that the hundred years since Shakespeare's time had witnessed a progressive increase in the sordidness and a progressive decline in the values of the culture. In love and marriage, as in any other arrangements of life, the highest premium was placed on acquisitiveness and material interests. Yet, if these pressures had become intensified, so had the obvious human contradictions of the culture. Because commerce and money dominated life, feeling and emotion—the idea of love itself—had not vanished from existence nor receded beyond the reach of human imagination. These are the values that were to form the positive pole of Jane Austen's comedy in the early nineteenth century. Out of the contradictions of the situation Richardson was to write his tragic novel *Clarissa* and Fielding his comedies only a few decades after Congreve and Farquhar.

Shakespearean comedy however, provides the most pertinent comparison. For while the intervening history had sharpened the thrust of naked reality, its accidents had also freshly revived some of the same traditional concepts that Shakespeare used as a dramatic counterweight to that reality. Faced by the triumph and steady advance of bourgeois culture, the reactionary court circles had, not unnaturally, turned for solace and entertainment to the old concepts of love and honor.[2] The result was the heroic drama which first occupied the stage after the formal reopening of the theaters. As Dryden, the chief promulgator and exemplar of this drama, put it in the epilogue to *The Conquest of Granada,* perhaps the best remembered of his heroic verse plays:

> If love and honour now are higher raised,
> 'Tis not the poet, but the age is praised.

A related development of the 1630s, associated with the French tradition of préciosité, was in essence a renewed expression of the centuries-old desire to free love from the limitations of its social existence. As propounded in the salons of Madame de Rambouillet, which Wycherley frequented during his years of early adulthood in Paris, it became an amalgam of refined manners and "Platonic love." Its code-book was D'Urfé's pastoral romance, *Astrée.* The cult became something of a craze in the English court and was reflected in such plays as Davenant's *The Temple of Love* and *The Platonic Lovers.*

Common to both these escapist impulses is the desire to marshall some sort of opposition to the materialistic attitudes

---

2. A recent "semasiological" researcher has calculated the steady upswing in the use of the word honor in the dramatic literature of the seventeenth century, "the range in single plays being from 0 *(Midsummer Night's Dream)* to 86 *(The Country Wife)."* C. L. Barber, *The Idea of Honour in the English Drama, 1591-1700,* Gothenburg Studies in English, VI (Göteborg, Elanders Boktryckeri Aktiebolag, 1957), p. 88, and passim.

of the age, and the point about them is that, as ideal and romantic configurations, they offered Restoration comedy the opportunity that comedy thrives on. Here, made available in readily tractable literary form, was a system of values that stood in perfect comic opposition to the realities of the day. Here was the initial literary situation, from which comedy might conceivably proceed to a definition of real values, but which at the very least could be exploited for adding some sense of drama even to the depiction of valueless reality.

Precisely this possibility is hinted at, though certainly not seized, by George Villiers in his otherwise insignificant play, *The Rehearsal.* Conceived as early as 1663 and acted in 1671, this literary parody considered Davenant and Sir Robert Howard, Dryden's early collaborator, as possible targets before settling on Dryden himself. In proposing that "prose and sense" henceforth replace the drama of rhymed nonsense, it was naming the two possible poles of a new comedy of love and honor.[3] But the succeeding playwrights, with their one-track imaginations, never awakened to the drama of the situation; by ignoring the high-flown rhyme of love they failed to grasp its true prose as well. Exceptions aside, they did not even conceive any heroic or Platonic lovers—if only to offset the real, brutal ones.

On the other side, bourgeois culture had itself developed a whole system of values as a protective covering around its realities. And, indeed, the sentimental virtues crowded the air far too densely to be wholly neglected by anyone. But, as we shall see, far from bringing them into the center of the action, most Restoration comedies relegated these virtues to the sentimental corner of their plots. Thus another dramatic possibility was missed, a possibility again hinted at in an early play of the period—Sir Robert Howard's unsuccessful anti-Puritan satire, *The Committee* (1665). Here too one thinks inevitably of

3. See p. 78 above.

Shakespeare, of the conflict between the virtuous Malvolio and the pleasure-seeking Toby Belch. The conflict is only a part and almost a side-episode of *Twelfth Night;* yet, in comparison with a typical Restoration comedy, it seems a complete drama in itself. Restoration comedy has no true Malvolios. Its Puritans and citizens, if given a voice at all, are not given the slightest semblance of a case. Often, like Alderman Gripe, they are shown as rakes too—middle-class rakes, motivated as exclusively by pleasure-seeking as the courtly rake and lacking only the courtier's savoir faire. The amorous intrigues of Gripe are actually far less utilitarian in their calculation than those of his gentlemanly rival and man-about-town, Dapperwit. With the line between Malvolios and Tobies thus blurred, even the peculiar version of cakes and ale philosophy, asserted everywhere, acquires nowhere any dramatic definition or meaning.

For their determined effort to ignore both the ideas of the past and the reigning concepts as well as the possible values of the present and still write a comedy of love, Restoration playwrights paid in the end a curious and unsuspected price. Blocking out all perspectives except the one leading to what they considered the naked truth had the effect of turning that truth itself into an abstraction. Grossly limited and partial to begin with, it became in their hands not merely the whole truth, but an axiom of universal applicability. Restoration comedy is sometimes looked upon as the final and most degraded expression of the Jonsonian comic tradition; indeed, to the extent that the relationship is valid, the degradation is undeniable. Jonson, concerned extensively with acquisitiveness, greed, and lust, recognized these symptoms of the age for the perversions of nature that they are and represented them as such. His theory of "humours" was a diagnostic theory. In a play like *Volpone* the rather insipid innocence of Celia and Bonario are not really needed to provide a perspective on the unnatural world of Volpone, Mosca, and their many equally depraved victims. The universal lust and greed are in themselves shown as abnormal and diseased. In Restoration comedy, by contrast, disease is treated as the natural human condition and abnormality as the norm. The theory of "humours" has become the philosophy of Man.

What is involved here is a dual process of universalization and inversion. So far from escaping abstractions, Restoration comedy succeeds only in inverting them. All those famous wicked maxims which regularly punctuate its dialogue are little more than virtuous truths turned upside down. This simple and rather monotonous trick of total reversal is, likewise, the secret behind the "daring" overall morality and philosophy of these plays. All pleasure is sinful: the only sin is to miss pleasure; love is a spiritual relationship: love is a carnal activity; love is deathless: love dies its natural death at the very moment of its satisfaction; marriage is an accepted bond of mutual esteem and fidelity: marriage is the recognized certificate of mutual distaste and infidelity; and so on. It is really a game, and the precise angry word for it, if one must be employed, is "profaneness" rather than "immorality"—the second rather than the first by which Jeremy Collier, its earliest critic and the harbinger of the sentimental reaction, described it on the title page of his blast. In fact, all that drama had to do in order to become moral was to take some of the same truths and set them on their feet again. For almost a whole century it did little else.

So much for the general picture. We now move to some of the exceptions—the plays which deal with, but are not exclusively dominated by, the way of the world; which bring the modish ideas of love and marriage not indeed to the bar of any radical judgment, but at least into some sort of play against other suggested ideas and perspectives. The most frequent of these alternative ideas—and also the most obvious, being in effect little more than the obverse of love à la mode—is the sentimental idea of love. As already mentioned, it appears on the stage with some regularity throughout the period. Even Etherege, the least sentimental of Restoration dramatists, makes ample provision for it through such characters as Young Bellair and Emilia, the side-lovers of his best play, *The Man of Mode.* In Wycherley, the burden of sentimentality is usually a woman's burden alone, carried by her singlehandedly until, close to the end, a male character is approved for the office and honor of sharing it with her (as in the case of Alithea and Harcourt in *The Country Wife*). In the earlier *Love in a Wood,* leaving aside the wholly Platonic and wooden affair of Christina and Valentine, there is the irreproachable Lydia whose main function is to punctuate the first four acts with the exclamation "False Ranger!" When Ranger finally stands converted at the end of Act IV, even though her periodic exclaiming has had little to do with the development, she plays the further part of becoming its inevitable beneficiary. "Lydia, triumph!" as Ranger now exclaims in his turn, "I now am thine again. Of intrigues, honourable or dishonourable, and all sorts of rambling, I take my leave; when we are giddy, 'tis time to stand still." If this is a false—that is to say, dramatically unmotivated and therefore unconvincing—echo of Benedick's "for man is a giddy thing, and this is my conclusion," there is more than a Shakespearean echo in Wycherley's last play, *The Plain Dealer.* Fidelia, its official heroine, is a close reworking of Shakespeare's Viola—but a Viola sentimentalized out of all credibility. A paragon of virtue and dullness, she surpasses even Alithea and Lydia in sheer lack of vitality just as she surpasses them in the superior truthfulness, constancy, and feminine humility of her love.

Wycherley exemplifies one Restoration approach—perhaps the most honest one—to the idea of sentimental love. He recognizes its claim on any contemporary comedy of love and dutifully incorporates it into all his plays. But Wycherley gives it a compartmentalized existence, presenting it frankly as an idea available to his mind but not to his imagination. Hence the detachability of his sentimental characters, his Truth or Fidelity, which exist in the world of the play but never on the same imaginative plane as that world itself. As in the case of Etherege's *The Man of Mode,* the sentimental lover and the rake are firmly separated, with the doings of one having no influence on the doings of the other. Like two sides of a coin, the two ideas of sentimental and rakish love may be inseparably rooted in the same hard metal of contemporary reality, but they cannot rub against each other and must always face in opposite directions. Except for the early case of "False Ranger," no characters are shifted from one side of the play to the other, and even Ranger's changing sides is less a case of conversion than a quick volte-face.

The difference becomes clear if we return briefly to Congreve's *The Way of the World.* For, with basically the same materials and an imaginative reach no greater than Wycherley's, Congreve was attempting something like the drama of an elaborate, adequately motivated, and spiritually convincing transformation. A new coin was to be forged, not the old one flipped over. A single action, leading to the marriage of Mirabell and Millamant, was to exemplify the creation of a true human relationship that would both include and at the same time transcend the two antithetical concepts of sentimental and rakish love. The results of this attempt—the sentimentalizing and satirizing by turns of the one unchanging and unchangeable way of the world—we have already seen.

The one Restoration dramatist who really exploited the opposition between sentimental love and love à la mode was Vanbrugh. In *The Relapse* the sentimental idea is given much more than token recognition; it is, in fact, treated with some seriousness and dignity. Unlike Congreve, Vanbrugh attempts no ambitious portrayal of transcendence, but, unlike Wycherley, neither does he leave the two opposed ideas on two separate planes. In the conflict experienced by more than one

character, the two ideas clash. And however inherently superficial and limited the significance of such a clash, he nevertheless explores it for all it is worth and is enabled thereby to put
the two concepts to a mutual test. In this, Vanbrugh alone
among Restoration dramatists can be said to have put the
ubiquitous sentimental perspective to some dramatic use. In
his play alone, in fact, it is a perspective rather than an inert
idea.

Before turning to *The Relapse,* however, two other examples
of the accommodation of the sentimental view may be noted.
The first is the well-known case of Colley Cibber's *Love's Last
Shift,* often regarded as the first sentimental comedy of the
type which was to become popular in the following century,
even as Cibber himself was to become a literary target of the
greatest comic writer of that century, Henry Fielding. What
Cibber did in this play was to write a comedy with many of
the usual materials and motivations of the Restoration model,
but also with a built-in device for turning the whole story into
a virtuous lesson at the end. For his hero Cibber took a rake,
Loveless, who, having deserted his wife Amanda several years
earlier, fails to recognize her so completely that he gladly takes
up with her again as a mistress. Repentance, however, follows:
the mistress reveals her identity as the former discarded wife,
and Loveless thenceforth vows to become a constant and virtuous husband. This is in effect the flip-of-the-coin device
again, though transferred to the basic conception of the entire
plot and cunningly executed. The other type of accommodation takes the form of more or less isolated statements in the
course of the play, such as the following in Farquhar's *The
Beaux' Stratagem:* "You and your wife, Mr. Guts, may be one
flesh, because ye are nothing else; but rational creatures have
minds that must be united."

Marriage of minds as against carnal appetite, the happiness of
constancy as against the pleasures of waywardness, coming to
rest in a "noble" love as against the giddy pursuit of endless
sexual conquest—this is the theme which, fragmentarily ex-

pressed elsewhere, is concentrated in the main action of *The Relapse* and there given as sustained and dramatic a treatment as it can possibly bear. Of course, Vanbrugh's play was intended as an answer to *Love's Last Shift,* expressly undertaken in order to refute what Vanbrugh considered Cibber's sentimental and opportunistic falsifications. Where Cibber had left his hero secure in the final vow of repentance and reform, Vanbrugh carried Loveless's story forward a few paces to show how skin-deep such vows of penitence usually are and how brittle the matrimonial future based on them. In comparing the two plays, however, it should be noted at the outset that Cibber's sentimental message was connected inextricably with the more tangible issues of money and prudence. He makes a point of Amanda's inheritance, which she has come into during Loveless's absence and which now accompanies her renewed offer of constant love. Vanbrugh carefully separates the issues and relegates the theme of money to the independent subplot involving Hoyden's fortune and the battle of wits between the brothers Fashion over its possession. Jeremy Collier would later attack *The Relapse* for violating the unity of action by having two plots instead of one. But the division enabled Vanbrugh to devote the story of his principal characters to the "pure" issue of love: the conflict between weak human "nature" and the strong human "soul."

The Relapse, subtitled *Virtue in Danger,* begins its action where *Love's Last Shift* ends. In the opening scene we find Loveless rehearsing—in blank verse—the primary tenets of his new-found philosophy: the "true philosophy which says / Our heaven is seated in our minds." Proposing a visit to London, the scene of his previous dissipation, he assures Amanda that there is no danger of his ever reverting to the weakness of his unreformed days. For

> The rock of reason now supports my love,
> On which it stands so fix'd
> That rudest hurricane of wild desire

> Would, like the breath of a soft slumb'ring babe,
> Pass by, and never shake it.

But this rock, to which Cibber had fastened his play, turns to quicksand when Loveless encounters Berinthia, a pretty widow, and after some further philosophical debate, goes straight into that relapse which he had earlier ruled out as an impossibility.

Thus the outcome of the action involving Loveless, Amanda, and Berinthia, taken together with the more or less abstract discussion of the issues that accompanies it, sufficiently demonstrates the point Vanbrugh set out to make against the shallow resolution of the problem in Cibber's play. But this is not Vanbrugh's own resolution of the problem, just as this part of *The Relapse*—the straight answer part—is not the whole play. Against this simple refutation of Cibber, Vanbrugh sets up a counter-demonstration, another action again involving the two principal women but this time in relation to Mr. Worthy and not Loveless. As Loveless pursues Berinthia, this other hero, a discreet rake, develops designs of his own on Amanda; to further those designs, he enlists the aid of Berinthia herself—his former mistress. The two intrigues, though running parallel to each other for the most part, nevertheless point eventually in opposite directions. By virtue of the second intrigue, the conflict that Loveless experiences is reproduced in Amanda and through her finally in Worthy as well. But while in Loveless's case it proves to be the prelude to a relapse, it leads Worthy to an impassioned renunciation of vicious love, with the further clear suggestion that in his case the change or the reformation is anything but shallow. In other words, though Worthy ends where Loveless began, we are meant to see a profound difference in the two cases—the difference between the true process and fact of change and the mere baseless assertion of it. Accordingly, when Worthy in his turn rehearses the new philosophy toward the end of the play, although he too uses blank verse and some of the same terms that Loveless had used in the first scene, we are not meant to take it ironically, as might be supposed. We are meant to take it as tested and proven—now, in this case, in this manner.

The idea, I think, is interesting enough to be pursued in some detail. Clearly the catalyst of this counter-demonstration is Amanda—and attempt is made to show her as a catalyst rather than as a mere touchstone or point of reference. By refusing to change herself—or rather her idea of love—she makes change possible. For she is shown not only resisting temptation but also experiencing it. The issue is brought to a clear practical point through the periodic discussions between Amanda and Berinthia in the first half of the play. At an early stage Amanda reveals that it is not Sir Novelty Fashion alone who has made advances to her; the apparently virtuous Worthy "has been tampering too." It is true, she admits, that Worthy's advances were not half so repulsive to her as those of the foppish Sir Novelty. But she has no fear in either case: "My love, my duty, and my virtue are such faithful guards, I need not fear my heart should e'er betray me." To this Berinthia counters the philosophy of worldly wisdom. Amanda, she argues, had shut herself up in the country following her husband's desertion. She had thus brought upon herself much sorrow as well as an illusion of virtuous strength—not to mention a naïve notion of love. "When your husband ran away from you, if you had fallen into some of my acquaintance, 'twould have saved you many a tear." She discounts the kind of love that Amanda insists can only find satisfaction in marriage and constancy—the possibility, as she puts it, that you "grow so passionately fond that nothing but the man you love can give you rest"—with the comment: "Ah, poor Amanda, you have led a country life: but if you'll consult the widows of this town, they'll tell you you should never take a lease of a house you can hire for a quarter's warning." At any rate, as Berinthia adds in a later scene, "'tis a presumptuous thing in a

woman to assume the name of virtuous till she has heartily
hated her husband and been soundly in love with somebody
else, whom if she has withstood—"

This is precisely the test that Vanbrugh arranges for Amanda, with the help of Berinthia, Worthy, and Loveless. The
situation is deliberately engineered by Berinthia and Worthy.
Amanda is to be shown from a distance a secret rendezvous
taking place between Loveless and his mistress, and she is thus
to be made a firsthand witness to her supposedly reformed
husband's betrayal of her love and confidence. When she returns home—"her spirit enflamed against her husband for his
treason, and her flesh in heat from some contemplations upon
the treachery; her blood on a fire, her conscience in ice"—
Worthy is to make his appearance for a final assault. Given her
previous signs of favor and happy predisposition toward him,
this scheme is certain to succeed.

And yet, when the scheme is put into effect and Worthy
encounters Amanda alone, certainty of outcome, one way or
the other, is precisely what we do not get. Does Amanda now
hate her husband and love Worthy instead? Is she in fact in the
situation proposed by Berinthia, and does her ability to withstand Worthy prove her title to "the name of virtuous"? If so,
what exactly is meant by "withstanding"? Amanda certainly
seems inclined to scorn her unworthy husband, and she is
equally firm against the plea of the sort of love that Worthy
has in mind. But at the same time she is prepared to "purchase" his heart "with a part of mine." The scene (V, iv) quite
obviously involves the contrast between virtuous and vicious
love throughout, but how this contrast is to be understood
does not become clear until the final passages when Amanda,
her vacillation over, states her position in terms of "the soul"
and "the mind" on the one hand and "Nature" on the other:

> The soul, I do confess,
> Is usually so careless of its charge,

> So soft, and so indulgent to desire,
> It leaves the reins in the wild hand of Nature,
> Who, like a Phaeton, drives the fiery chariot,
> And sets the world on flame.
> Yet still the sovereignty is in the mind,
> Whene'er it pleases to exert its force.

This is the climax of the counter-demonstration—indeed the resolution of the issues raised in the play. As Amanda exits, Worthy follows her statement with a soliloquy which closes the scene (the play, if we leave out the final scene devoted to the winding up of the Fashion-Hoyden plot) and shows the rake's transformation that she has wrought:

> Sure there's divinity about her;
> And sh'as dispens'd some portion on't to me.
> For what but now was the wild flame of love,
> Or (to dissect that specious term)
> The vile, the gross desires of flesh and blood,
> Is in a moment turned to adoration.
> The coarser appetite of nature's gone,
> And 'tis, methinks, the food of angels I require:
> How long this influence may last, heaven knows.
> But in this moment of my purity
> I could on her own terms accept her heart.
> . . . .
> When truth's extorted from us, then we own
> The robe of virtue is a graceful habit.

With the weight of the two intrigues behind it, this conclusion does not strike us as altogether an exercise in empty rhetoric. It even possesses a certain measure of force and dignity of its own as the final statement of a theme explored in various direct and indirect ways throughout the play. Yet the source of whatever strength it possesses is also the source of its patent weakness. For the passage reveals, above everything else, the inherent limitation of the terms in which the issue is conceived and the consequent falseness of the choice it offers. Berinthia, in proposing the test of virtue cited above, had completed the sentence as follows: "whom if she has withstood—then—much good may it do her!" Suggested in this is a question that Amanda's noble and otherwise complete victory leaves unanswered. In fact, the manner in which she withstands Worthy confirms Berinthia's cynical implication that virtue does no good; that the nobler it is, the more sterile it becomes. For what after all is the reality, let alone the value, of Amanda's final offer to Worthy? She seems to promise him her heart on certain conditions, and he seems to understand both what is promised and on what terms. But do we? The truth of the matter is that Vanbrugh is invoking an idea of pure love which he cannot define because it has no reality, in his imagination or anywhere else. It is a pure abstraction. The dissection of "love"—"that specious term"—into the "coarser appetite" of nature and "the gross desires of flesh and blood" is forthright and admirable, but the alternative turns out to be nothing better nor more definite than "adoration" and "the food of angels."

This is the dead end of sentimentality. While Vanbrugh uses the sentimental idea effectively against the Restoration concept of love, he has no perspective on sentimentality itself. Thus the action becomes impaled on the horns of a dilemma: abandonment of one abstraction involves acceptance of another at the opposite extreme. What the play seems to be crying out for is a concept of love that can at one stroke put the two opposed ideas into their proper place, bring the debate down from the detached elevation of blank verse, and show the essential falseness of the assumptions in which the issue has locked itself. Vanbrugh does not attempt this, but something like it Fielding was to do in the following century. By that time, of course, the sentimental rather than the rakish view of love reigned supreme. However, while he used the rake to expose the sentimental hypocrite, Fielding had resources other than "adoration" and "the food of angels" when it came to the reformation of the rake himself. The love in which *his* comic heroes come to rest is neither angelically pure nor bestially gross. Rejecting both these as equally reductive and absurd, Fielding shows love to be simply whole, wholesome, and human.

This human or natural perspective, as we may call it, enters into two major Restoration comedies: briefly at the end of Etherege's *The Man of Mode,* and perversely throughout Wycherley's *The Country Wife. The Man of Mode,* perhaps the most brilliant and ruthless of Restoration comedies, exemplifies par excellence the fundamental characteristics and limitations of the type. In fact we see its motifs, characters, and even situations reproduced and diluted throughout the period. While, however, its main distinction lies in its concentrated expression of the new theme of love à la mode, it strikes a few notes that we strain for but seldom catch in any of the plays that followed and imitated it. The play depicts, for instance, at least in the case of one character, that natural passion which we would expect to be the occasional accompaniment or consequence or even accident of modish love. Characteristically, the passion is not one of love but rather of fury experienced by a cast-off mistress. Yet, in experiencing it, Etherege's Mrs. Loveit ceases to be a mere figure of stage convention, a necessary cog in the machinery of Restoration intrigue. She puts forth a recognizable human face. Of course, her frustrated passion and pride bring her dangerously close to a moment of sentimentality—the moment when she adjures the friend who has witnessed, and been the immediate cause of, her being jilted by Dorimant: "Take example from my misfortunes. Bellinda, if thou wouldst be happy, give thyself wholly up to goodness." This might seem a false note. It is; but only so far as Mrs. Loveit is concerned. Etherege knows better and has

Harriet administer the following immediate rebuke to Mrs. Loveit: "Mr. Dorimant has been your God Almighty long enough; 'tis time to think of another."

It is, however, the case of Dorimant and Harriet, as it finally develops, that we must consider. For the most part these two characters are true to type, nor is there anything exceptional about their love or even their contemplated marriage. Only at the end does Harriet introduce something of a variant note. There is a great temptation to pass directly from vicious to virtuous love, from its low reality to its high-flown rhetoric, but Etherege makes Harriet steer clear of both. As her retort to Mrs. Loveit shows, this country girl is no creature of sheltered ignorance; she knows the world too well and takes too much pleasure in its pleasures to put herself forward as a votary of virtue. When, in a show of his ultimate subjection and devotion, Dorimant offers to "renounce all the joys I have in friendship and in wine, sacrifice to you all the interest I have in other women," we recognize this as a declaration that might have met the requirements of the heroine of *The Relapse.* But Harriet checks the flight in midair: "Hold! Though I wish you devout, I would not have you turn fanatic." Unlike Amanda, she at least makes her terms clear:

> Could you neglect these [joys] a while and make a journey into the country? . . . To a great rambling, lone house that looks as it were not inhabited, the family's so small. There you'll find my mother, an old lame aunt, and myself, Sir, perched up on chairs at a distance in a large parlour, sitting moping like three or four melancholy birds in a spacious volary. Does not this stagger your resolution?

When Dorimant replies, again with high-flown statements about "pangs of love" and his soul which has "quite given up her liberty," she turns away with words combining three-quarters of mock-despair with a quarter of genuine sense and sadness: "This is more dismal than the country! Emilia, pity

me, who am going to that sad place. Methinks I hear the
hateful noise of rooks already . . . There's music in the worst
cry in London—My dill and cowcumbers to pickle!"

There is a good deal of playfulness about all this, but there is
also symbolic power in the picture of the lone country
house—a picture of the reality or the ordinary quality or the
normalcy of married life. The picture is not sentimentalized,
to say the least. It lacks the pleasures of London, which is to
say of the sort of world with which Restoration comedy habitually deals. The very idea of the country is more attractive
when one is not there, when it is only an idea—like the green-
vendor's musical cry in the streets of London. Yet Harriet is
clearly overdrawing the picture in this direction for Dorimant's
benefit—to stagger his resolution, to counter his notions of
love's bondage which she finds "more dismal than the country." The journey to the lone house need not be a journey into
a joyless wilderness; it has an equal chance of becoming a
journey into quiet happiness and contentment, depending on
who makes it and with what motivation. At any rate it is a
necessary part of what coming to rest from the giddy pursuit
of pleasure means.

Is this idea or image of normalcy an authentic resolution? To
the extent that Harriet proposes and Dorimant accepts it, as he
clearly seems to do, it is. Yet this is an interpretation whose
weight the rest of the play can hardly bear. Harriet herself,
though natural and strong and even truly witty and wise here
at the end, is elsewhere far too conventionally drawn to make
this final picture of marriage altogether convincing. She is no
Sophia Western. Worse, the man with whom she must reckon
is Dorimant. It is true that the facts of his past do not by
themselves disqualify him from the future that Harriet offers
him—going on the analogy of *Tom Jones,* those facts could be
a comic argument in support of that future. At one point, in
fact, he closely resembles Fielding's hero when, having fallen
in love with Harriet, he still remembers the assignation with

Bellinda and makes haste to keep it. His "I am not so fop-
pishly in love here to forget. I am flesh and blood yet" is not
significantly different from Tom Jones's early philosophy of
one in the hand being better than two in the bush. But then
Dorimant is a Restoration not a comic hero. His faults are not
the faults of good nature. They are not even faults. They *are*
nature. He even adds to them as much gratuitous cruelty as he
can summon, and by his own admission finds the cruelty as
pleasurable as love. I have already discussed the Restoration
treatment of unnaturalness as nature, of abnormality as the
norm. But even in the context of such a philosophy Dorimant's treatment of Mrs. Loveit stands out as a peculiar, a
recognizably psychopathic case of perversity. Small wonder
then that although he seems to accept he cannot in reality
even understand the idea of normalcy held out at the end—
which thus becomes an idea with an uncertain, uneasy relation
to the rest of the play.

From the country house as a picture of normalcy in Etherege's play, we can pass over to the country girl as a picture
not of innocence but of inexperience or ignorance of the way
of the world in Wycherley's *The Country Wife.* In Vanbrugh
also, as we have seen, the country is a place of worldly ignorance, but in a wholly virtuous sense—it is the place, as Bellinda says, "to make any woman break her heart for her husband." Wycherley's country wife, Margery, loses no time in
ridding the play of this notion of country virtue. In the very
first letter she writes to Horner she declares: "I'm sure if you
and I were in the country at cards together I could not help
treading on your toe under the table or rubbing knees with
you, and staring in your face, till you saw me and then looking
down, and blushing for an hour altogether." And Margery
takes exactly this sort of initiative in the town, too—for
instance, in the very act of writing this clandestine letter under
the nose and supposed dictation of her husband. The first

thing to notice about *The Country Wife,* then, is that its country-town opposition is not simply the customary one between virtue and vice.

Yet the opposition exists, and the idea of the country is more important here than anywhere else in the Restoration period. In fact, although Wycherley's play is, like most other Restoration comedies, set entirely in London, the idea of the country enters the action at the very beginning and plays a part right up to the end. The best way to understand this part is to see it as the application of the natural perspective in reverse. We have seen how *The Man of Mode* shifts the emphasis briefly at the end from the town to the country, as though the play was headed suddenly toward the naturalness and normalcy associated with the distant picture of the house in Hampshire. The action of *The Country Wife* moves steadily and systematically in the opposite direction. Through the adventures of Mrs. Margery Pinchwife, it shows untutored nature yielding to and being finally corralled by the inescapable conventions of the beau monde.

Clear as the outline of the play is, the manner in which the underlying issue of nature and artifice is handled presents some difficulties, all of which have to do with the play's scheme of values. There is little doubt that, when all is said and done, Margery stands out as a creature of vital impulse, simple but strong. Although she readily joins the game that everyone else is playing and eventually even agrees to play it strictly according to the book, she brings to it, in the words of a recent critic, "the directness of a natural force."[4] To her the game is not quite a game, perhaps not even at the very end. She thus introduces a real sense of value into the play, far more so than the sentimental Alithea, whose virtue is as technical and artificial as the vice of the rest of the characters. To

4. Vivian Mercier, "From Myth to Ideas—and Back," *Ideas in the Drama,* ed. John Gassner (New York and London, Columbia University Press, 1964), p. 51.

describe Margery Pinchwife as a "natural force" can, nevertheless, prove misleading; it might suggest the idea of a sort of
earth goddess, the embodiment of instinctual and natural
energy wholly unamenable to quotidian regulation. Such a
conception would be alien to any comedy at all, for even when
comedy deals with nature and instinct it must deal with them
in their social and cultural manifestations. This is particularly
true of *The Country Wife,* the deliberate purpose of which is
to show the universality and impregnable strength of artifice
and convention, not of nature.

There is thus a double view of Margery that results in the
marked, often crude, ambiguity surrounding the valuation of
her character right up to the last curtain. Her innocence is seen
as ignorance, her naturalness as naïvete, her impulsiveness as
childish eagerness, her vitality as clumsiness, and her simplicity
as monumental stupidity. Not only Pinchwife—whose maxim
is that "he's a fool that marries; but he's a greater fool that
does not marry a fool"—but other characters as well look upon
her as a witless person. Even Horner, who says of her letter:
"'tis the first love-letter that ever was without flames, darts,
fates, destinies, lying and dissembling in't," is nevertheless confirmed by this very directness in his opinion of her as "a silly
innocent." He knows that her silliness will cause him trouble,
which it does. So strongly is this point of view established that
there are moments when we are ourselves uncertain about the
nature of the heroine, when we begin to wonder if she is not
just a natural after all.

The truth of the matter is that Wycherley's reversal of the
natural perspective involves an equally systematic reversal of
normal valuations. This can hardly fail to be the case, indeed,
in a play whose hero is Horner (the "Machiavell in love," as he
calls himself) and whose central strategem (Horner's false report of his own impotence) is tailor-made to bring out the
power and supremacy of the unnatural and the artificial. In
this world of total artifice, the country wife is deliberately

represented as an awkward child or novice to be duly instructed in the ways of the world, not spoiled by them. The picture
is overdrawn to the point of inconsistency and caricature. We
have already seen the kind of letter that Margery can write to
Horner and how the sentiments she expresses mock the lisping
language in which they are couched. Yet she is shown raising
in perfect earnestness the most incredibly childish questions
and objections. She is unfamiliar with the word *jealousy* and
wonders how her husband can possibly be stricken with it
when she is "sure there's no such disease in our receipt-book at
home." She believes that in asking her to draft a letter to
Horner, her husband can only be mocking her; for is she not
well aware "that letters are never writ but from the country to
London, and from London into the country? Now he's in
town, and I am in town too; therefore I can't write to him,
you know." She cannot understand why her husband should
insist on describing Horner's kisses as nauseous and loathed
when she has plainly informed him that Horner "has the
sweetest breath I ever knew."

It is the instruction of this girl, then, that constitutes the
action of the play; and it is the husband himself who, through
being in a fever of anxiety to prevent her from being instructed, becomes unwittingly her most efficient and consistent in-
structor. This is one of the more effective and sustained ironies
of a play famous for the ironic twists and turns of its plot. It
cuts right across the entire action. In the first scene Pinchwife
is already trying to throw his friends off the scent by reporting
his wife as ugly, while at the same time representing his friends
as lewd and worthless to his wife. To this he adds the further
precaution of keeping her safe under lock and key. Being
locked in the house, however, has the effect of whetting her
curiosity about the town; being constantly warned against its
dangers makes her wish to court them. Later, when Pinchwife
forces her to write to Horner, though he would have her write
in contempt and anger, the sentiments change easily enough

into love and compliment. Moreover, she learns a new and
necessary art: "now he has taught me to write letters," Margery writes to Horner, "you shall have longer ones from me."
The second and longer letter contains a declaration and the
importunity for a decisive assignation. When Pinchwife unluckily intercepts this letter, she rescues herself through yet
another art of his teaching—the art not just of dissembling, but
of disguise and impersonation. To protect her from the attention of the gallants, he had earlier led her through town
dressed in a suit intended for her brother. Now she hits upon
the idea of impersonating his sister and, wrapped up in
Alithea's clothes from top to toe, makes Pinchwife himself
escort her to Horner's doorstep and deliver her personally into
his waiting and welcoming arms.

   With this (at the end of V, ii) Pinchwife has succeeded in
accomplishing the two things he dreaded most: his own
cuckolding and his wife's transformation into a standard town
wife. However, only in the last scene of the play, which takes
place a short while later, is the action brought to a head and
the underlying issue finally defined and settled. The issue that
needs settling primarily is, of course, the long-standing question of Margery's nature. But we must first look at some of the
other characters involved, especially Pinchwife. In this scene,
which assembles the whole cast around Horner, most of the
principal characters are led to make a discovery of one sort or
another. Horner alone knows everything and needs to discover
nothing; although responsible for precipitating the entire ado,
like the true catalyst that he is, he himself remains unaffected
and unchanged. His is that perfect knowledge of the world
which inevitably causes the less cynical and hard-boiled to
correct the defect in their own knowledge and, accordingly,
readjust themselves to the prescribed ways of the world and
the established rules of the game.

   Pinchwife's discovery is somewhat singular in that it comes
closest to being a self-discovery. He is both a classic type of

comic gull and a humor character. As an embodiment of jealousy his reward is to reap in sober truth what he has first sowed in wild imagination; thus he both aids and deserves the deception practiced on him. There is, however, a further irony involved in Pinchwife's story. A jaded and aging debauchee, his constant boast is that he "knows the town"—but he does not. His apprehensions about Margery are accurate, and although the attempt to forestall her proves him foolish, the fact that in the end she does take the course he feared only confirms his claim to knowledge. But this is clearly not all that is needed; it is in his lack of self-knowledge—that is, of the part that he himself is equally fated to play—that he reveals how little he really "knows the town." The last scene brings him face to face with inevitability. There is no doubt in his mind that Horner has at last done what he had all along known and feared Horner would do—cuckolded him. But what he must be made to realize is that the important thing is not fact but appearance. Deceptions are not prevented but countered by further deceptions; what saves him is what has saved his fellow-cuckolds before. As they inform him, the whole town "has heard the report"—of Horner's impotence. The only further question is the one that he asks: "But does all the town believe it?" With the world happily deceived, the trick now is to deceive oneself: "For my own sake fain I would all believe; / Cuckolds, like lovers, should themselves deceive." From now on Pinchwife will be as well-adjusted and routinely jealous a husband as Sir Jasper Fidget. He can now agree with Congreve's Fainall: "Ay, ay; I have experience: I have a wife, and so forth"—with, however, the important difference that in his case we have not the statement about experience but something like that experience itself.

Earlier in the scene, during the Bacchanalian encounter between Horner and his mistresses, a comparable act of adjustment has taken place on a mass scale. The discovery that the assembled ladies make, the *veritas* that in this instance *vino*

brings forth, is simply that Horner, so far from being the exclusive and secretly monopolized gallant that each of his mistresses had supposed him to be, is in fact the general and
impartial lover of them all. But the problem is quickly and
amicably resolved, and by reference to the same ultimate court
of appeal. "Well then, there's no remedy," as Lady Fidget
observes; "sister sharers, let us not fall out, but have a care of
our honour . . . the jewel of most value and use, which shines
yet to the world unsuspected, though it be counterfeit." To
which Horner rejoins: "Nay, and is e'en as good as if it were
true, provided the world think so."

In this otherwise harmonious scene, Margery appears to
make, as it were, her last-ditch stand. By now she too is a
sharer, a fully initiated member of the sisterhood. Technically
there is no reason why she should make any more trouble than
the other assembled ladies, and indeed everyone expects her to
act according to the way of the world in which she has been so
thoroughly instructed. But she raises strange questions instead,
and it becomes obvious that, powerful as the world's view of
her is, it is not entirely the play's view. About the two paramount issues—honor and love—she shows a spirit that threatens to put everything into confusion. The first, honor—"the
jewel of most value and use"—that is to say, reputation, she
holds in such scant respect that not merely does she refuse to
withdraw "the back way," as Horner implores her to do, but
she voluntarily bursts forth from concealment in order to announce everything, including her "certain knowledge" that the
report about Horner is false, that it is in fact a wicked dis-
paragement. Likewise, her ideas of love and marriage. Early in
the play she had declared that her unfortunate match with
Pinchwife was not of her choice or making and that she had
fallen in love with Horner. But this was to be expected, since
these were the sentiments of her salad days when she was only
a "silly innocent." It now transpires that she really meant
what she had said. When Horner advises her to save her reputa-

tion by withdrawing from his chambers and quietly returning to her husband, she answers: "What care I? d'ye think to frighten me with that? I don't intend to go to him again; you shall be my husband now." To Horner's objection that he cannot marry her since she is married already, she counters: "Oh, would you make me believe that? Don't I see every day, at London here, women leave their first husbands, and go and live with other men as their wives?" She loves Horner, as she adds to the whole company later, "with all my soul, and nobody shall say me nay."

The irony here lies in Margery's notion of London—in her belief that in coming to the large town-world, she has left behind her old status as a country girl and come instead to a place of freedom and open choice. What she does not realize is that the much-vaunted freedom of town wives, which she has observed, is not essentially different from but only a more brazen version of the sort of freedom which she herself would enjoy, according to her first letter to Horner, in the country. For town wives too only take surreptitious freedoms; and town or country, it only adds up to a slave's freedom—the freedom not to break out of captivity but to do messy little things, on the side, on the sly, and on purpose. As Lady Fidget states the case for town wives:

> Why should our damn'd tyrants oblige us to live
> On the pittance of pleasure which they only give?

In mistaking this for true freedom, Margery reveals her real ignorance of the world. And in a sense she never learns any better, not even at the very last when she is finally brought round to play the game and declares to herself: "And I must be a country wife still too, I find; for I can't, like a city one, be rid of my musty husband, and do what I list."

The city as Margery imagines it does not exist in Wycherley's play or anywhere else in Restoration comedy; and with her abandonment of this outlandish concept, the world of denatured artifice rules supreme. The curtain comes down on a crowded stage that has freshly ratified the counterfeit ideas of love and honor. To this extent *The Country Wife* can be called an anti-comedy, a play that shows not the discovery of value against the grain of convention, but the surrender of potentially normative values to the power of collective abstraction. The abstract ideas are the same that we find elsewhere in Restoration comedy. But the distinction of Wycherley's play lies in the fact that it is not merely built around them; it dramatizes the process by which they are formed. In this it gives us not truth so much as the truth about Restoration comedy. It can be regarded as a play about the plays which preceded and followed it, a sort of master key to the whole period.

Chapter 4

A Note on Sheridan

Sheridan's comedy need not detain us for long. The purpose of this note is, in fact, to round out the picture thus far rather than to add anything of significance to it. And considering Sheridan at this point has one further advantage: when we are done with him we are virtually done with stage comedy until the time of George Bernard Shaw, more than a hundred years later. The history of English comic drama records a steady decline from Shakespeare and Jonson to the perversities of Restoration comedy, and then it further deteriorates into the monotonous vapidity of sentimental drama. Nevertheless, throughout these two centuries (with, of course, the exception of the brief Commonwealth period) there is a certain sense of continuous activity—the stage is more or less constantly plied with comic pieces which, even when destitute of literary merit, still retain some interest as a cultural manifestation or symptom. But with Goldsmith and Sheridan in the late eighteenth century, the story comes to an abrupt end, and stage comedy remains a thing of the past until the new beginnings in the last quarter of the nineteenth century.

The place of Sheridan in this history is not difficult to define. It is not an important place; quite obviously he originates nothing of any importance, and he leads nowhere. More markedly than Goldsmith, he is a backward-looking dramatist. Even this, however, can suggest an exaggerated importance unless we remember that the comic past was not at this point easily recoverable on the stage. It is conceivable that a greater or more serious dramatist than Sheridan might have succeeded in reanimating the traditions rather than simply and haphazardly borrowing from them, as Sheridan did. But on the whole this would seem to have been very nearly a hopeless task in the given theatrical situation. Marvin Mudrick puts the case well in his incisive essay, "Restoration Comedy and Later": "Sheridan, the presumptive inheritor of the tradition of Congreve, found his inheritance dissipated before he could lay his hands on it." The result of this, Mudrick goes on to add, was that when he came to write *The Rivals,* his first play, he wrote in effect a "candid and melancholy epitaph on the comedy of manners, indeed on the English comic drama."[1]

A major reason for this theatrical situation lies, of course, in the character and taste of the audience. "Bottle-fed," as Mudrick puts it, for three-quarters of a century "on sermons and sentimental comedy," it simply refused to recognize, let alone demand, any vitality or freshness in the theater it patronized.[2] To this, however, we must add another and perhaps a more signal reason—the rise of the novel. In any history of English comedy, the emergence of prose fiction as a well-defined and realistic genre must surely count as the most decisive single

---

1. *English Stage Comedy,* ed. W. K. Wimsatt, Jr., pp. 115, 116. It is beside the point here to quarrel with some of Mudrick's particular judgments, to argue against his summary dismissal of all Shakespeare's comedies, for instance, or his case in support of Restoration comedy which, though careful and selective, seems to me still far too strong and enthusiastic. Mudrick's essay is remarkable for the brevity and precision with which it documents the decline of comic drama from Jonson to Oscar Wilde and also for the attempt it makes to analyze the developments that led to, or at least abetted, the steady deterioration from one period to the next. His brief comments on Sheridan seem to me fair and shrewd, with the exception of one or two seemingly small but rather basic points which I will take up later in the chapter.

2. Ibid., p. 115.

event separating Congreve from Sheridan and lying between the old comic traditions and the unavailing attempts of Goldsmith and Sheridan to revive those traditions on the stage. The point of transition, the exact moment at which comic energy passed from the drama to the novel, has been traditionally fixed with nice precision. It came soon after 1740 when Fielding, having already written something like a score of comic pieces for the stage, turned to the writing of *Joseph Andrews,* his first novel or, as he termed it, his "comic epic-poem in prose." The rise of the novel was, of course, neither so simple nor so instantaneous a phenomenon. Even Fielding himself had to write *Shamela* before he could write *Joseph Andrews.* Nevertheless, the two parts of Fielding's career dramatize the fact that the English novel was in its origins, as it has remained in much of its history, a lineal descendant of the English comic drama. While this is a subject that will be taken up more fully in the following chapter, it may be pointed out here that the advantages of the novel over the drama included its being addressed not so much to an audience as to a wide reading public. No doubt the reading public was not only wider but also more amorphous and incalculable in its response than a theatrical audience. But for this very reason it could be taken as not set in its tastes, as at least capable of divergent attitudes. Both Richardson's *Pamela* and Fielding's parodies of this novel could reasonably compete for its ear and favor. Its very newness and amorphousness made it, in fact, a promising audience for fresh comic experiment and revival. Thus, returning to Mudrick's argument, if Sheridan found the stage a disinherited institution, it was not because the inheritance of comedy had altogether disappeared from English literature but because it had been preempted by the English novel.

With comic energy rehabilitated in the novel, Goldsmith and Sheridan could only lament on the stage the dead hand of sentimentality and write sentimental comedy even as they decried it. At the beginning of *The Rivals* Sheridan, for instance, has his Prologue point to the figure of Comedy on the stage and exclaim:

> Look on her well—does she seem form'd to teach?
> Should you *expect* to hear this lady preach?
> Is gray experience suited to her youth?
> Do solemn sentiments become that mouth?
> . . . .
> Must we displace her? And instead advance
> The Goddess of the woful countenance—
> The sentimental Muse!

The question raised in these jaunty lines is not only much too hopefully phrased, it is blissfully anachronistic. A Vanbrugh might have addressed it to a Cibber with greater timeliness, even though in Vanbrugh himself, as pointed out in the preceding chapter, the preachy sentimental Muse was already on the point of elbowing out the gay Restoration goddess that Sheridan so plainly wishes to invoke. The question a century later was hardly whether the Muse of Comedy was to be displaced from the stage, since she was in fact virtually defunct there; it was rather whether anything at all could be done to displace the other—the "Goddess of the woful countenance"—who had long usurped the theater as her own exclusive realm. And the very manner in which Sheridan raises the issue shows that, try as he might to brighten her countenance with a jest or two, he has no intention of challenging her authority.

Goldsmith, too, had professed himself (in the preface to *The Good-Natured Man*) "strongly prepossessed in favour of the poets of the last age. . . . The term, *genteel comedy,* was then unknown amongst us." But though he "strove to imitate" the poets of the last age, he knew, as he says in the note dedicating *She Stoops to Conquer* to Dr. Johnson, that in his own age "undertaking a comedy, not merely sentimental, was very dangerous." Garrick's prologue to this play puts the situation more accurately than Sheridan's lines quoted above:

Pray would you know the reason why I'm crying?
The Comic Muse, long sick, is now a-dying!
. . . .
One hope remains,–hearing the maid was ill,
A Doctor comes this night to show his skill.
To cheer her heart, and give your muscles motion,
He, in Five Draughts prepared, presents a potion:
A kind of magic charm; for, be assured,
If you will swallow it, the maid is cured:
But desperate the Doctor, and her case is.

Aside from the assurance about the Muse's magical recovery, this is rather well said, for what Dr. Goldsmith and even Sheridan did was indeed to doctor the comedy of the time by administering a few potions derived from a more daring theatrical past but themselves first carefully doctored and made harmless and agreeable.

This is quite obviously true of Goldsmith who, by comparison with Sheridan, dealt openly and exclusively with goodness and good nature and strained less to modify the sentimental formula by peppering his plays with contradictory suggestions. Of the Restoration playwrights he looked to Farquhar rather than to Wycherley or Etherege. (*She Stoops to Conquer* has many resemblances to *The Beaux' Stratagem;* in fact for some time Goldsmith, at Reynolds's suggestion, thought of calling it *The Belle's Stratagem.*) His theme in theory can be summed up in a sentence spoken by one of the characters in *The Good-Natured Man:* "There are some faults so nearly allied to excellence, that we can scarce weed out the vice without eradicating the virtue." This certainly sounds like a modification, however slight, of what might be called the pulpit view of life. But, then, what

Goldsmith concedes in theory he takes away in practice. Indeed, the only vice of his hero, Honeywood, is the false reputation of being a vicious rake; his only fault is an excess of
virtue. In the more dangerous ("not merely sentimental") *She
Stoops to Conquer,* the hero is tongue-tied in genteel company
while free and easy with ladies of another stamp, including
those in an inferior social rank. But even here the vice is less a
vice than a device—primarily a device for turning and twisting
the plot—and the turns and twists of the plot are very nearly
the whole play.

At first sight Sheridan appears to be an altogether different
kind of dramatist, and his comedies seem a healthy and realistic comment on the "Virtue Rewarded" formula of sentimental plays. For one thing, he ranged more freely and farther in
the past, exerted much greater virtuosity, and no doubt briefly
enlivened the jaded stage with a sense of novelty. He also
wrote more various kinds of drama. In addition to his three
comedies, his two farcical pieces (one of them, *The Critic,*
with obvious affinities to Villiers's 1671 play *The Rehearsal*)
exploited the minor strain of what was called "laughing comedy," a type that enjoyed some popularity at the time in
reaction against the uniform solemnity and preachiness of genteel comedy. In *The Duenna* he turned to another minor
eighteenth-century dramatic type—the comic opera. And as his
final contribution to the stage, he even wrote a tragedy,
Pizarro, which was a reworking of Kotzebue's spectacular
thriller.

It was in his comedies that Sheridan went beyond his age
and attempted to press into service some of the forgotten
themes and traditions of the sixteenth and seventeenth centuries. If we look at these comedies, however, we find again
the device of making daring suggestions against the sentimental
formula without supporting or even meaning them in the least.
Consider, for instance, *A Trip to Scarborough*—an adaptation
of an adaptation which provides, because of this very historical

background, the clearest test of Sheridan's position on the question of sentimentality. Sheridan's model, *The Relapse,* though itself a concession to the sentimental view of love, nevertheless shows the "reformed" Loveless entering into a characteristic Restoration intrigue with Berinthia; it thereby disputes Cibber's easy view of reformation and the power of domestic virtue. In reworking *The Relapse,* Sheridan not merely returns to the spirit of the original behind the original but in fact improves on Cibber. While he retains the intrigue with Berinthia, the lovers are now guilty of nothing worse than exchanging a few sly words, and the whole affair becomes ultimately a red herring drawn across the straight path of sentimental love. In a final scene, arranged in a moonlit garden, it transpires that Berinthia had never even "entertained a thought," and Loveless himself is only too willing to rush back into the arms of his wife. Nor is Sheridan content with just one pair of virtuous lovers. In the same moonlit scene it dawns on Worthy (here called Townly) that he still loves only Berinthia, just as Berinthia has already made clear that despite her intrigue with Loveless she only loves him. Thus at one stroke Sheridan smooths out not only the difficulties of life but also the very real complications of Vanbrugh's play.

The difficulties in *The School for Scandal,* Sheridan's best known comedy, are certainly not smoothed out at one stroke. Nevertheless they are eventually resolved in the approved fashion. *The School for Scandal* is in fact a good play, but only in the sense that it is actable and funny and has, moreover, several well-rounded characters. But it is also in some ways a remarkably trifling play. "The school for scandal" idea itself is largely ornamental: it has little functional importance, much less the sort of importance one might expect of an idea proclaimed in the title. It is supposed to have been directed at a widespread contemporary vice, but neither this fact nor any amount of cleverness on Sheridan's part can conceal its basic triteness and triviality.

More important, of course, is the play's attack on the sentimental tradition. It is supposed to be a head-on collision, with
Sheridan protected by the sturdy old armor of Restoration
comedy. Yet the attack turns out to be another red herring,
though one much more cleverly manipulated. The center of
the attack is Joseph Surface—"a sentimental knave," as Lady
Sneerwell calls him—whose grave maxims and virtue conceal
what is supposed to be a many-sided villainy. He is cold, calculating, and avaricious. The play also wants us to believe him
an inveterate intriguer in love, a sort of latter-day Horner.
Neatly balanced against him is his brother, Charles, who resembles Goldsmith's Honeywood and may well have been modeled
after that good-natured man. Exactly reversing Joseph's attributes, Charles has the surface appearance of a dissolute rake
but is at bottom a perfectly good and generous man. And yet
the realities underneath are as unreal and schematic as the
surfaces or the masks, so that in the end they cancel each
other out equally effectively and leave us with the usual
nullity of sentimental comedy. The villainy and the virtue are
both discovered and respectively defeated and rewarded. The
good Charles, like Goldsmith's Honeywood, even promises to
purge himself of his generous little faults in the play's last
speech: "Why, as to reforming, Sir Peter, I'll make no promises, and that I take to be a proof that I intend to set about
it."

The trickery that characterizes the play is manifest in this
speech itself. The good man is really irreproachable, but then
he will make no promises to reform himself, reformation being
no easy matter, and yet indeed he has already started reforming. This is the sort of attack that Sheridan's play makes on
sentimentality, in big matters as well as small. Sheridan might
himself have made Lady Sneerwell's admission: "Pshaw!—
there's no possibility of being witty without a little ill nature."
And indeed very little ill nature enables Sheridan to show his
wit as well as his indebtedness to the witty "poets of the last

age." This is even true in the case of the arch-villain, Joseph
Surface—though we see the virtues and vices of his sentimentality, we see nothing of his amorous knavery. The famous
screen scene obviously owes its inspiration to *The Country
Wife,* yet it should rightly be called the smokescreen scene. It
is true that the screen in Joseph's chamber conceals a lady, a
young country wife at that, and one whose husband is Joseph's old guardian and benefactor. Furthermore, this husband, Sir Peter Teazle, is shown himself discussing the uses of
the screen with Joseph even as his lady hides behind it. There
is also the suggestion that various other ladies may well have
taken their turn behind the screen at various times in the past.
Yet to compare this most salacious and daring of Sheridan's
scenes with Wycherley's play, or even with the more timely
Tom Jones, is to see all the more clearly Sheridan's genius for
peppering a tale without really spicing it, for raising much dust
without allowing any traffic. For, when the screen is removed
at last, it proves not merely Lady Teazle but virtually the
whole play entirely blameless. Lady Teazle, the country wife,
herself proves the point conclusively. Starting out with ideas
remarkably like those of Wycherley's Margery Pinchwife, she
soon makes us realize that in reality she, like Sheridan's Berinthia, has hardly so much as "entertained a thought," and in
any case she is prepared not only to remain a virtuous woman
but become a model wife to her aging husband. The dust
raised in the interim goes nicely with the titular idea, showing
up the activities of the "school" of which she herself had been
a reputed member.

These plays, while clearly expressing a mild dissatisfaction
with the contemporary theater, seem to have gained little
other than their reputation from the recourse to older drama.
Curiously enough they strike us in some ways as more sentimental than even Steele's thoroughgoing sentimental comedies. Furthermore, where they appear to diverge from the set
formulas of sentimentality in the interests of realism, in a

sense they only become more unrealistic—idiosyncratic, unrelated to anything except what they relate, too often dependent on a character or situation that signifies nothing but itself. In other words, the sort of departure they attempt makes
them more lively but at the same time more trifling and less
relevant.

The Rivals alone can claim a certain amount of significance
and limited originality within the larger comic tradition to
which it belongs. It also exhibits, more than any other play of
Sheridan's, a pastiche of motifs, character patterns, situations,
and theatrical devices drawn from various comedies of the
preceding two centuries. To the extent to which it is an epitaph on the English comic drama, it is one of those jaunty
epitaphs that delight in rehearsing and summarizing the main
features and signal achievements of that which has passed from
the world. Or, to change the metaphor, the play may be
viewed as a sort of archaeologist's surface, an open and remarkably uncomplicated facade showing layer beneath layer
of literary history. This side of the play has its own interest
and to it we must briefly turn.

To begin with there is the immediate past, or rather the
immediate present—the sentimentality of Sheridan's own day
and age. "When hearts deserving happiness would unite their
fortunes, Virtue would crown them with an unfading garland
of modest hurtless flowers." This, one feels, ought to be
tongue in cheek, but, being spoken by Julia, one simply cannot be sure. It may be meant quite seriously as the moral of
the play. True, in the epilogue (spoken by the same actress
who plays Julia) we have a different moral, which is better in
that it indicates some of the better things that have gone
before:

> Man's social happiness all rests on us:
> Through all the drama—whether d—n'd or not—
> *Love* gilds the *scene* and *women* guide the *plot.*

Nevertheless, the problem of sentimentality looms large within the play, in the shape of Julia and her lover, Faulkland. It is a problem only because here, as in his later plays, Sheridan is not content to offer sentimental love straight but must trifle with it a little. The trifling lies in the character of Faulkland, through whom Sheridan clearly means to ridicule mildly the contemporary notion of the good and sensitive though self-doubting and therefore overly jealous lover. Julia, on the other hand, is presented without question as the epitome of goodness, patience, sense, sensibility, and all the other desirable feminine virtues. The heroine of weighty maxims and moral lectures, she is the play's unequivocal tribute to the sentimental formula; though Lydia once calls her "my grave cousin," Lydia, as much as everyone else, is made to look up to her as to a mentor of undisputed moral authority.

Julia and Faulkland are, of course, important inasmuch as they share the theme of love on almost equal terms with Lydia and Captain Absolute, the real comic heroine and hero of the play. But sentimentality likewise colors certain subsidiary characters and situations of otherwise older ancestry and inspiration. The hero's father, Sir Anthony Absolute, and the heroine's aunt, the famous Mrs. Malaprop, for example, are both character parts in the old tradition of humors. Sir Anthony is parental tyranny or absolute authority: "If not, z—ds!" as he threatens his son in one of the better expressions of his supposedly blind absolutism, "don't enter the same hemisphere with me! don't dare to breathe the same air, or use the same light with me; but get an atmosphere and a sun of your own!" The bluster and "country" rudeness being clearly reminiscent of more than one character in Restoration comedy, we can view him altogether as Sheridan's rendering of a Jonsonian humor after the manner of Restoration playwrights. On the other hand, Mrs. Malaprop, whose humor is vanity, goes back in a straight line through Fielding's Mrs. Slipslop to Shakespeare's Dogberry. With Dogberry she shares not merely the habit of malapropism but that unshakable sense of personal worth which is the common source of their aspiring locutions. Her short scene with Captain Absolute (III, iii), where she cheerfully asks him to read aloud the letter that refers to her as a "she-dragon" and a person of "ridiculous vanity," owes much to Dogberry's involvement with the villains of *Much Ado* and his total shock that even self-confessed villains can take it into their head to call him an "ass." "Me, sir—*me*—he means *me* there," Mrs. Malaprop repeats to Captain Absolute, much as the outraged constable keeps insisting that the examining officers not forget to write him down an ass. As the comparison with Dogberry shows, these characters—the fierceness of their humors notwithstanding—are at bottom good-natured. Sir Anthony's tyranny is evident throughout as the bluster of good intentions. And the she-dragon, whom the plot reveals as softer in the heart than in the head, is prepared in the end to swallow her vanity and bless her niece's marriage with the secret reviler of her parts of speech.

With two other peripheral characters Sheridan moves a step closer to Shakespeare. Bob Acres—the country wooer caught in a town world, the pale squire on whom are thrust both the idea of courage and the laws of honor and dueling—is, of course, reminiscent of Sir Andrew Aguecheek. His new domicile being what it is, his gulling becomes an entirely humane affair, and he emerges from the duel not merely without fighting it, but also with the laugh on the other side. The trait of cowardice is in fact transformed into the virtue of good sense; and a major part in the transformation is played by Acres's servant David, who thus becomes a Falstaffian expounder of common sense against the pretentious claims of honor.

> *Acres.* But my honour, David, my honour! I must be careful of my honour.
> *David.* Ay, by the mass! and I would be very careful of

it; and I think in return my *honour* couldn't do less than to be very careful of *me*. . . . Look'ee, master, this *honour* seems to me to be a marvellous false friend: ay, truly, a very courtier-like servant.—Put the case, I was a gentleman (which, thank God, no one can say of me); well—my honour makes me quarrel with another gentleman of my acquaintance.—So—we fight. (Pleasant enough that.) Boh!—I kill him—(the more's my luck.) But put the case that he kills me!—by mass! I go to the worms, and my honour whips over to my enemy.

    Acres. No, David—in that case!—Odds crowns and laurels! your honour follows you to the grave.

    David. Now, that's just the place where I could make a shift to do without it.

Much can be cited in this same vein, but it is time to change the argument. For all this borrowing helps to define, even as it hems in, the originality of *The Rivals*. The originality lies in the Lydia-Absolute plot, which is the heart of the play. There is no deliberate borrowing here such as we have seen elsewhere in Sheridan. Yet the story of Lydia and Captain Absolute is not for that reason an idiosyncratic story, unrelated to any other love stories both before or after. On the contrary, its originality lies precisely in its relation to a continuing tradition. It does not imitate older comedies; it shares their critical purpose, and in so doing even foreshadows the point of departure for the later comedy of Jane Austen.

The critical purpose of *The Rivals* can, of course, be exaggerated if not actually misrepresented. It is, for instance, tempting to claim that Sheridan is concerned with nothing less than the problem of a woman's freedom in a society that looks upon its women as property and upon marriage as a business transaction. This, after all, can be said to be the point of the play's two authoritarian figures, Mrs. Malaprop and Sir Anthony Absolute. Both assert a view of marriage fiercely opposed to the idea of independence and choice—opposed, in fact, to the very idea of young people's thinking or reading or engaging in anything and everything that is supposed to subvert, however indirectly, their own business philosophy. The point is best expressed by Sir Anthony when he urges on his son an advantageous marriage which the son finds unacceptable on the ground that the lady who goes with the advantages remains unknown and unseen. "Odds life, sir!" explodes the father, "if you have the estate, you must take it with the live stock on it, as it stands." And if the young man's heart is engaged elsewhere:

> *Sir Anth.* Then pray let it send an excuse.—It is very sorry—but *business* prevents its waiting on her.
> *Abs.* But my vows are pledged to her.
> *Sir Anth.* Let us foreclose, Jack; let her foreclose; they are not worth redeeming.

Lydia has already been subjected to the same argument through the combined might of Sir Anthony and Mrs. Malaprop and, being a woman, without the opportunity to marshal a complete objection in return. Mrs. Malaprop's objections: "You thought, miss! I don't know any business you have to think at all—thought does not become a young woman. . . . What business have you, miss, with *preference* and *aversion?* They don't become a young woman," are reinforced by Sir Anthony: "It is not to be wondered at, ma'am,—all this is the natural consequence of teaching girls to read. . . . Madam, a circulating library in a town is as an evergreen tree of diabolical knowledge! It blossoms through the year!—And depend on it, Mrs. Malaprop, that they who are so fond of handling the leaves will long for the fruit at last."

Given all this, we can readily sympathize with Lydia's resolution not to allow herself to become "a mere Smithfield bargain" and with her own opposing ideology of love. As she says, recollecting the days of romantic wonder:

How often have I stole forth, in the coldest night in January, and found him in the garden, stuck like a dripping statue!—There would he kneel to me in the snow, and sneeze and cough so pathetically! he shivering with cold and I with apprehension! and while the freezing blast numbed our joints, how warmly would he press me to pity his flame and glow with mutual ardour!—Ah, Julia, that was something like being in love.

Yet, as is clear from this passage itself, what animates Lydia is the spirit not of love but of pure bookish romance. She is not the radical critic of her culture that she imagines herself to be; she is rather its mildly self-deluded comic heroine. Her enemies are not Mrs. Malaprop and Sir Anthony, whom she condemns, but, as Sheridan presents the case, herself and that same circulating library which they condemn.

Thus the theme marriage for love against marriage for money, although Sheridan suggests it indirectly, is not the comic problem of *The Rivals*. In Restoration comedy, as we have seen, money and marriage on the one hand and love on the other are treated as two separate issues. The problem of Lydia and Captain Absolute is that for them the two happen to be identical. As Absolute pithily summarizes the situation: "My father wants to *force* me to marry the very girl I am plotting to run away with." What, then, keeps the lovers apart—what introduces the element of conflict into their situation—can be seen by comparing them with the other pair of lovers in the play. For in both situations love happens to coincide happily with material advantage and filial duty, so that in each case caprice alone can be said to constitute the lovers' difficulty. The difference, however, is that Faulkland's caprice, self-doubt, is precisely that—a caprice, an idiosyncrasy not unlike the personal idiosyncrasies of the other heroes of Sheridan and Goldsmith, carried here to a still more absurd and tiresome length. Little is needed to subdue it except a turn in the plot at the appropriate moment. By comparison, Lydia's caprice is more in the nature of a comic idea, and something more or less like comic experience is needed to free her from its hold.

Lydia's story is both singular and representative. She imagines her lover, known to her as Beverley, to be an impoverished but romantic young officer—or rather she imagines him romantic because impoverished. As we are informed in the first scene, she is "a lady of a very singular taste," a lady who likes her lover "better as a *half-pay ensign* than if she knew he was son and heir to Sir Anthony Absolute, a baronet of three thousand a year." And in the very second scene we know the reason for her singular taste: she is a devourer of romances. Her maid, returning from her errand to the circulating library, reports her failure to procure *The Reward of Constancy, The Fatal Connexion, The Mistakes of the Heart,* and *The Delicate Distress;* nevertheless, she has brought to her mistress an armful of other equally tempting titles along with *Peregrine Pickle, Humphrey Clinker,* and *The Sentimental Journey.* Marvin Mudrick, regarding the scene with some severity, comments that it is a poor way "of expressing Lydia's affectation . . . to feed the audience on curiously mixed, interminable catalogues of lending-library fiction, in which Smollett is equated with Sterne and both with the true-romance writers of the time—as if Sheridan, acquiescing in the eighteenth-century snobbery toward the novel, is himself incapable of making the distinctions."[3]

This comment, I think, completely misses the point. For, whether or not Sheridan was "himself incapable of making the distinctions," the "curiously mixed" titles reflect not his confusion but that of his characters (to whom at least one of the reputable titles would seem immediately promising just because of its use of the word *sentimental*). Indeed, it is the fact of confusion as well as affectation that needs to be expressed

3. Ibid., p. 117.

here, the point being not merely that Lydia's taste runs to romance but equally that she is incapable of distinguishing romance from real life—that to her all experience, whether in life or literature, can only be the experience of "fatal connexions" and "delicate distresses." Nor is this confusion expressed only through the book catalogue device; it is expressed elsewhere through dialogue and situation as well as the whole Lydia-Absolute action in the play. In Lydia's long speech cited above, for instance, we see the same undiscriminating combination of sneezes and coughs on the one hand and flames and ardors on the other. Likewise, what follows the catalogue of romances shows the extent to which Lydia's sense of reality has faded into the nonsense of her reading. For, as she and Julia bring each other up to date on their respective situations, Lydia constantly filters the facts of both through the haze of romance, making every item coincide with the sort of sentiment expressed in one or the other of the titles mentioned earlier.

The importance of the catalogue, however, is not simply that it expresses confusion by mixing up romances and novels cheek-by-jowl. What the emphasis on books makes clear at the outset is that Lydia is a female Quixote—that, in Sir Anthony's words, "the girl's mad!—her brain's turned by reading." If not mad, she certainly suffers in a mental sense from that imaginary squint whose physical existence or absence provides much laughing matter in various ways at various times in the play. What the interminable catalogue does also is show how little Lydia's "singular taste" is in reality to be considered singular. For, as we learn in the same early scene, not just Lydia but all fashionable ladies are after the same romances and devour them with equal avidity. Lydia's caprice is thus something more than a caprice; it is a fashion, a general squint in the culture of which she is the representative comic heroine.

Lydia's lover, Captain Absolute, is what might be called the positive hero of this culture. He knows what he wants and

knows also how to get it all. Initially his problem is that if he
agrees to elope with Lydia in the character of Beverley, he
loses two-thirds of her fortune; yet if he offers to marry her in
his own character and with the recommendation of his own
name and fortune, he stands to lose the girl herself. His solution is not to attempt anything rash or precipitate but instead
to "prepare her gradually for the discovery, and make myself
necessary to her, before I risk it." This sounds unheroically
cool and calculating, and so it is. But within the value-scheme
of the play—in contrast, that is, with Lydia's absurd illusions,
Julia's vapid sentimentality, and Faulkland's "exquisite
nicety"—Absolute becomes the embodiment of manly confidence and good sense. He accepts from the outset the play's
thesis that financial interest and filial duty are not opposed to
love but are rather its necessary supports and blessings;
through his success at the end, Sheridan underlines the same
thesis regarding the basic health and harmony of the culture
depicted in the play.

In the meantime Sheridan does his best to protract suspense
through the flimsiest theatrical devices and through having
Absolute play up to Lydia's fantasies at great length. "Will you
then, Beverley, consent to forfeit that portion of my paltry
wealth?—that burden on the wings of love?" asks Lydia in the
phraseology of her lending-library gospel. "O, come to me—
rich only thus—in loveliness," he replies, humoring the same
gospel: "Love shall be our idol and support! . . . Proud of
calamity, we will enjoy the wreck of wealth; while the surrounding gloom of adversity shall make the flame of our pure
love show doubly bright." To this Lydia exclaims in a rapturous aside: "Now could I fly with him to the antipodes! but
my persecution is not yet come to a crisis." When the crisis
does come at last, it is, of course, not of the expected sort.
Discovering that the romantic Beverley and the eligible Absolute are one and the same suitor, Lydia's first reaction is:
"So!—there will be no elopement after all!" Later, developing

the sentiment, she complains: "when I thought we were coming to the prettiest distress imaginable, to find myself made a mere Smithfield bargain of at last.—There, had I projected one of the most sentimental elopements!—so becoming a disguise!—so amiable a ladder of ropes!—Conscious moon—four horses . . . O, I shall die with disappointment."

What she does, of course, is not die but straighten out her romantic squint and look somewhat within herself and somewhat upon the realities of the world outside. "What, you have been treating *me* like a child!—humoring my romance," she says to Absolute. *"I* am myself the only dupe at last!" To which he replies: "Come, come, we must lay aside some of our romance—a little *wealth* and *comfort* may be endured after all."

Chapter 5

The Adjudication of
Fielding's Comedy

Fielding's place in literary history has a double importance. By
creating what he called the "comic epic-poem in prose," he
helped to establish the main features of the English novel as it
was to be written for at least the next century and a half. But
he also gave, in this new form, a fresh lease on life to English
comedy. The tying of the comic and the epic no doubt delim-
ited markedly—even regrettably if one considers some of Fielding's successors—the chief concerns as well as the formal procedures of the novel. There are, for instance, subjects which
we recognize today as among the legitimate concerns of the
novel; which in fact we prize as the deeper and truer concerns
of this or that novelist in the Fielding tradition itself; and
which yet are treated by that novelist in an unrecognized and
disconcertingly incidental fashion, as though clearly beyond
the novel's proper business. At the same time there are other
subjects which, no matter how perfunctory in his particular
case, he continues nevertheless to treat routinely as that
proper business. This in turn has the consequence frequently
of detaching what then becomes "plot interest" from the
other interests of the novel. Indeed, one cannot doubt that the
example of Fielding has proved powerful, both for better and
worse. And yet it is of some importance to distinguish the
man's influence from the man himself. This is particularly true
with regard to a subject that concerns us most directly in the
present context—the subject of love. It is a real subject in

Fielding's comedy, not the mere love interest that it was to become later—the notorious sine qua non of nineteenth-century fiction. Here, in fact, Fielding should be seen as inheriting and evaluating a past as well as bequeathing a future. For in his work love is what it had been in the best comedy before him—both a recognized value in itself and a way of testing the assumptions of a culture through its main love conventions.

These main conventions are the two that have been noted previously. One was made immediately available to Fielding in Richardson's *Pamela*—the story of a virtuous girl whose exemplary character lay not in the quality of her virtue, but in its material and matrimonial outcome, which was vastly advantageous to herself. Richardson, however, was by no means the first writer to consider profitable marriage to a rake a suitable reward for virtue. The history of sentimental literature, as Joseph Wood Krutch has pointed out, is full of comparable devices denoting the same "hypocritical rage for the moral."[1] On the other hand, there was the older convention of libertinism—from the literary point of view, once potent but still available which had formed the central convention of Restoration comedy and which Fielding himself had attempted when he first began to write plays after the manner of William Congreve.

How exactly does Fielding place himself with regard to these two conventions? It used to be thought once that, in his reaction against sentimental love, Fielding had only reverted to the stock Restoration idea of love as sensuality and licentiousness. Today it seems that he is being held guilty of the exact opposite, of not reacting against sentimentality at all but instead furthering its cause under a superficially deceptive color. In this latter view Fielding's novels become nothing less nor

1. Joseph Wood Krutch, *Comedy and Conscience After the Restoration* (New York, Columbia University Press, 1924), p. 211.

more than a sad landmark in the progressive degeneration of English comedy from Congreve to Sheridan. For instance, Marvin Mudrick, in discussing the dissipation of the Congreve tradition—a discussion already referred to in the last chapter—sees Fielding as a precursor of Sheridan inasmuch as Sheridan was putting back on the stage those "good-natured sentimental dramas of comic intrigue and situation, which Fielding had acclimated to fiction, in the guise of anti-sentimentalism, a generation before."[2]

Having discussed the case of Sheridan at some length, I need say here only that insofar as Fielding counts in Sheridan's background, he counts there as something of a saving grace, along with such other lesser or greater background figures as Wycherley and Shakespeare. If Sheridan still remains by and large a sentimental dramatist, it is not because but rather in spite of whatever recourse he took to these writers. And in any case the future effect of Fielding's novels is better judged not by what happened on the stage—where nothing much seemed capable of happening anyway—but by what happened in prose fiction itself, and particularly by the later comic novels of Jane Austen. Returning, however, to the question of Fielding's relation to his own literary background, it is not at all surprising that he should be condemned by turns as either a sentimentalist or an advocate of sensual delights and libertinism. Indeed, his comedy depends on both almost equally, though only for the sort of interplay through which comedy usually makes its own final and distinct affirmation. But if we miss this comic interplay, it is then an easy step to conclude that either of the two sides represents Fielding's true position while the other is only a color. In reality Fielding is an advocate of neither. He is a judge over both; and such is the nature of his adjudication that it leads him in the end to an idea of love in whose light both sentimentalism and libertinism stand convicted for what

2. *English Stage Comedy,* ed. W. K. Wimsatt, Jr., p. 115.

they are: partial and misleading theories of love, each pleading in place of a real and possible good a different but equally reductive alibi.

That the establishment of this judgment is the principle behind Fielding's comedy can be shown only through a systematic discussion of his novels, especially *Tom Jones*. But by way of a preface it is useful to pursue a little further his idea of love as simply an idea or, as Fielding himself would call it, a philosophy or a doctrine. Of course to Fielding, as to any other comic writer, philosophical doctrines meant little except as active principles of conduct. "By philosophy," a minor character says in *Amelia*, "I do not mean the bare knowledge of right and wrong, but an energy, a habit, as Aristotle calls it." Or, as Dr. Harrison in the same novel asks of another doctrine: "Are we like Agrippa, only almost Christians? or, is Christianity a matter of bare theory, and not a rule for our practice?" It is on this basis of practical energies and habits engendered that Fielding judges the two philosophies of love, the spuriously virtuous as much as the vaguely hedonistic. This too explains why he seems to judge acts of undisciplined passion and impulse leniently, while reserving unqualified censure for those of sentimental calculation. In the first place, a sin of passion is not an irrevocable evil precisely because it is not doomed in every case to lead to a settled habit. As Fielding observes in the introduction to Book VII of *Tom Jones*, with a glance at the naïve faith in the truthfulness of contemporary plays, "A single bad act no more constitutes a villain in life, than a single bad part on the stage." Calculation and hypocrisy, on the other hand, are habits; they reflect not an error of the energy of love but its negation, its perversion into a passion for material and social ambition. Furthermore, these involved a question larger than that of individual morality; as Fielding saw the situation, calculation and hypocrisy had come to usurp the energies of the whole culture and were now almost its unquestioned habits. It is a mistake, he concludes in another introductory chapter of *Tom Jones* (Book XIV), to affix "the character of lewdness to these times. On the contrary, I am convinced there never was less of love intrigue carried on among persons of condition than now. Our present women have been taught by their mothers to fix their thoughts only on ambition and vanity, and to despise the pleasures of love as unworthy their regard."

This being so, Fielding might well have taken the sentimental formula as the object of his comedy and lewdness and pleasure as his answer to it. But this is not what he did. It must in fact be credited to his judgment that, despite the difference which he recognized between the two philosophies, he regarded them as not at all opposed to each other in one fundamental respect. The quarrel between Restoration and sentimental drama notwithstanding, he saw both kinds of love as arising from a common social root, and alike in one basic objective. Richardson had romanticized his age by holding up, as its paradigmatic image, the marriage of a rakish squire and a maidservant. Fielding realized that, for the rake no less than for the sentimental hero, marriage was a matter of interest, not of love or pleasure. When we think of the world of Restoration comedy as it enters into Fielding's novels, we think only of such aspects as the bawds, the duels, the masquerades, and the intrigues that color the later portion of *Tom Jones* and permeate the otherwise sad and seedy world of *Amelia*. We forget to take into account what Fielding shows us everywhere—the unswerving principle of matrimonial calculation which is as much a part of this beau monde, and which its sense of gaiety and abandon is never allowed to compromise. A stalwart representative of this world is introduced early in *Tom Jones* in the person of Mrs. Western, the fashionable town lady, whom we find lecturing her niece frequently "on the subject of matrimony; which she treated not as a romantic scheme of happiness arising from love, as it hath been described by the poets; nor did she mention any of those purposes for which we are taught by divines to regard it as instituted by sacred authority: she considered it rather as a fund in which prudent women deposit their fortunes to the best advantage, in order to receive a larger interest for them than they could have elsewhere." And it is, of course, on the strength of the same principle that Tom Jones, anxious toward the end of the novel to break his connection with Lady Bellaston, is able to win all by apparently risking all; for, as he is correctly advised, no matter how irresistible the lady's passion for him, she is sure to break with him rather than accept the marriage proposal of a penniless young man.

To this extent, then, there was little difference between the two conventions. Both reflected the paramount importance of material interests and prudence, but from this common prudential base the two diverged consciously into different and opposed doctrines concerning the nature and purpose of love. And it was these rationalized superstructures that, more than anything else, engaged the comedy of Fielding. For the sentimentalist the object of love was material advantage; for the libertine this was the object of marriage only, the purpose of love being to satisfy an appetite. In one case, accordingly, love became an elaborate apology; in the other, a cynical reduction. Fielding was too realistic a writer to disregard the part played by material interests in life and too serious a writer to deny the place of appetite in sexual love. To him, however, love ultimately had no object but itself. As the hero of *Amelia* declares: "Beauty is, indeed, the object of liking, great qualities of admiration, good ones of esteem; but the devil take me if I think any thing but love to be the object of love."

On the nature of this love, which is its own cause and justification, Fielding has inserted a brief essay in the opening chapter of Book VI of *Tom Jones*. The essay arrives through expository argument at the same judgment that is the key to the meaning and organization of his best comedy. Fielding sets out playfully and yet with complete seriousness by taking issue with "that modern doctrine, by which certain philosophers" claim to have discovered that "no such passion" as love exists "in the human breast." He replies to this Hobbesian argument by pointing out that "there is in some (I believe in many) human breasts a kind and benevolent disposition, which is gratified by contributing to the happiness of others," and that "if we will not call such disposition love, we have no name for it." But this is a general definition that applies as much to philanthropy, to friendship, to filial and parental affection—all of them among the minor themes of Fielding—as it does to sexual love, his major concern. Sexual love, he goes on, is not "what is commonly called love, namely, the desire of satisfying a voracious appetite with a certain quantity of delicate white human flesh." That is only its familiar reduction. Sexual love is still the love for which he is "an advocate," the disposition that he has designated by that name, but now with this difference: that "when it operates towards one of a different sex, [it] is very apt, towards its complete gratification, to call in the aid of that hunger which I have mentioned above; and which it is so far from abating, that it heightens all its delights to a degree scarce imaginable by those who have never been susceptible of any other emotions than what have proceeded from appetite alone."

This, I think, is a succinct answer to the sort of dilemma presented by Worthy's final speech in *The Relapse* already noted in a previous chapter:[3]

> For what but now was the wild flame of love,
> Or (to dissect that specious term)
> The vile, the gross desires of flesh and blood,
> Is in a moment turned to adoration.
> The coarser appetite of nature's gone,
> And 'tis, methinks, the food of angels I require.

The dilemma, of course, went beyond the resolution of Van-

3. See pp. 117-19 above.

brugh's play and even beyond the impasse of sentimental and libertine literature foreshadowed there; it was eventually the dilemma of a whole culture polarized between the claims of body and soul, passion and virtue, pleasure and happiness. Nor is Fielding's answer merely a matter of right precept; it is the basic truth of his novel, and upon it he stakes the novel's emotive force. If you will accept these matters, he concludes to the reader in this early chapter, "you may now proceed to their exemplification in the following pages; if you do not, you have, I assure you, already read more than you have understood; and it would be wiser to pursue your business, or your pleasures (such as they are), than to throw away any more of your time in reading what you can neither taste nor comprehend."

Thus Fielding saw this love, the central tenet of his doctrine, as the summum bonum of life—transcending all the business and pleasures (such as they were) of men in his world. It was, as Middleton Murry puts it, "the thread of gold in the sordid texture of society."[4] Not merely Fielding's readers, however, but his heroes have to comprehend the meaning and value of this love. Herein, as a matter of fact, we can see the nature of Fielding's development as a comic novelist—all the way from burlesque to dark comedy. For though love is the one constant value behind all his works, it is not enforced or dramatized in the same way in all of them. In *Shamela* its standing is naturally that of an implication, the unformulated issue behind the one that is formulated. In *Joseph Andrews* it enters the story itself, but so far as the hero is concerned, it is his happy possession from the outset—he needs to comprehend nothing further but rather defend what he already possesses. It is only in the two novels after *Joseph Andrews* that the hero himself is caught in the issue, called upon to discover and recognize it

4. J. Middleton Murry, "In Defense of Fielding," *Unprofessional Essays* (London, Jonathan Cape, 1956), p. 40.

for himself, and enabled to do so only after first wandering
and being almost lost in a labyrinth of sentimental falsity,
sensual temptation, and the many prudential sophistries leading thereto. Needless to add, the development, while primarily
in the direction of greater dramatization, represents also a development in the clarity and meaning of the value thus dramatized.

Before turning to the novels a word may be said concerning
Fielding's method, which is the method of comedy adapted to
the problems and opportunities of the new province of writing. Basically it involves confronting romance with reality.
While realistic fiction was written before Fielding, he was the
first writer to undertake realistic fiction that conducted itself
deliberately as anti-romance. His insistence everywhere on the
historical truth of his novels is thus, in the first place, an
argument against the romantic make-believe of other fiction
writers. In offering the definition ("comic epic-poem in
prose") as well as further explanation of his work in the preface to *Joseph Andrews*—the critical starting-point in this
respect both for him and us—his whole effort is to distinguish
it firmly from "the productions of romance writers" and align
it instead with comic literature of the past, whether in dramatic or epic form. Misunderstanding, he feels, may arise from
the fact that "those voluminous works commonly called Romances" (such as *Clelia, Cleopatra, Cassandra*) resemble his
own book in that they are all fictions in prose. But this is an
irrelevant consideration, and Fielding is at pains repeatedly to
warn the reader against being misled by the superficial resemblance. A novel is for him—as he puts it in one of the introductory chapters of *Tom Jones* (Book IV)—a "narrative of
plain matter of fact . . . a newspaper of many volumes," unlike
the "idle romances which are filled with monsters, the productions, not of nature, but of distempered brains." And yet, on
the other hand, historical truth is not confined to everyday

fact, to minute realism. Like the comedy of the past, his fiction is concerned at the same time with some measure of the
truth about a whole age. It is after all an epic poem as well as a
newspaper—in his own words, a "heroic, historical, prosaic
poem."

To the extent, then, to which a comic novel opposes romantic pretense with the truth of reality, to the extent to which it
is a newspaper of the age, it can easily adapt for its own use
the method of dramatic comedy, which is what Fielding does.
The novel, of course, allows for—though it certainly does not
demand, as witnessed by Jane Austen's novels—the exploitation of the principle on an epic or simply large and panoramic
scale. The one new requirement, however, is the management
of the narrative presence, something that has no real place on
the stage but without which no novel can exist. This presence
need not be substantively that of the author; it may be that of
a designated fictional deputy, as it is in James's *The Ambassa-
dors* for instance. Such a step represents a further dramatization of the narrative necessity. But even so, in *The Ambassa-
dors* as in *Pride and Prejudice* or *Tom Jones,* there are strictly
nondramatic portions of the novel which communicate directly either simple information or impressions, reflections,
and analyses, be they those of the author or of one of his
characters.

The new province of writing conferred this added necessity
or freedom on the author, to be used by him as he chose. The
point I should like to make here is that Fielding used it in a
manner which was not only consonant with the purpose of
comedy in general, but which enabled him to carry out that
purpose in the moment to moment detail that forms the continuous fiber of a novel. By developing the twin principles of
narrative irony and ironic analysis of motive, he was able to
devise innumerable small wheels, as it were, to turn within and
support at every point the primum mobile of comic art. "In
particular," as A. R. Humphreys pointed out several years ago,

"his irony reinforces the scorn for 'theory' and subtle ratio-
cination so typical of his empirical and practical age."[5] Consider, for instance, the following two passages occurring within
a few pages in the first book of *Tom Jones,* the first relating to
Doctor Blifil and the second to his brother Captain Blifil. Both
are concerned with the subject, entertained by each brother in
turn, of marriage with Miss Bridget—Squire Allworthy's sister
and, at that time, his only possible heir:

> As sympathies of all kinds are apt to beget love; so expe-
> rience teaches us that none have a more direct tendency
> this way than those of a religious kind between persons of
> different sexes. The doctor found himself so agreeable to
> Miss Bridget, that he now began to lament an unfortunate
> accident which had happened to him about ten years be-
> fore; namely, his marriage with another woman, who was
> not only still alive, but, what was worse, known to be so
> by Mr. Allworthy. This was a fatal bar to that happiness
> which he otherwise saw sufficient probability of obtaining
> with this young lady; for as to criminal indulgences, he
> certainly never thought of them. This was owing either to
> his religion, as is most probable, or to the purity of his
> passion, which was fixed on those things which matrimony
> only, and not criminal correspondence, could put him in
> possession of, or could give him any title to.

> He [Captain Blifil] was one of those wise men, who regard
> beauty in the other sex as a very worthless and superficial
> qualification; or, to speak more truly, who rather choose
> to possess every convenience of life with an ugly woman,
> than a handsome one without any of those conveniences.

5. A. R. Humphreys, "Fielding's Irony: Its Method and Effects,"
The Review of English Studies, 18 (1942), pp. 183-96. See *Fielding: A
Collection of Critical Essays,* ed. Ronald Paulson, Twentieth Century
Views (Englewood Cliffs, Prentice-Hall, 1962), p. 13.

If we regard these two passages as a roundabout way of saying that the two men were after Bridget's money rather than Bridget herself, we will have little patience with Fielding's ironical way of saying so. Of course, the passages do say this; but that is only the obvious part of their irony—and comedy. Among other things, they also turn upside down, insofar as is possible within the space, the meaning of such value-charged words and concepts as "sympathy," "love," "religion," "happiness," "purity," and "wisdom." The achievement thus does not lie in just laying bare the obvious prudential motive of the two men. It lies rather in associating the motive with all these values; in showing on a small scale the process of deception, including possible self deception, by which a sordid truth gets converted into the most high-sounding abstractions.

However simple the effect may seem to us today, by devising it Fielding was not only meeting his own needs but suggesting further possibilities which he did not himself fully exploit. He was creating the basic working method of not just his but other kinds of comic novel—a "species of novel," as Ronald Paulson concludes after his own fine discussion of Fielding's irony, "in which an author consciously sets the real conduct of everyday against the large abstractions of moral values, classical literature, or myth."[6]

Fielding is among those writers who make little display of the effort, literary or otherwise, that lies behind their work. This sense of decorum in the finished work can easily lead to the mistaken belief that no serious effort has in fact gone into it. In Fielding's case there is an assumption that all his concerns and effects as a novelist were an easy possession of his from the outset, and the only question worth deciding is whether this or that work best exemplifies those fixed and limited effects. Thus in the introductory chapter to *The Great*

6. Paulson, *Fielding*, pp. 9-10.

Tradition F. R. Leavis, dismissing *Tom Jones* as a bloated novel so much the worse for being stretched to epic proportions and *Amelia* as evidence that by this time Fielding had "gone soft," observes that what Fielding *"can* do appears to best advantage in *Joseph Andrews.*"[7] The truth is that Fielding's concerns were not rigidly determined at the outset, but continued to develop from one work to the next, so that what we see in him is a process of thinking, learning, and experimenting until the very end. *Joseph Andrews* is no doubt an exemplary work, but only with reference to Fielding's rather limited purpose at the time; similarly, even *Shamela* shows to great advantage what the author wanted to and could do in that kind of work. The biggest single extension of interests is to be seen in *Amelia;* if this is a weak and disorderly novel, in places careless and sentimental ("soft" in that sense), it is also his most experimental. In it Fielding was pioneering into relatively unfamiliar territory: the problems of public administration, social justice, economic hardship—a whole world of not incidental but systematic harassment and deprivation. While still concerned with the art of love, he was attempting here to place it in a new context, to relate it to what he calls in the opening chapter the "ART OF LIFE." Much that is interesting in the so-called "social" novel of the following century may in fact be said to derive from Fielding's general picture in *Amelia* of honest but powerless, and therefore dispirited and dismal,

7. F. R. Leavis, *The Great Tradition* (New York, Doubleday Anchor, 1954), pp. 11-13. It may be mentioned here that critics who have taken issue with Leavis's judgment of Fielding disregard and occasionally even misrepresent his high estimate of Fielding's historical importance. Compare, for instance, Ronald Paulson's comment: "Leavis sees J. B. Priestley and the rowdier aspects of Dickens as the only Fielding tradition" (Paulson, *Fielding,* p. 9) with Leavis's own careful words: "Fielding deserves the place of importance given him in the literary histories . . . He is important not because he leads to Mr. J. B. Priestley but because he leads to Jane Austen . . . Fielding made Jane Austen possible by opening up the central tradition of English fiction."

endeavor in a world that seems to have shut its doors and windows and substituted instead a series of hidden traps.

To say that Fielding was constantly enlarging the scope of his experiment is not, however, the same as saying that none of his works can or should be judged adversely; it only means that each of them needs to be judged in its own terms and not as an unsuccessful or unneccesarily bulky redoing of the one essential *Joseph Andrews*. Even *Shamela*—with which we must begin—is not, for all its obvious connections with *Joseph Andrews*, an unsuccessful or lesser version of that novel. It is a different thing: not a comic novel but an example, perhaps the best known example, of the sort of exercise through which a comic writer finds his vocation. A parody of Richardson's *Pamela*, it represents the point of Fielding's entry into the sort of bookish battle which leads eventually to the true and more comprehensive perspective of comedy, and with that to what can more properly be called a comic action. Richardson, by writing of a serving-maid unwilling to part with her charms for less than the price of profitable marriage, had preached a prudential ethic under the guise of a virtuous love story. It was clearly "a nonsensical ridiculous book," as Parson Oliver of *Shamela* calls it in his concluding note, yet there was more to it than that. The stir that *Pamela* created, the "epidemical phrenzy" with which it was received, showed equally clearly how sympathetic the theme Richardson had struck was and how widespread the assumptions he had voiced.

Here, then, was what Fielding regarded as a false book playing the part, significant for comedy, of revealing the nonsensical make-believe of a whole culture. That happiness in marriage was dependent on strict previous chastity could be considered a possible though not incontrovertible moral view. But Pamela, and the readers whom she took by storm, were interested in neither marriage nor happiness; love and virtue were to them not even subordinate interests but sham names for the one purpose of material advancement. Richardson had

subtitled his novel "Virtue Rewarded" and claimed that it was
published "in order to cultivate the Principles of Virtue and
Religion in the Minds of the Youth of Both Sexes" and that
the narrative had "its Foundation in Truth and Nature." To
Fielding the book might more justifiably have borne the subtitle: "a lecture on prudence and matrimonial politics," a
phrase which he was to use in *Tom Jones* to describe one of
Mrs. Western's many discourses to Sophia on the subject, or
"the folly of love" and "the wisdom of legal prostitution for
hire," phrases he used a little later in the same novel. As for
the "Principles of Virtue and Religion," they were rather what
he declared them to be on the title page of *Shamela*—"the
matchless Arts" of a "young Politician." But above all it was
the Richardsonian "Truth and Nature" which were to be
shown up as "notorious Falsehoods and Misrepresentations."

All this is well known and often repeated, and one need
comment further only on the kind of truth-telling Fielding
undertook in his parody. Basically it involved little other than
what may be called a motivational readjustment of Richardson's story. Thus Pamela's virtue becomes Shamela's determination to make "a good market," and the honorable designs of
the one girl are openly revealed as calculating designs by the
other. In short, the career of Fielding's heroine—"I thought
once of making a little fortune by my person. I now intend to
make a great one by my vartue"—shows the extent to which
the ideology of virtue in *Pamela* was a mere camouflage for
legal prostitution.

Even in this parody, however, Fielding was not attacking just
the theory of virtuous love. By associating it closely with the
rival theory of love as sensual pleasure, he was already beginning to engage in that process of larger adjudication which has
been mentioned above as the central theme of his comedy.
For, although his heroine claims resolutely that she prefers her
"vartue to all rakes whatever," he makes her frigid only in the
marriage bed while a lively pleasure-seeker elsewhere, at the

same time altering Parsons Williams into her lewd and incorrigibly hedonistic paramour. The point, of course, lies in the fact that Shamela and Parson Williams are in no way troubled by what the world around them would regard as the irreconcilability of the two theories of love and of the conduct they entailed. The divine, in fact, proves the two to be perfectly in harmony. The "Flesh and the Spirit were two distinct matters, which had not the least relation to each other," as Shamela recalls and reproduces the doctrine:

> That all immaterial substances (those were his very words) such as love, desire, and so forth, were guided by the Spirit: but fine houses, large estates, coaches, and dainty entertainments were the product of the Flesh. Therefore, says he, my dear, you have two husbands, one the object of your love, and to satisfy your desire; the other the object of your necessity, and to furnish you with those other conveniences.

The discourse, directed at Shamela's conscience, turns out to be altogether unnecessary, however; for, as Shamela replies with forthrightness, "A fig for my conscience, said I; when shall I meet you again in the garden?"

In recasting the relationship between the heroine and her mentor, Fielding made the reward of virtue include sensual as well as material conveniences. Where desire would commonly be considered an attribute of the Flesh and love of the Spirit, the twist that Fielding's divine gives to the doctrinal screw has the effect of elevating both to the same spiritual standing. For both desire and love, as he argues, are "immaterial substances" "those were his very words" and therefore one is fully as justifiable as the other, provided of course that neither is confused with (or, more important, permitted to stand in the way of) estates, coaches, and such other material considerations. Through this absurd rationalization, through its neat logic and deliberate confusion, Fielding strikes home the point of his parody in all its irony. He demonstrates not merely how each of the two theories of love conceded primary importance to worldly or prudential interest, but he also shows how close the two are even as disembodied principles and how little philosophy is needed to make one as conscientious as the other.

By reconciling the sentimentalist's idea of love with that of the libertine—that is, by playing them against each other and neutralizing them—Fielding reveals them as equally empty and unreal. The very spirit, however, in which *Shamela* points at the underlying emotional void makes it a wholly negative book. As a parody it could be very little else. But then the insights of parody, while of great value to a comic writer, are not in themselves sufficient for the purpose of comedy, which calls out for a positive statement to complete the argument. In the three following novels Fielding set out to explore, grasp, and express the reality and the experience of love.

The element of parody is carried over into *Joseph Andrews.* In this novel Fielding is still taking issue with *Pamela,* though now with a strategy that might at first appear only slightly different. He informs us in the opening chapter that the reason for undertaking the "authentic history" of Joseph, Pamela's brother, is to demonstrate how "it was by keeping the excellent pattern of his sister's virtues before his eyes, that Mr. Joseph Andrews was chiefly enabled to preserve his purity in the midst of such great temptations." And, indeed, for several chapters it seems as though the trick is going to consist entirely in taking up Richardson's claim—"to cultivate the Principles of Virtue and Religion in the Minds of the Youth of *Both* Sexes"—and making his example of female chastity ridiculous by devising a comparable case of male chastity. Joseph would thus be not only Pamela's brother but her conscious pupil, and his conduct would reveal the beneficent moral influence envisaged by Richardson. As Joseph writes to his sister just after his dismissal from Lady Booby's service: "O most adorable

Pamela! most virtuous sister! whose example could alone enable me to withstand all the temptations of riches and beauty, and to preserve my virtue pure and chaste for the arms of my dear Fanny." And yet the difference is already evident. In *Shamela* Fielding had taken over Richardson's characters more or less intact, revising only their motivation to make it correspond with their conduct. But in *Joseph Andrews* the spirit of *Pamela* is not only exposed but also dramatically opposed. Even in the early chapters, where Fielding seems to be following a simple line of parody, Joseph is clearly no male Pamela. The parody in fact goes little beyond the opening situation and such rhetoric as Joseph's statement above. And Joseph's motivation owes nothing to Pamela's example, although he attributes it to that alone. While resisting his employer, as Pamela had resisted hers, he has withstood the temptation both of riches and beauty. He has, in a word, resisted Lady Booby herself, not just her dishonorable—that is to say, materially unprofitable—advances. And the reason is obviously not Pamela's example but, as he casually lets fall, "the arms of my dear Fanny."

If we look at the novel as a whole, it is clear that Joseph and Fanny stand at its moral center. Thus, while we can say that much of *Joseph Andrews* gives us the world of *Shamela* enlarged into a realistic and continuous narrative, it is no longer that world because Fanny represents a new element in it, and Joseph's love for her introduces a new perspective. Indeed, if we do not wish to regard the novel as simply a concatenation of variously introduced comic incidents and episodes, if we would rather see its comic plot, the three principal women in the story furnish us our best index. Pamela is, of course, still the original heroine of virtue well rewarded. But the other idea of love, the salacity which Fielding had earlier combined with "vartue" in the single person of Shamela, is now embodied in Lady Booby. This lady, whom Fielding at one point calls "the heroine of our tale," is in fact a figure straight out of Restoration comedy. When she says to Joseph:

> Answer me honestly, Joseph; have you so much more sense and so much more virtue than you handsome young fellows generally have, who make no scruple of sacrificing our dear reputation to your pride, without considering the great obligation we lay on you by our condescension and confidence?

it is the very accents of Lady Fidget to Horner that we hear. And yet, as the broad irony of her reference to virtue makes clear, this is a Lady Fidget trapped in a Richardsonian rather than Restoration situation. She can speak like Pamela, too— which, given Fielding's idea of Pamela, means that to some extent she is like Pamela. But this sort of limited judgment on the contention between Spirit and Flesh had already been arrived at in *Shamela*. What Fielding now introduces through Fanny is a love that makes the entire contention meaningless.

Not merely the three heroines but much of what happens in the novel can be seen along the same lines. The plot of *Joseph Andrews* consists of three stories put into one narrative. On the one hand, we have the original Pamela story of virtuous love, which is present in various implicit and explicit ways throughout the novel. On the other hand, there is the story heralded by Lady Booby, which is not so much a single and continuous narrative as it is an assemblage of all those incidents and episodes, taking place in mansions as well as on the road, where gentlemanly seducers and rapists introduce us to the incontinent and sadistic ways of the world of fashion and pleasure. And running through the entire narrative, as much above the other two stories as it is snarled with them at every point, is the story of Joseph and Fanny.

The exemplary tales of Mr. Wilson and Leonara, likewise, address themselves to the same basic comic theme. Whatever evaluation of the fashionable world and its illusions that Fielding cannot accommodate into his quick-paced narrative, he provides in the interposed tale of Mr. Wilson. This tale is in many ways like the Man of the Hill's story in *Tom Jones*. It has, of course, a direct bearing on the final unraveling of the mystery element in the plot, a function that the Man of the Hill's story does not possess. But its part in the plot machinery is a flimsy justification for the length and elaboration of the tale, since in this respect it need have been given no more space or thought than the revelations of the Irish drummer which turn out to be equally crucial at the end. Nor can one see it as altogether a diversionary tale if only because in truth it is among the least diverting parts of the novel. It is, however, enormously interesting in that it provides not merely a nutshell summary of the attitudes that dominate the world of fashion, but reflection and commentary on those attitudes. For it was this world, half real and half literary, that had enticed Mr. Wilson in his youth.

> The character I was ambitious of attaining was that of a fine gentleman . . . The reputation of intriguing with them [women of distinction] was all I sought . . . Here I met with smart fellows, who drank with lords they did not know, and intrigued with women they never saw. Covent Garden was now the farthest stretch of my ambition; where I shone forth in the balconies at the playhouses, visited whores, made love to orange-wenches, and damned plays.

This is obviously a comment not so much on the real world —not even the real world of Wilson's youth—as on the world of literary convention. And that is precisely the point. It is curious how Fielding, while packing these interposed narratives with great factual detail, gives them at the same time a remote quality, the quality of a dated romance. This has the effect of making what is described seem both true and illusory, or rather true only as illusions can be true. Thus Wilson makes

clear that the character of the man of mode, the character
which as a youth he was anxious to assume, had little reality
even then, just as the world of fashion was itself largely a
matter of make-believe; yet, as consciously adopted ideals or
conventions, both held great power over the real destinies of
individual men and women. At one point, when Parson Adams
interrupts him with: "Good Lord! what wicked times these
are!" he replies: "Not so wicked as you imagine," and goes on
to relate how he had himself made a practice of addressing
letters to himself which he then advertised as the "billets" of
ladies of distinction. *"Write letters to yourself!"* Adams exclaims in wonder. But Wilson knows that not only can illusions
be thus sustained by the individual, but they can be collec-
tively perpetuated by a whole culture, especially when assisted
by suitable literature. "O Sir, answered the gentleman, *It is the
very error of the times.* Half our modern plays have one of
these characters in them."

Leonara's tale is relatively simple, though more to the point
inasmuch as it involves not only the seductions of the beau
monde but equally the temptations of the other mode of love.
It is the "tragic" tale of a girl lost through wavering between
two kinds of suitors: the patient lover Horatio, the man of
"sighs and tears"; and "the French-English Bellarmine" with
his rakish "gaiety and gallantry." Seen as an interposed narrative, however, and in its quality of romance, it becomes simply
an exemplum of the false contention between two mere ideas
or literary conventions.

While these are the two main ideas or conventions of love
with which Fielding surrounds the central story of Joseph and
Fanny, it is worth emphasizing that neither idea constitutes in
any sense their temptation. This is in fact the point at which
one can turn to Parson Adams, the great and original character
whose role vis-à-vis Joseph has been sentimentalized and even
misinterpreted by recent critics. It is often argued that if
Joseph is able to escape untouched (unlike Tom Jones) the

many temptations with which he is surrounded, the reason can be found in the teachings of Adams, his constant friend and spiritual mentor. But this argument has proved misleading. One has to insist first of all, that even as a character Adams is not as simple a creation as such a reading makes him out to be. He is not only a good shepherd, a portrait of exceptional goodness in a rogues' gallery of self-seeking divines, like Chaucer's good parson; he is also fundamentally a comic character—almost a comedy in himself—who derives his true originality from his combination of real and spontaneous virtues on the one hand and the most stilted, absurd, and even mildly self-deceptive principles and doctrines on the other. In his conduct he is always exemplary; in his preaching, often impossible. His comedy lies in the fact that he cannot tell the difference between the two. But Fielding can and invariably does. At one point he even puts Adams's preaching on the same shelf as that of his primary target, Pamela, declaring that Joseph's perfect modesty—as evinced by his determination to die naked in the cold rather than offend the decency of a lady in the coach by entering it—was among the "mighty effects" wrought upon the young man by "the spotless example of the amiable Pamela, and the excellent sermons of Mr. Adams."

Aside from his formal and doctrinal teachings, his sermons, there is no doubt that Adams is meant to function as a moral counterweight to all those examples of depravity, hypocrisy, and cupidity with which this picaresque novel is so densely strewn. But even this role is unnecessary insofar as Joseph is concerned. One can, of course, build an elaborate but rather pointless hypothesis about Joseph's upbringing before the novel opens and about the part played by Adams's influence. But Joseph, as presented within the novel, hardly needs to learn anything from anyone. If he did not consider it disrespectful, he could even correct his friend and mentor on certain points; on one crucial point, as we shall see, he does consistently try to do so. Adams's value to Joseph lies, in short, not in any moral instruction that the former can impart, but in his deeds, in his practical support and the courage—both physical and moral—with which he renders it. Nor is the proper comparison with Tom Jones the one that is commonly made. The fact that Tom both lacks the friendship of a man like Parson Adams and succumbs to the temptations he encounters proves nothing that is relevant here. For if we go a step further to *Amelia,* we find a hero who succumbs despite the help and guidance of the wise and kindly Dr. Harrison. And even Tom is provided with the example of Squire Allworthy who, though not a Christian minister, does exemplify a goodness which, to Tom at least, is both powerful and without blemish. The comparison would thus reveal that Joseph is by nature immune to the sort of dangers to which the other two heroes are prone—which is in fact how Fielding saw and presented his heroic character at this stage in his development.

What the argument comes to is that, while Parson Adams occupies a commanding place in the ethical scheme of the novel taken as a whole, he has little part to play in the "education," as it is often called, of the novel's hero. This is particularly true of that hero's basic situation. Consider, for example, Adams's judgment on Wilson's early career as a libertine and man-about-town: "Sir, this is below the life of an animal, hardly above vegetation," which is as forthrightly severe as it is just. But the temptation of Wilson's youth is never for a moment Joseph's temptation, just as the danger represented by Leonara's history is never Fanny's danger. Likewise, the example of Pamela carries for them no threat of sanctimonious confusion of issues. When toward the end Mr. Booby argues that, among other things, marriage with Fanny "would break the hearts of your parents, who now rejoice in the expectation of seeing you make a figure in the world," Joseph proves himself bolder than even Sophia Western and certainly far more clear-sighted than Tom Jones. "I know not," he replies, "that my parents have any power over my inclinations; nor am I obliged to sacrifice my happiness to their whim or ambition." The point again is that the Joseph who makes this declaration is in no way different from the Joseph of the earliest pages. His belief is the same as it was then, and he holds to it no more resolutely now than he did before; the only difference is that, having no longer to play a part in the original parody, he can be allowed to formulate the idea directly.

The happiness—the love for Fanny—which Joseph thus defends throughout is to him naturally and indistinguishably virtuous, tender, and passionate, just as Fanny herself is at once good, loving, and physically desirable—a beautiful girl for whom undressing, as Fielding says at one point, "was properly discovering, not putting off, ornaments: for, as all her charms were the gifts of nature, she could divest herself of none." This being so, Joseph can hardly accept Parson Adams's constant sermonizing on the virtues of other-worldliness, the importance of Christian resignation, and, above all, the sin of carnal as against spiritual love. Indeed, he cannot always succeed even in turning a deaf ear. To the canting Barnabas he says straight out "that neither in this world nor the next could he forget his Fanny." But he interrupts similar discourses from Adams only at particularly trying moments, as at one point with: "O sir! all this is very true, and very fine, and I could hear you all day, if I was not so grieved at heart as now I am." It is not, however, until that late and justly famous scene in the novel where Adams's son is reported drowned that Fielding finally trips the good parson by his doctrinal heels. For, as Adams abandons himself to uncontrolled lamentation, Joseph reverses roles with him for the moment and counsels Christian resignation. But "do not go about impossibilities" is all that Adams can answer. Of course, as soon as the "drowned" child is safely returned, Adams returns to his familiar role and picks up his sermon to Joseph where he had left it. Joseph, however, remains unyielding—utterly unimpressed by the distinction that

Adams proceeds to make between Joseph's carnal love for Fanny and his own parental love which, being spiritual, need fear no sinfulness through excess and immoderation. Joseph declares that, sin or no sin, he "shall love without any moderation," and Mrs. Adams has the final word and describes her husband's doctrine as "wicked nonsense." Her speech, in fact, not only provides the final word on this whole question of Spirit and Flesh but also gathers to a fine conclusion the comedy of Parson Adams himself:

> I am certain you do not preach as you practice; for you have been a loving and a cherishing husband to me, that's the truth on't; and why you should endeavour to put such wicked nonsense into this young man's head, I cannot devise. Don't hearken to him, Mr. Joseph; be as good a husband as you are able, and love your wife with all your body and soul too.

Joseph has, of course, always meant to. In this sense *Joseph Andrews* is not a novel of education, much less one of experience. It is a novel of external and fixed contrasts, a comedy that deals with cultural conflicts which it does not allow its hero and heroine to share. If only for this reason, it is not finally so interesting a comic novel as *Tom Jones,* where the culture's opposed temptations are equally the temptations of the hero, and where the hero is made to discover and not merely defend his own values.

During the course of *Tom Jones,* Fielding declares at several points that the *expected* outcome of Tom's story can only be a bad end for Tom. Even at the first appearance of his hero as a foundling infant the narrator is constrained to "declare honestly . . . that it was the universal opinion of all Mr. Allworthy's family, that he was certainly born to be hanged." Nor would Tom's subsequent conduct—conduct for which he is himself responsible—be considered as calculated to alter this early opinion or in any way mitigate its force. On the contrary, as Fielding concludes several hundred pages later, the intervening narrative must have served to convince even the reader that his "main design" in writing the history of Tom Jones could indeed be no other than "to bring Mr. Jones to the gallows, or, if possible, to a more deplorable catastrophe."

It is thus against the background of certain assumed expectations that Fielding consciously sets forth the actual and very different fate of his hero. His interest, one can say, is not only in truth but in truth as opposed to "abstracted considerations" (his own phrase used twice in the novel) or simply in comic truth. As such it is a truth that can ultimately be enforced through the dramatic and emotional power of his story. But he also canvasses it through direct reflection and reasoning—philosophically, so to speak. For example, he argues in the introductory chapter to Book XV, addressing himself to the purpose of wiping off (as he puts it) a doctrine that lies in his way: "There are a set of religious, or rather moral writers, who teach that virtue is the certain road to happiness, and vice to misery, in this world. A very wholesome and comfortable doctrine, and to which we have but one objection, namely, that it is not true." Or again, regarding what he thinks is sure to be certain readers' astonishment at the discrepancy between what should have happened and what has actually taken place in the novel: "I must remind such persons that I am not writing a system, but a history, and I am not obliged to reconcile every matter to the received notions concerning truth and nature."

Fielding, however, did not regard his truth as only truer than the various abstracted considerations and received notions of it; he also considered it morally superior. As I have pointed out, he could defend it as a philosophy, the more so since it did not consist of "the bare knowledge of right and wrong" but was a matter of practical conduct, "an energy, a habit." In Chapter 6, Book IV of *Tom Jones* he makes the same point by invoking an "active principle" which "doth not content itself with knowledge or belief only" and which, he adds, "may perhaps be said to constitute the most essential barrier between us and our neighbours the brutes." This principle— whose only name can be the one that Fielding gives it elsewhere in the novel: love, and love as both a social and a sexual emotion—manifests itself as the spontaneous energy of generous feeling, or, at the very least, as a habit of human reciprocity. This is Fielding's essential philosophical defense of his hero. Tom, as he goes on, "was very strongly under the guidance of this principle; for though he did not always act rightly, yet he never did otherwise without feeling and suffering for it. . . . Such can never receive any kind of satisfaction from another, without loving the creature to whom that satisfaction is owing, and without making its well-being in some sort necessary to their own ease."

True, the principle of love does not prevent Tom from falling into difficulties. It, or rather its misunderstood guidance, actually leads to his most serious confusions and conflicts. But then it is through a clearer understanding of the same principle that he is also able to extricate himself from them in the end. With this, however, we leave general philosophy behind and enter the particular issues of Fielding's comedy in *Tom Jones*. The above discussion itself, though developed in general terms, arises from the specific question of Tom's relationship with Sophia—something that will become the central theme of the novel but which, as a relationship, can hardly be said to exist as yet. For while there are signs already that Sophia is in love with Tom, Tom is not in love with her. He is in fact carrying on with Molly Seagrim, the gamekeeper's daughter, and pays no attention to the signals emanating from Sophia. Fielding's failure to even rebuke his hero for the affair with Molly is well known and often commented upon. But the real focus of interest here, as elsewhere, is on Sophia. Fielding is concerned less with Tom's taking advantage of Molly's present offerings than with his failure to take advantage of the future rewards promised by Sophia's signals. That is to say, he sees with real comic penetration that at bottom the world is more likely to judge Tom for his sin of omission than for the sin he actually commits. The jury will be divided—along the lines familiar by now—and though both factions will convict, they will do so on different grounds:

> The former of these will blame his prudence in neglecting an opportunity to possess himself of Mr. Western's fortune; and the latter will no less despise him for his backwardness to so fine a girl, who seemed ready to fly into his arms, if he would open them to receive her.

To this the chapter title has already added a special note by declaring that the proceedings recorded in the chapter are bound to lower Tom's character in the estimation of those very people "who approve the heroes in most of our modern comedies." This is to say that Tom is to be neither a sentimental nor a libertine hero but, for these very unconventional or anti-conventional reasons, a truly comic one.

Not merely the hypothetical jury of Chapter 6, Book IV, but much of the actual cast of characters in the novel divides along the same lines. Although, as we have seen, Fielding recognized the basic identity between the two factions, for purposes of comedy he also habitually separated them into the faction of prudence and virtue versus that of prudence and pleasure. Often, of course, the same character is openly of one party and covertly of the other, and this is part of Fielding's point. Nevertheless, judging by appearance or professed philosophy, the main representative of the first faction is Master Blifil himself—the rival and "moral" scourge of Tom Jones and the type of hypocrite whom Sheridan was to identify somewhat mildly as the unerring "man of sentiment," a man whose self-seeking is camouflaged by maxims or sentiments of religious and secular virtue. Behind him stand not only the two Blifils of the first generation but, in a more commanding position,

the two tutors, Square and Thwackum—one an absurd champion of rational philosophy ("the unalterable rule of right, and
the eternal fitness of things") and the other a time-serving
voice of religion ("Christian religion; and not only the Christian religion, but the Protestant religion; and not only the
Protestant religion, but the Church of England"). To their
favorite pupil, love means self-love and sexual love a species of
sadism, as witnessed by his reaction to Sophia's strong but
helpless aversion toward him. This, as Fielding tells us, did not
lessen his desire, but "served rather to heighten the pleasure he
proposed in rifling her charms, as it added triumph to lust;
nay, he had some further views, from obtaining the absolute
possession of her person, which we detest too much even to
mention."

The other faction includes, in varying degrees, Mrs. Western,
Mrs. Fitzpatrick, her discarded husband as well as the Irish
lord who is her present protector, Lady Bellaston—in short,
the citizens of the gay town world. Even Nightingale, "one of
those young gentlemen who, in the last age, were called men
of wit and pleasure about town," very nearly sacrifices his
happiness to the code of this world. Although in love with his
landlady's daughter, whom he has made pregnant, he is ready
to write her off as an affair of pleasure and marry instead a
wealthy but unseen girl selected by arrangement. In reality,
however, poor Nightingale is no worse than a superficially deluded young man; he has none of the feeling, or rather the lack
of all feeling, which characterizes the people he has sought to
imitate. Accordingly Tom has little difficulty in persuading
him that marriage to the girl he loves will satisfy the claims of
both happiness and honor—the latter especially, since on this
point Nightingale is as scrupulous as he is ludicrously confused: "I know you are a man of honour," he appeals to Tom,
"and would advise no one to act contrary to its rules; if there
were no other objection, can I, after this publication of her
disgrace [her being made pregnant by himself] , think of such

an alliance with honour?" This is the sort of parody of the code of honor (or whatever of it remained associated with the courtly libertine tradition) that Fielding takes up more extensively in *Amelia,* especially in the character part of Colonel Bath—"old honour and dignity," as he is called.

The comic exposure of the sentimental and libertine conventions is something that *Tom Jones* shares, on the surface, with Fielding's other novels. But the new feature of this novel is the manner in which the conventions are brought to bear on the hero himself. The relationship between the hero and the heroine here is not what it was in *Joseph Andrews*—an accomplished thing before the novel opens, and one, therefore, that exists as a perfect and detached example. Possessing neither this perfection nor this static quality, Tom's love for Sophia has to grow and find itself; something of its emotional power and much of its meaning are developed through the very real confusions and conflicts experienced by the hero. For instance, at the very time we find him advising Nightingale to such good purpose, Tom himself is nearly in the situation of "those young gentlemen who, in the last age, were called men of wit and pleasure about town." Indeed, in the scene in which he has to hide one lady in order to receive the messenger of another, he might well be acting the part of a latter-day Dorimant or Horner. True, his motivation is not the same as theirs. Fielding, as is well known, defends even this last and least defensible intrigue with Lady Bellaston in terms of Tom's sense of gratitude and generosity, misguided though it is in the present case. He always has basic scruples of conscience which he cannot disregard. He says quite truthfully to Nightingale: "I have been guilty with women, I own it; but am not conscious that I have ever injured any. Nor would I, to procure pleasure to myself, be knowingly the cause of misery to any human being"—something a Dorimant, exulting precisely in such misery caused to others, would never say. Nevertheless, the possibilities inherent in such a course of conduct are incalculable, and of this too Fielding makes us aware. "Jones had never less inclination to an amour," he tells us, than at the time he took up with Lady Bellaston; "but gallantry to the ladies was among his principles of honour; and he held it as much incumbent on him to accept a challenge to love, as if it had been a challenge to fight." In fact, Tom's three affairs disclose a diminution of animal spirits and a steady progression of principle, and not only we but Tom himself has to recognize the dangers ahead in this direction. In the same way, Sophia's one real anxiety at the end is to ascertain how far along the road to perfect and cynical libertinism this principle has actually carried her lover.

While the rake's progress idea, or at least the warning of it, in *Tom Jones* is widely appreciated—indeed, overemphasized—we do not always recognize the extent to which Tom reveals himself in the other conventional role, the role of a sentimental hero. The novel in fact carefully weighs his animal spirits together with their consequences against his many long-winded, self-pitying, noble speeches to Sophia and the pose he often adopts of a sighing, self-sacrificing lover. Sophia is to him a goddess before whom he is forever ready to abase himself but to whom he is entirely reluctant, until the end, to make the proposal that she desires and would welcome. She herself once pulls him up sharply for his "affected contempt of life," as she calls it, while to do so constantly and pointedly is among the more delightful functions of Partridge. At the root of this posture of Tom's lies, of course, his inability to distinguish the question of love and marriage from that of fortune. Honour Blackmore's sly comment on Sophia: "If I was in love with a young man, and my father offered to lock me up, I'd tear his eyes out, but I'd come at him; but then there's a great fortune in the case, which it is in her father's power either to give her or not; that, to be sure, may make some difference" is made to Tom but could with greater justice be applied to him. However, it cannot really be applied even to Tom because, though the thought of fortune indeed weighs heavily with him, it does so not for his own sake but for Sophia's. Yet this prudence, however unselfish, is still misguided—the more so since Sophia herself is restrained only by her sense of filial duty (Joseph Andrews would have known better than even that) and has no thought of the "fortune in the case." See, for instance, the following exchange between the lovers during the accidental but to them crucial meeting at Lady Bellaston's:

> "That, did not her duty to her father forbid her to follow her own inclinations, ruin with him would be more welcome to her, than the most affluent fortune with another man." At the mention of the word ruin he started, let drop her hand, which he had held for some time, and striking his breast with his own, cried out, "Oh, Sophia! can I then ruin thee? No; by heavens, no! I never will act so base a part. Dearest Sophia, whatever it cost me, I will renounce you; I will give you up; I will tear all such hopes from my heart as are inconsistent with your real good. My love I will ever retain, but it shall be in silence; it shall be at a distance from you; it shall be in some foreign land, from whence no voice, no sigh of my despair, shall ever reach and disturb your ears. And when I am dead"—

This is certainly no answer to Sophia's problem; nor, however pleasing to the partisans of virtue and sentiment, is it one calculated to please her. Underneath its heroics—and critics who are inclined to go to the other extreme and make a sentimentalist out of *Fielding* should note that these are presented, clearly and deliberately, as comic heroics—is Tom's superficial but cocksure notion of what constitutes Sophia's real good. But what does constitute real good is the central question of the novel, and neither Sophia nor Fielding would decide it so summarily or so foolishly.

There is thus some justification for Sophia's exclamation on hearing the news of Tom's departure from Somersetshire: "O

Honour! I am undone. . . . I have thrown away my heart on a
man who hath forsaken me," though none for Honour's rejoinder, the way she means it: "And is Mr. Jones such a perfidy
man?" Through much of the novel, in fact, it is Sophia who
brings to the central love relationship whatever clarity and
courage it possesses. By comparison with Tom's confused actions, the part she plays, like the parts of many other heroines
of English comedy, is one of boldness and intelligence. "Sophia," as Fielding so well puts it, "with all the gentleness
which a woman can have, had all the spirit which she ought to
have." She holds out against Blifil under the combined threats
and blandishments of her father and Mrs. Western and, in pursuit of her vagabond lover, sets out into an unknown world as
resolutely as any Shakespearean heroine.

A whole essay could be written—as in fact essays have been
written—on this journey of Sophia's and the manner in which
Fielding arranges to have her path crisscross that of her lover's.
But the point to be made here is that it is during this journey
that Tom's and Sophia's love story becomes persuasive and
powerful, as we are shown the emotion and experience of love
taking shape before our very eyes. There are no doubt varied
ways of recreating emotion in art, but the one that Fielding
uses depends most on a process of externalization. It is not the
minds and declarations of the lovers that reveal to us, and to
themselves, the existence and growth of their love; it is rather
the recurring appearance of objects like Sophia's muff or wal-
let, the coincidences and disappointments of particular places
and spots, the overheard mention of each other from random
people, the indirect reports of each other's movements, and
such little happenings and associations, all of which create a
vibrant echo and counter-echo of emotion.

And it is the reality of this emotion—once it thus becomes a
reality—that enables Tom Jones to see his way through the
confusions into which he has fallen. In the letter of dedication
appended to the novel, Fielding declares that it was his pur-

pose "to make good men wise" rather than "to make bad men good."[8] In fact, making of good men wise was not only his purpose but the purpose of comedy generally, as he understood it; and what it involved we can see from the following passage in his invocation to the comic Genius in Chapter 1, Book XIII:

> Teach me, which to thee is no difficult task, to know mankind better than they know themselves. Remove that mist which dims the intellects of mortals, and causes them to adore men for their art, or to detest them for their cunning in deceiving others, when they are, in reality, the objects only of ridicule, for deceiving themselves.

The passage can be taken as a paraphrase of that Delphic motto to which Socrates insisted was also the true motto of comedy; the task of enforcing it, however easy it may seem, is in no way less difficult than the task of tragedy. As Fielding concludes playfully in the introductory chapter of the penultimate book, he has by now "contrived much greater torments for poor Jones" than the devil himself could have devised. "What then remains to complete the tragedy but a murder or two, and a few moral sentences? But to bring our favourites out of their present anguish and distress, and to land them at last on the shore of happiness, seems a much harder task."

Of course, providence can aid the author in this task. Together they can save the favorites from the cunning and deceptions of others. But from deceiving themselves the favorites must at least to some extent be left to save themselves. Indeed, in this novel, as in *Amelia,* the happy accidents at the end are presented as an endorsement of, rather than a substitute for, that self-discovery in which the comic hero finds his highest task. Critics who recognize this aspect of the comedy of *Tom*

8. It is worth noting here that Sophia means wisdom; thus the pursuit of Sophia is the pursuit of wisdom. I am indebted to Richard S. Sylvester for this suggestion.

Jones usually content themselves by pointing out that Tom's eyes are opened at last when he comes to suspect, though mistakenly, that his free and easy way with women may have caused him unwittingly to commit incest with his mother. In reality, however, the process of discovery begins earlier and involves the errors of sentimentality as much as the dangers of libertinism.

The single event that precipitates the sharpest awareness of the former is the marriage proposal from Mrs. Hunt. This is for Tom a crucial and tempting moment. At this point he has virtually lost all hope concerning Sophia; he is also at the very nadir of his financial difficulties. The proposal is from a lady whom he likes "as well as he did any woman except Sophia," and who, moreover, possesses a fortune that "would have been exceeding convenient to him." But above all he sees an opportunity of freeing Sophia from the threat of ruin which she has incurred on his account and which, as we have seen, weighs heavily on him. All things considered, Tom is "almost determined" to accept the proposal and forsake Sophia, as Fielding puts it, "from a high point of honour." And yet the moment actually proves a turning point in the other direction. For the very reasons that Tom gives himself show him how little he is capable of acting on them: "But to abandon Sophia, and marry another, that was impossible; he could not think of it upon any account." The realization dawns upon him that fortune is not after all the real good and the lack of it cannot therefore be ruin. He is led very soon to write a letter to Sophia in which for the first time, despite his habitual phraseology while addressing her, he makes a proposal to her.

> Can the most perfect admiration, the most watchful observance, the most ardent love, the most melting tenderness, the most resigned submission to your will, make you amends for what you are to sacrifice to my happiness? If they can, fly, my lovely angel, to those arms which are

ever open to receive and protect you; and to which, whether you bring yourself alone, or the riches of the world with you, is, in my opinion, an alternative not worth regarding.

On the other side, the first firm resolution comes not after the false discovery of incest but earlier, when Tom resolves to see nothing more of Mrs. Fitzpatrick, to whom he has turned as the only available source for news of Sophia. During the entire meeting this attractive woman has made the usual sort of signals; nor could she "forbear making him a present of a look at parting, by which if he had understood nothing, he must have had no understanding in the language of the eyes." Here in short is the sort of challenge to love the acceptance of which, as we have already learned, had become one of Tom's chief principles of honor. But this kind of honor and its temptations he has learned to put behind him. The parting shot from Mrs. Fitzpatrick's eyes only

confirmed his resolution of returning to her no more; for, faulty as he hath hitherto appeared in this history, his whole thoughts were now so confined to his Sophia, that I believe no woman upon earth could have now drawn him into an act of inconstancy.

Tom even announces "his resolution to sin no more" to the incredulous Mrs. Waters during their prison interview, before there is any suspicion that she may be his unknown mother. Thus it is on grounds prepared beforehand that the alarm of incest is rung finally to complete the process: "I am myself the cause of all my misery. All the dreadful mischiefs which have befallen me are the consequences only of my own folly and vice."

Not *only*, or entirely, as is soon made clear by that "nice train of little circumstances" which, having hitherto gone against him, begins now to turn full speed in his favor. But, while providential assistance returns him to Allworthy's favor and thereby also reduces the question of fortune to one of academic interest, he still has the other question to clear with Sophia. Tom certainly exaggerates matters when he says to Allworthy: "I have sinned against her beyond all hope of pardon," but he is right, as he goes on to say, that his "guilt unfortunately appears to her in ten times blacker than the real colours." Sophia is anxious to ascertain the extent to which her lover has assumed "the character of a libertine" and the attendant "profligacy of manners" which, in her words to Mrs. Miller, "will corrupt the best heart in the world." She believes wrongly that she has seen an unmistakable sign of such degradation in Tom Jones—namely, his spreading word of an amour with her with the cynical nonchalance, the combined vanity and levity, of a man of pleasure and fashion. This is the decisive reason behind what has seemed to some readers her puzzling behavior during the crucial episode at Upton; for, as Fielding puts it, she

> was much more offended at the freedoms which she thought (and not without good reasons) he [Tom] had taken with her name and character, than at any freedoms, in which, under his present circumstances, he had indulged himself with the person of another woman; and to say truth, I believe Honour could never have prevailed on her to leave Upton without her seeing Jones, had it not been for those two strong instances of a levity in his behaviour, so void of respect, and indeed so highly inconsistent with any degree of love and tenderness.

To us this may seem a pedantic point: convicting a man for the shadow of folly while acquitting him for the substance of vice. But here Sophia reflects her author's knowledge that, in its eventual outcome, a species of folly can prove more vicious than what commonly passes for vice. This knowledge is confirmed by the story of her cousin, Mrs. Fitzpatrick—Miss

Giddy to Sophia's Miss Graveairs, according to their early nick-names—whose whole life is an example of the dangers inherent in fashionable folly. Sophia's comment at the conclusion of her cousin's narrative is both significant and touching: " 'Can no man,' said Sophia, in a very low and altered voice, 'do you think, make a bad husband, who is not a fool?' "—and we know what she is thinking about.

Indeed, the whole tradition that gives libertine folly its comic weight in *Tom Jones* is expressly invoked in that last scene where Sophia assures herself on this point. Are Tom's present passionate entreaties the usual declarations of a fashionable rake? Is this a rake's conversion, as ephemeral as his desires of the moment? "After what is past, Sir," she asks, "can you expect I should take you upon your word?" What, on the other hand, about the teaching of those sentimental authors from Cibber onwards who had shown virtue permanently triumphant over vice, but of whom Fielding may have said what Cowper (in his "Progress of Error") was to say of popular novelists:

> Who, kindling a combustion of desire,
> With some cold moral think to quench the fire.

No, virtue in such cases is not so simple a matter. It should be born precisely where the temptation to vice has its origin—in the passions. In a stroke of insight, justly famous, Fielding makes his hero seize a mirror, hold it up to Sophia, and thus give her the "better security" she demands—a lasting pledge:

> There, behold it there in that lovely figure, in that face, that shape, those eyes, that mind which shines through these eyes; can the man who shall be in possession of these be inconstant? Impossible! my Sophia; they would fix a Dorimant, a Lord Rochester.

With this Fielding has at last brought his hero to those promised shores: "for what happiness this world affords equal to

the possession of such a woman as Sophia, I sincerely own I
have never yet discovered."

Not very much need be said here about Fielding's last novel,
Amelia, which is often regarded as a sort of sequel to *Tom
Jones.* I have already mentioned some of the interests and
concerns which make this novel a new departure in Fielding
and also more absorbing in its own right than is usually conceded. It is, however, a sequel in that it extends the theme of
love beyond the point to which Fielding had earlier brought
it—beyond in fact its conventional terminus in fiction generally. The subject of *Amelia,* as we are told in the opening
sentence, is the "various accidents which befell a very worthy
couple, after their uniting in the state of matrimony;" the idea
behind the subject is that more difficult art of love which does
not cease to be relevant after marriage but is rather cotermi-
nous with the art of life itself.

Amelia is still concerned with the happiness of love, a happiness which is still possible. Yet, like the last works of some
other comic writers, it is a somber book. "A match of real love
is indeed truly paradise; and such perfect happiness seems to
be the forbidden fruit to mortals"—this statement might almost be said to sum up the mood of the novel. It is made by
Mrs. Bennet, a character who has not only found her own
paradise destroyed, but who in this respect foreshadows the
fate that seems inescapably in store for Amelia as well. For the
same anonymous noble lord who has accounted for Mrs. Bennet's paradise now has his eye on Amelia and has set the same
apparently respectable bawd, Mrs. Ellison, to entrap her. Indeed, this noble lord stands at the dark center of power which
he exercises virtually unchallenged through various covert
agencies. If we compare him with a character like the Irish
lord, Mrs. Fitzpatrick's protector in *Tom Jones,* we get some
idea of the closed and stifling quality of the world of *Amelia.*
He may be seen as something of a literary precursor of Thack-

eray's Marquis of Steyne, but though he possesses comparable power and ruthlessness, he lacks all Steyne's wit and dash and relies in his intrigues altogether on force and cunning. Moreover, his taste runs usually to ordinary, unwilling, chaste married women, none of whom is safe if once she comes within the orbit that he so invisibly and shabbily dominates. Not only the professional Mrs. Ellison but many others, including some of Booth's fellow officers and friends, are his willing tools and accomplices. It is Mrs. Ellison who openly contradicts Mrs. Bennet's view of the true paradise of love:

> "I shall never forget the beginning of a song of Mr. Congreve's that my husband was so fond of, that he was always singing it. 'Love's but a frailty of the mind, / When 'tis not with ambition join'd.' Love without interest makes but an unsavoury dish in my opinion."

The view is not only shared generally; but by some it is acted upon quite in Mrs. Ellison's way. Captain Trent, for instance, having sold his wife to the lord, is now employed by him to persuade Booth, by whatever means are necessary, to do the same with Amelia. Even Colonel James is not above taking a hand in the business, though in this case the "goods," as he puts it, happen to be not Amelia but "the charming person of Miss Matthews," for whom he is convinced "my lord would bid a swingeing price."

Thus the dangers of love in *Amelia,* while of the same general kind that Fielding had recorded earlier, are intensified and made more positively menacing. In fact, the accidents which befall Booth and Amelia are presented as virtually inescapable, not accidents so much as the results of a deliberate and web-like design. But what makes the novel truly somber is not in the last analysis the grimness of external circumstance; it is rather the real possibility of inner deterioration, the suggestion that not merely is love a nonexistent value in the world at large, but that it is threatened with extinction even where it

does exist. Love, as Fielding puts it at one point (using again
the metaphor of a garden), "sprouts usually up in the richest
and noblest minds;" yet it can there choke and kill "whatever
is good and noble" unless it is "nicely watched, pruned, and
cultivated, and carefully kept clear of those vicious weeds
which are too apt to surround it." And it is the growth of
something like rankness within Booth's mind that finally distinguishes his problems from those of Tom Jones. Booth's
affair with Miss Matthews during his imprisonment—his passing
an evening with her "in a manner inconsistent with the strict
rules of virtue and chastity"—though it adds infidelity to the
sort of unchastity of which Tom is guilty, is still an isolated
act. As even the phrase quoted above shows, Fielding is prepared to defend it against an overly censorious view more or
less on the lines on which he had defended the lapses of Tom
Jones. What interests Fielding here is, in fact, not the morality
of the act but the mental and emotional state to which it leads
just when Booth is struggling against other external difficulties
and beginning to feel the general helplessness of his situation.
Thus, while Tom Jones is conscious of nothing worse than
error, Booth is stricken with a sense of guilt and panic. He
becomes surreptitious, hurriedly transfers Miss Matthews to
Colonel James, and loses money at gambling to Captain Trent,
thus laying himself open, among other things, to the bawdy
propositions of the two men. Indeed, as these acts interact and
multiply, it becomes a serious question whether the weeds
sprouting in Booth's inner landscape will not in the end destroy its once rich and noble prospect.

That this does not in fact happen, even though Booth turns
for a while into a "seriously miserable man," his mind seized
by a "deep melancholy," is owing to an immense resource
from which he is able to draw strength even in his worst ex-
tremity. "Our lives resembled a calm sea—" he attempts to
describe the extent and harmony of conjugal love, but Miss
Matthews cuts him short: "The dullest of all ideas." To this

Booth can only reply: "I know, it must appear dull in description." This is, indeed, an idea that not many novelists have ventured to describe and the readers of *Amelia* who go no further than these early chapters will wish Fielding had not tried it either. Not that there are not weaknesses in the novel. Amelia herself becomes one at several points: Miss Matthews considers her a prude, and Mrs. Bennet calls her one to her face. Indeed, in the scene with Mrs. Bennet, she is unquestionably a champion of prudery rather than purity. In that chapter—as in many other moments when Fielding, in the very act of challenging sentimentality, becomes crassly sentimental himself—she might well be a mid-Victorian heroine. Thackeray's Amelia, for instance, rather than Fielding's. Nevertheless, readers who have the patience to go through the novel will certainly not agree with Miss Matthews, who has only the description (not to mention her own designs of the moment) to guide her. For even this description is not of what happens in the novel (though most readers think it is) but of what lies behind those happenings. What Booth recapitulates to Miss Matthews is past felicity; what is dramatized within the novel is almost its irrevocable loss.

A more accurate idea of the novel's action can be conveyed by citing two phrases from Chapters 1 and 3 of Book IV. The first occurs when Booth, having just concluded his narrative with an account of his and Amelia's many present distresses, is astonished that Miss Matthews can still call his wife "the happiest of women." Of course, Miss Matthews is in part using her each word with ulterior design, but nevertheless she can answer with complete sincerity: "O Mr. Booth! there is a speck of white in her fortune, which, when it falls to the lot of a sensible woman, makes her full amends for all the crosses which can attend her." Fielding then goes on to use a counterphrase in opening the chapter that launches Booth into the action proper of the novel after his release from prison:

There is nothing more difficult than to lay down any
fixed and certain rules for happiness; or indeed to
judge with any precision of the happiness of others
from the knowledge of external circumstances. There is
sometimes a little speck of black in the brightest and gay-
est colours of fortune, which contaminates and deadens
the whole.

Amelia is not all platitude and sentimentality. Its action is
concerned essentially with the play of these specks of black
and white: with (if we think also of the metaphor of the calm
sea in the background) the sort of cloud which, though no
bigger than a man's hand at first, can in time obliterate the
noblest and sunniest of prospects; and with that speck of
white on the other hand which, when all seems lost, still be-
tokens the bright though hardly visible sea. Indeed, it is this
metaphorical or symbolical quality of its vision that distinguishes *Amelia* from Fielding's earlier works and links it with
the last works of such other comic writers as Shakespeare and
Jane Austen. The same can be said of the threat of negation at
the novel's core, the sense of both external stress and crisis and
inner weakness, guilt, loss—and yet somehow ultimate resilience. It is through these means rather than through harping on
some fixed idyll of domesticity that Fielding is able in the end
to dramatize persuasively the idea of conjugal love—"the dullest of all ideas"—as a source of enviable happiness and tran-
quillity.

Chapter 6

Jane Austen

Jane Austen's novels are the central achievement of English comedy. She sums up and perfects a tradition that goes back through Fielding to Shakespeare and whose history includes that internal split which resulted in the opposed movements of Restoration and sentimental drama and, later, such minor and indeterminate figures as Goldsmith and Sheridan. On the other hand, there are novels of hers, or at least elements within certain novels, that clearly anticipate a radical dilemma in the work of Henry James and thus suggest that clouding of the modern comic vision which has developed into something of a total eclipse in recent years. In Jane Austen comedy is still confident—confident of itself and of the culture it reflects— but it is now confident only at the cost of that culture's deep-seated complacency.

From the lighthearted juvenile burlesques to the autumnal ripeness of Anne Elliot's story in *Persuasion,* Jane Austen's work explores all the major possibilities offered by this par- ticular tradition. The prentice-work of the juvenilia is in itself exemplary and provides the proper starting point for any understanding of her comedy. It is no accident that Mary Lascelles, who first discussed the importance of this prehistory, so to speak, of Jane Austen's literary career, thereby also laid the foundation of all modern Austen criticism.[1] She did this by demonstrating how necessary it is to examine Jane Austen's burlesque writings—the whole question in fact of her response to her reading—in order to discover what Miss Lascelles rightly calls "the root of her intention as a novelist." But such examination, as we have seen, is instructive in understanding the intentions of other comic writers such as Fielding and Shakespeare no less than Jane Austen. In Jane Austen's case the battle against books began almost as soon as she could read and write, and we find it still going on in her last unfinished fragment, *Sanditon.* Of course in the completed novels, with the exception of *Northanger Abbey,* the issue is never formulated overtly or with sustained reference to specific books. As Miss Lascelles puts it: "allusions to books run like an undercurrent through Jane Austen's writing; her preoccupation with them is constant, but it is seldom, if ever, quite directly expressed."[2] What Jane Austen in fact does after *Northanger Abbey* is to shift her focus from literary conventions to those areas of life which are responsible for having engendered the conventions in the first place. She constructs plots, that is, in which she can directly confront the cultural superstructure and test its abstractions (chiefly in the sphere of love and marriage) against its possible realities. This, of

1. Lascelles, *Jane Austen.* The important chapter in this study is "Reading and Response," pp. 41-83. See also Lascelles's earlier essay, "Miss Austen and Some Books," *The London Mercury, 29* (1934), pp. 527-39. For subsequent discussions of the subject, see Q. D. Leavis, "A Critical Theory of Jane Austen's Writings," *Scrutiny, 10* (June 1941), pp. 61-87; *10* (October 1941), pp. 114-42; *10* (January 1942), pp. 272-94; *12* (Spring 1944), pp. 104-19; Mudrick, *Jane Austen,* pp. 1-36; B. C. Southam, *Jane Austen's Literary Manuscripts* (London, Oxford University Press, 1964); A. Walton Litz, *Jane Austen* (New York, Oxford University Press, 1965), pp. 3-57; Frank W. Bradbrook, *Jane Austen and Her Predecessors* (Cambridge, Cambridge University Press, 1966).

2. Lascelles, *Jane Austen,* p. 49.

course, gives her mature work a "novelistic" consistency—a sense of unmediated and unbroken contact with real living—that we find lacking even in parts of *Northanger Abbey*, let alone her juvenilia. But it also makes her comic position vis-à-vis her culture somewhat difficult to define. Hence the value of starting with a consideration of the earlier writings, particularly the earliest juvenilia, where the manipulation of the illusory world of popular fiction makes the issues stand out with relative simplicity.

Specific novels have been brought forward as the targets of Jane Austen's burlesque—novels such as Charlotte Smith's *Emmeline* and *Ethelinde* in "Love and Freindship" and Mrs. Radcliffe's *Udolpho* (or, more recently, a minor Gothic tale, *The Midnight Bell* by Francis Lathom) in *Northanger Abbey*. Following up specific parallels, however, should not obscure the larger diagnostic purpose of her burlesque. Jane Austen, as Miss Lascelles has pointed out, "very seldom aims merely at this or that wretched novel or novelist. It is her way to strike through a particular novel, or type of novel, to the false conventions that govern it, and through these conventions to the false taste (in writer and reader alike) that have allowed them to come into being."[3] Nor should this idea of "taste" be narrowly understood. Miss Lascelles herself speaks of the "community of literate but unliterary readers, which was then awakening to a new consciousness of the part that reading plays in the growth of the ordinary persons mental constitution."[4] Thus Jane Austen's literary quarrel was not just a quarrel about literature. As in the case of other comic writers, it reached beyond the literary issue to the question of education in its widest sense—to the question of conduct and ultimately the conduct of life itself. In this respect novels bore greater

3. Lascelles, "Miss Austen and Some Books," p. 530.
4. Lascelles, *Jane Austen*, p. 50.

responsibility and were to be held more accountable than other forms of literature. As Dr. Johnson observed in *The Rambler,* No. 4:

> These books are written chiefly to the young, the ignorant, and the idle, to whom they serve as lectures of conduct, and introductions into life. They are the entertainment of minds unfurnished with ideas, and therefore easily suscep- tible of impressions; not fixed by principles, and therefore easily following the current of fancy; not informed by experience, and consequently open to every false sugges- tion and partial account.

The class of the young, the ignorant, and the idle included, of course, many persons of quality and many more who aspired to that standing and thought novel-reading one way of pre- paring for it. Fanny Burney's diary is full of instances such as that of Lady Louisa Stuart who, looking back on the days of her youth, recalled particularly her first reading of *The Man of Feeling* and her "secret dread [lest she] should not cry enough to gain the credit of proper sensibility."[5]

It is, of course, this cult of feeling—whether fostered by the novel of sensibility or the novel of Gothic sensation—that Jane Austen burlesques. If we turn to "Love and Freindship," the most exemplary of the early burlesques, and note how she attacks the substance of the novel of sensibility and ridicules its conventions—how, in fact, she shows its entire world as a world of illusion—we might well conclude that her purpose is to deny the value and existence not just of this sort of feeling but of any feeling in the world of reality. Told in letters, "Love and Freindship" glances satirically at several stock ad- ventures and devices of popular fiction such as love at first sight, spontaneous exchange of confidences, miraculous identi- fications, coincidental reunions of long-lost relatives, and the

5. Quoted in ibid., p. 54.

creation of "suspense" through otherwise unmotivated concealment of true names and identities. The underlying moral purpose of the burlesque is made clear at the outset by invoking the tale openly as a deliberate lecture on conduct and an introduction to life. An account of the "Misfortunes and Adventures" that befell one lady in her life, it is solicited and offered for the benefit of a younger woman as "a useful lesson for the support of those which may befall her in her own."

The misfortunes and adventures are, of course, principally the misfortunes and adventures of sensibility. The heroine, Laura, being possessed of a "sensibility too tremblingly alive to every affliction of my Freinds, my Acquaintance and particularly to every affliction of my own," is quite naturally predisposed to romantic suffering. Thus, while she almost forgets to mention the trifling circumstance of her parents' death, she is overcome by the plight of a young stranger who has lost his way. This starts her on her adventures, for since it becomes obvious at once that the youth's sensibility matches her own, the two are immediately united. The young man's sister brings forward the possibility that, barring their father's consent and generosity, the couple is likely to want for "Victuals and Drink." But to the lovers this is a contemptible suggestion. "Victuals and Drink! (replied my Husband in a most nobly contemptuous Manner) and dost thou then imagine that there is no other support for an exalted Mind (such as is my Laura's) than the mean and indelicate employment of Eating and Drinking? . . . Does it appear impossible to your vile and corrupted Palate, to exist on Love?" To prove the point the lovers betake themselves to the abode of Augustus and Sophia, a similarly disposed and married couple, where they are able to add to the joys of love the further undying "mutual Protestations of Freindship." This state of affairs, however, does not last; the cash "which Augustus had gracefully purloined from his unworthy father's Escritoire" having long run out, the two males are presently seized for debt, while the two female

friends journey to Scotland to the house of Macdonald, a relation of Sophia's. Here, in addition to converting their host's
daughter to sensibility and thus breaking up her impending
marriage, Sophia emulates her husband's example and sets
about making free with Macdonald's escritoire. But Macdonald
comes in just "as Sophia was majestically removing the 5th
Bank-note from the Drawer to her own purse," and the two
ladies are promptly shown the door. On the open road they
encounter their husbands again, only to see their carriage over-
turned and both of them expire instantaneously. The two bereaved ladies seize the opportunity to go into prescribed lamentations on the spot, but unluckily Sophia carries the exhibition a trifle too far, catches cold, and is soon dead. Laura,
who accidentally falls in with her husband's family, is hand-
somely pensioned off by her father-in-law and thus survives to
tell the tale.

It is obvious that the cult of sensibility displayed by Laura
and her friend is for Jane Austen the most dangerously silly
aspect of the current fashion in both love and literature. The
question, however, is to what extent the plot of "Love and
Freindship" turns on the issue of sensibility versus prudence—
particularly prudence, or the lack of it, in matters of money. It
would seem from the above summary that while popular fiction ruled out any worthwhile motives for conduct other than
those of feeling, Jane Austen's purpose was to show that in
real life no motives exist except the prudential ones. She does
indeed show that beneath their postures and their rhetoric, the
exemplary friends and lovers are not only devoid of the feelings they profess, but are actuated at all necessary moments by
the very motives they claim to despise. Their delusive fantasy
of love and friendship notwithstanding, they are perforce as
much in the worldly business as anyone else, perhaps less pru-
dently than other people but in the end more hypocritically.

Yet it seems to me that this is not at all the main point of
the burlesque, that Jane Austen is not merely turning the argu-

ment of popular fiction upside down, but that her position even in this slight childish piece is far more interesting. True, she shows that the kind of sensibility Laura advocates can only exist in the "Vale of Uske," in "one of the most romantic parts" of which the heroine meets and marries the hero. Such sensibility, that is, can be bred only in the more fantastic regions of the literary imagination and can have no place in any real world, prudential or otherwise. But for Jane Austen, the total separation of Uske from the ordinary world does not answer the issue between feeling and prudence; it evades that issue. Thus, while her characters assume as axiomatic the incompatibility of love and fortune and choose love and the Vale of Uske rather than the everyday world of money and prudence, she does not merely show the folly or hypocrisy of their choice. Instead she questions the basic assumption itself: the fantasy of the Vale of Uske aside, are the claims of feeling irreconcilable with the facts and duties of ordinary life? What Jane Austen does quite simply in "Love and Freindship" is to have these facts themselves ridicule the question. Quite consistently she shows that it is the lovers who are bent on flying from a world that is prepared to embrace them and accommodate all their claims; that should the lovers' vigilance flag even for a moment, they are sure to find themselves trapped into the humiliating situation of being both happy in love and prosperous in fortune. This is the main joke throughout "Love and Freindship." Thus the point about Laura's being granted an annuity is that the accidental meeting with her father-in-law is absolutely the first opportunity that he has ever had of showing his generosity toward her, indeed the first opportunity he has had of coming anywhere near her. Or take the situation right at the beginning of the tale, the situation that has led his son Edward to lose his way in the Vale of Uske in the first place. Edward is running away from the prospect of a marriage. He highly approves of the lady and has, in fact, no objection to the marriage except that it has unluckily merited the approval of his father as well. As he recounts the situation to Laura: "My Father, seduced by the false glare of Fortune and the Deluding Pomp of Title, insisted on my giving my hand to Lady Dorothea. No never exclaimed I. Lady Dorothea is lovely and Engaging; I prefer no woman to her; but know Sir, that I scorn to marry her in compliance with your Wishes." The same logic is responsible, of course, for breaking up the marriage in the tale's subplot. Laura and Sophia persuade Macdonald's daughter to elope with a worthless scoundrel, almost a complete stranger to her, by convincing her that she cannot possibly be in love with, and therefore cannot marry, a man who has the approbation of her father.

Jane Austen traces this perverse theory of love and marriage to its source when she makes Edward's father exclaim in response to the young man's outburst cited above: "Where, Edward in the name of wonder . . . did you pick up this unmeaning gibberish? You have been studying Novels I suspect." Obviously the inspiration here is quite close to the crux of Lydia's comedy in *The Rivals,* which was performed at Steventon some time before "Love and Freindship" was written. For, as pointed out in Chapter 4 above, Sheridan's heroine is a creature of the same perverse romantic logic, fed from the same source—the "mere Trash of the common Circulating Library," as Jane Austen describes it in *Sanditon*—as Laura. Like Edward and Macdonald's daughter after Laura and Sophia have worked on her, Lydia spurns any idea of love and marriage that does not involve at the same time the certainty of family displeasure and loss of fortune—until, of course, the recognition dawns on her that "a little *wealth* and *comfort* may be endured after all."

No doubt "Love and Freindship" treats the whole issue in extraordinarily simplistic terms. The reason for this is that not only is the tale a juvenile effort, but, more important, it is a burlesque and answers the blatant either/or theory which it ridicules with an equally blatant both/and. In the later novels, as we shall see, the answer is never quite so simple; the world is never quite so willing to accommodate the claims of lovers. Nevertheless it remains true that in the end not one of the heroines is required to win love at the cost of material comfort or material comfort at the cost of love. Not one of them labors under the theory that would hold wealth to be a taint on the good life and a source of danger per se—a sentimental theory by no means confined to the worst writers of cheap fiction. Take, for example, the mysterious old man in Fanny Burney's *Cecilia* who makes a nuisance of himself throughout the novel by frequenting the haunts of the rich and issuing prophecies of imminent doom unless they submit to the petty claims of charity that he lays before them—as though the future of the moneyed classes depended upon the giving (or witholding) of sixpence to the poor.

That the doom of wealth could so easily be averted would seem to the clearheaded Jane Austen a self-indulgent and even hypocritical notion. It is inconceivable that she would ever introduce a character like this "prophet," much less allow him to have on her heroines the influence he exerts on Cecilia. She knew that no matter how the moneyed middle class might itself declaim against the dangers of wealth, in reality money remained the necessary source of its culture and vigor in her time. On this question she was prepared to stand against no less a person than Dr. Johnson—her moral tutor as well as Fanny Burney's. While Johnson warned in *The Rambler* (No. 38) against superfluity in health and riches, Jane Austen could write pointedly in the last paragraph of her last finished novel: "Mrs. Smith's enjoyments were not spoiled by this improvement of income, with some improvement of health . . . she might have bid defiance even to greater accessions of worldly prosperity. She might have been absolutely rich and perfectly healthy, and yet be happy."

The point is worth emphasizing because Jane Austen's position with regard to the culture of which she wrote has been misconstrued by some of her best and most influential recent critics. Hers is far from an uncritical position, but both the nature and the extent of her criticism can be exaggerated. For instance D. W. Harding, who comments that Jane Austen's books are read and enjoyed precisely by the sort of people she disliked, goes on to characterize her as ironically "a literary classic of the society which attitudes like hers, held widely enough, would undermine."[6] Undermine? The idea is surely misleading, for Jane Austen is not (however we may regret the fact) a writer of that sort at all. She does not question any of the basic arrangements of her world: its economic structure, the power and prestige of money, the financial dependence of women, the insistence on marriage as the only permissible form of love. Her subject is not the basic structure of her society but only that of a few of the topmost chambers of the cultural edifice that is further erected upon it. She calls for no impossibilities, no resolution of fundamental contradictions or irreconcilable conflicts and is concerned only with those values—love above all—which she considers attainable in her society even as it stands. She is a classic of bourgeois comedy.

Jane Austen's belief in the real possibility of love—here and now, or, to use Wordsworth's lines:

> Not in Utopia,—subterranean fields,—
> Or some secreted island, Heaven knows where!
> But in the very world, which is the world
> Of all of us,—the place where, in the end,
> We find our happiness, or not at all!—

is, as I have suggested, the main point of her quarrel with the

6. D. W. Harding, "Regulated Hatred: An Aspect of the Work of Jane Austen," *Jane Austen: A Collection of Critical Essays,* ed. Ian Watt, Twentieth Century Views (Englewood Cliffs, Prentice-Hall, 1963), p. 167. The essay first appeared in *Scrutiny, 8* (1940), pp. 346-62 and has since proved widely and on the whole deservedly influential.

fantastic novel of sensibility. The belief indicates likewise, though from the opposite end, her divergence from the other burlesque writers of the time, who also were arguing against the rampant romancing of popular literature. Charlotte Lennox's *The Female Quixote,* for instance, is dedicated not to questioning but rather to reversing a proposition which, as we are told in the opening chapter, her heroine had learned from the writers of fiction—the proposition "that Love was the ruling Principle of the World; that every other Passion was subordinate to this; and that it caused all the Happiness and Miseries of Life." Jane Austen, although she rejected as emphatically as Charlotte Lennox the notion that love ruled the world, did not for this reason regard love as a quixotic fantasy. She thought it only one among several possible and contending passions, but she did insist that upon it depended not all but certainly much of the true happiness of life in the world she knew. Her novels, like those of Fielding before her, held up before the common love of prosperity the uncommon prosperity of love.

One realizes, of course, that this love—both as a value in itself and, more specifically, as it is expressed in Jane Austen's novels—has come under extensive criticism and questioning. It is possible that modern readers, torn in opposite directions by sentimentality and sex, have to some extent lost the older feeling for the emotion of love. For if love changes, it does so not in its basic facts but only in the emotional accompaniments which used to be meant by the term itself. Indeed, when once we see rightly what Jane Austen is expressing, we will not, I think, quarrel with her expression of it—for love, like any other emotion, is often best rendered in literature through suggestion rather than explicit statement. Jane Austen is, as Virginia Woolf puts it, "a mistress of much deeper emotion than appears upon the surface. She stimulates us to supply what is not there."[7] If, however, this is as obvious a fact as

7. Virginia Woolf, "Jane Austen," *The Common Reader,* First and Second Series (New York, Harcourt, Brace, 1948), p. 197.

I take it to be, why have so many critics of Jane Austen disregarded it? Aside from the real possibility mentioned above of a cultural gap that makes understanding difficult, there are certain other obstacles which can perhaps be more easily put out of the way. Consider, for example, the following statement of Marvin Mudrick's: "The bourgeois world is safe for Jane Austen because—formalizing all personal relations—it makes no provision for feeling . . . It is no accident that whenever social maneuvering ceases and lovers must come face to face in a moment of love, Jane Austen makes a joke."[8] Behind this statement lie not only the old assumption of the comic writer's hostility to emotion, but also a misunderstanding of the true relation between comedy and culture. For this joke, when it does occur in a Jane Austen novel, occurs there for the same reason as do the jokes in *Much Ado* or the joke at the end of *Tom Jones* when Sophia and Tom come finally and happily together: they are all jokes at the expense not of love, but of the absurd conventions of love. When, for instance, at the end of *Sense and Sensibility* Jane Austen tells us that Edward Ferrars, although now made "one of the happiest of men," showed very little of his happiness "in the rapturous profession of the lover," what she ridicules is neither love nor feeling but only the raptures and professions of sensibility—the counterfeit emotions of such a hero as the Edward of "Love and Freindship." The relative reticence that Jane Austen enforces upon the lovers themselves in moments of love is likewise a considered and deliberate gesture against the profuse and empty rhetoric required by contemporary fashion. But the reticence, unlike the joke, is not always merely negative in its effect: in most situations, as in the meeting after a long interval between Darcy and Elizabeth at Pemberley, it proves a more eloquent statement of true emotion than any open declarations could be. Such situations, however, need a depth and

8. Mudrick, *Jane Austen*, pp. 19, 30.

art of preparation which are little appreciated today. To be effective they can only come after a carefully and subtly woven web of previous happenings, of mutual apprehensions and misapprehensions, of reflection and speech, of meetings and absences, and even of partial avowals—the last, especially, since it would be ridiculous to suggest that Jane Austen brings her lovers together only through jokes and silences. What Mudrick calls the "moment of love" is in fact only the relatively unimportant moment of public or explicit acknowledgement. There is no one moment of love in Jane Austen. Love is rather an emotion that takes root and develops gradually, and she takes care to make it manifest and convincing to the reader long before she has the characters or the novel announce it formally.

Those who are moved by this emotion believe naturally that, though an invention of the few past centuries, it represents a value worthy of surviving the specific social order that first invented it. The point here, however, is that in Jane Austen's novels, where we see it coming to maturity, it is already a threatened value. As we move from "Love and Freindship" into the novels, we find love opposed increasingly not just by the illusions of literary fantasy but by forces more difficult to contend with. For if the world regarded its women as what Sheridan's Lydia calls "a mere Smithfield bargain," the fictionists of this world practically endorsed the same status for them: the "realists" by depicting love as a quixotic sentiment in the real world and the romancers by insisting on its reality but only in the Vale of Uske—"subterranean fields,— / Or some secreted island, Heaven knows where." The woman's choice thus was to submit, or submit and read Charlotte Smith. Accordingly Jane Austen had to fight on two fronts, as it were, though against the same enemy. She had to disabuse her heroines of the Vale-of-Uske notions, and at the same time make them resist the alternative of becoming mere Smithfield bargains in the ordinary everyday world—a task she held

capable of accomplishment but only through a sustained effort
of moral and emotional intelligence.

To dispel the illusory ecstasies and difficulties which formed
the stock-in-trade of popular fiction, and to substitute in their
place some of the real problems and possibilities of bourgeois
culture—this, then, is the double purpose of Jane Austen's
comedy. Both aspects can be seen with great clarity in *Northanger Abbey,* a novel in which the background of books continues to play an active part. As Marvin Mudrick has observed,
Jane Austen here "juxtaposes the Gothic and the bourgeois
worlds, and allows them to comment on each other."[9] The
Gothic novel was an extension of the novel of sensibility, but
not only because it pushed the theater of emotion or feeling
farther still into fantastic settings. The Radcliffean Gothic reduced feeling itself to fantasy by eliminating all common
psychological ground between its exquisite sensationalism and
any possible inner life of its readers. Thus, in treating *Udolpho*
comically, Jane Austen did not merely have to attack the
theory of feeling it proposed but at the same time define the
status and role of feelings in real terms.

Northanger Abbey is the story of a young girl's education, or
rather her double education: first through a selective and highly self-conscious course of literary readings, and then through
various experiences that teach her to differentiate the real
from the bookish world and thus cause her to readjust the
attitudes and expectations derived from literature. In the first
chapter, which offers the early history of the heroine and
which seems in many ways a simple piece of burlesque writing,
Jane Austen is already working toward this double comic purpose. On the one hand we are given in Catherine Morland an
ordinary girl, rather plain and tomboyish in childhood, with a
commonplace family background which as little as her per-

9. Ibid., p. 38.

sonal appearance can be said to mark her out as a future heroine of romance. Showing above all no aptitude for drawing or music or any of the other required accomplishments, her mind seems definitely "unpropitious for heroism"—up to the age of fifteen. But at fifteen appearances suddenly start mending, and Catherine, despite her disqualifications, considers herself from this point on as avowedly "in training for a heroine." She undertakes a preliminary study of the appropriate literature and is soon determined, not unlike the heroine of "Love and Freindship," to have the world live up to the romance she has developed out of her reading. She knows that the neighborhood contains neither lords nor baronets and that not even young men of mysterious origin or ordinary foundlings are to be found anywhere within reach. "But when a young lady is to be a heroine, the perverseness of forty surrounding families cannot prevent her. Something must and will happen to throw a hero in her way."

The emphasis here, as elsewhere in the novel, falls on the mind—on its vulnerability to illusion even in the most unlikely external circumstances. Catherine Morland's mind is a tabula rasa, a fact Jane Austen underlines before embarking on the story proper in the following chapter. Summing up her heroine's "personal and mental endowments, when about to be launched into all the difficulties and dangers of a six weeks' residence in Bath," she observes that although Catherine's "heart was affectionate, her disposition cheerful and open, without conceit or affectation of any kind," her mind was "about as ignorant and uninformed as the female mind at seventeen usually is." What the generalized comment about the female mind at seventeen makes clear is that Catherine Morland is to be regarded not as a subject for burlesque or satire, but essentially as a representative comic heroine—someone who is neither freakish nor abnormal, but rather typical. She is, however, also typical in a less universal and more important sense: she embodies the dangers of a cultural situation

in which the youthful mind is apt to be seduced by a peculiarly perverse variety of romantic delusion. This is in fact what
happens to Catherine as soon as she steps into the fashionable
world of Bath. But if a basically good-natured and unaffected
girl like Catherine can so easily fall prey to well-cultivated
illusions, her sound temperament also contains the promise of
eventual awakening and the possibility of a second and more
sound education. This is why Jane Austen gives us a stage-by-
stage history of her heroine's early years in the preparatory
first chapter. And herein we see, too, the advantage of an
omniscient point of view for a comic novel, a point of view
that can surround the consciousness of a character with a
larger consciousness, aware from the beginning of more than is
the character himself. Thus unlike "Love and Freindship,"
which is told in letters by the heroine throughout, *Northanger
Abbey* is not locked within the mind of a deluded character.
We are rather shown Catherine Morland in the process of deluding herself, being made witness at the same time to her
normalcy in other ways, so that for us her self-deception
carries at each stage its own seeds of final undeception.

Thus we are not surprised when, much later in the novel—at
the height of the Bath adventure—the author assures us that
Catherine, for all her submission to romance, still possessed
feelings "rather natural than heroic." By this time, however,
there is little need to direct our attention through authorial
comment. For with Catherine's arrival at Bath and her entering
into relationships with the novel's two other principal characters, the conflict between nature and heroism becomes a
dramatic issue. Mrs. Allen, under whose protection the girl has
come to Bath, is herself characterized by total "vacancy of
mind, and incapacity for thinking." The charge of educating
Catherine's mind falls accordingly to her two new acquaint-
ances: Isabella Thorpe, the "friend," who becomes the abettor
of romantic illusion; and Henry Tilney, the potential lover,
who assumes early the office of mildly but constantly ridi-

culing the visions of romance. The friend and the lover thus pull their weight in opposed directions.

To a large extent the plot turns on romance of the Gothic variety. Under Isabella's tutorship Catherine comes readily to believe that she could happily spend her whole life reading *Udolpho,* and very soon she learns to look upon the world as a scene expressly arranged for the purpose of corroborating the truth of Mrs. Radcliffe's imagination. She welcomes an excursion to Blaize Castle as an opportunity for "exploring an edifice like Udolpho," but this is only a preparatory touch for her later visit to Northanger Abbey, the family-seat of the Tilneys —a visit during which she develops around the old house a complete history of Gothic deeds involving her host, General Tilney, as the villain and his dead wife as the victim. This leads her to a series of blunders followed by humiliating discoveries, such as the well-known midnight perusal of a manuscript which Catherine takes for a record of secret crimes committed and suffered in the Abbey but which on examination turns out to be an inventory of linen: if "the evidence of sight might be trusted," actually a "washing-bill." And, of course, there is Henry Tilney's equally well-known final admonition of Catherine which brings this line of adventure to an end:

> "Consult your own understanding, your own sense of the probable, your own observation of what is passing around you. Does our education prepare us for such atrocities? Do our laws connive at them? Could they be perpetrated without being known in a country like this, where social and literary intercourse is on such a footing? . . . Dearest Miss Morland, what ideas have you been admitting?"

Among the many ironies of this passage, the one that has escaped attention is the most obvious and telling one: namely, Catherine's "education" and "social and literary intercourse" are precisely the factors that have paved the way to the trap into which she has fallen. Her disillusionment, however, is now complete: "The visions of romance were over. Catherine was completely awakened."

Yet the Gothic self-deceptions are not nearly so important as the deceptions of another variety—the deceptions of sensibility—with which they are connected in the novel. This aspect of romance cuts more vitally into Catherine's story, and while Isabella Thorpe and Henry Tilney remain the two other principal actors, this part of the story involves in one way or another the entire cast of characters. In it, furthermore, the roles of Isabella and Henry are not only opposed to each other but also doubled and at the same time reversed. As a sentimental tutor, Isabella is the Laura of "Love and Freindship" transferred from the world of burlesque to that of comedy. Her overt function is the same: to educate Catherine "in the finesse of love" and "the duties of friendship." Of course, in this respect Catherine is never quite as taken in as she is in the matter of *Udolpho.* The very fact that she can enter into a relationship with Henry Tilney assures us of her natural resistance to the attitudes of a sentimental heroine. The remark already cited about her being "rather natural than heroic" is made in relation to her feelings for Henry. Considering that, as Jane Austen tells us a little later, even her "passion for ancient edifices was next in degree to her passion for Henry Tilney," it is not surprising that given his presence on the scene, the passion for sensibility never takes firm root. As a matter of fact, Henry precedes Isabella in Catherine's acquaintance and has already burlesqued the fashionable sentimental attitudes in his first meeting with her, a short time before Isabella can start advocating them. Nevertheless in the end it is Isabella who first opens Catherine's eyes to that which "the finesse of love" and "the duties of friendship" are really meant to conceal: money and the matrimonial maneuver. For, profuse as have been her professions of friendship for Catherine and love for Catherine's brother, Isabella calmly throws both overboard the moment she fancies herself within reach of a better prospect—Captain

Tilney. Although earlier she had held up the ideal of love with as little cash to interfere as possible—the "ecstasy" of living in a "cottage in some retired village"—she now concedes with a facility that astonishes poor Catherine that "after all that romancers may say, there is no doing without money."

This is Catherine's first lesson in the realities of bourgeois life, and it is offered to her by the "romantic" Isabella Thorpe. Of course she learns how timely and plausible a lesson it has been when General Tilney—hitherto a model of courtly grace and hospitality—unceremoniously throws her out of the Abbey. This is the climax of the story—the true surprise of its surprise ending. Catherine's fate now seems identical with that of her brother, and for the same reason. The General, it turns out, had sought and entertained her as a suitable match for his son; but happening to discover his mistake in her, finding out that in fact she was "guilty . . . of being less rich than he had supposed," he now sends her packing with brutal abruptness. Her brother's situation had already caused the "anxieties of common life" to supersede "the alarms of romance" in Catherine's mind; her own present case drives the point home— "Yet how different now the source of her inquietude . . . how mournfully superior in reality and substance! Her anxiety had foundation in fact, her fears in probability."

By thus translating Gothic terror into real-life terms, Jane Austen removes its comforting quality of vicarious indulgence. "Oh! Mr. Tilney, how frightful! This is just like a book! But it cannot really happen to me," Catherine exclaims to Henry's playful description of Northanger Abbey and "the horrors that a building such as 'what one reads about' may produce." But in a surprising and to her unexpected—and therefore more terrifying—way, it does happen to her. She had always wondered about General Tilney, knowing that something "was certainly to be concealed," only to dissipate in Gothic fantasy rather than try to understand this persistent feeling caused by the General. The monster of avarice, when she finally recognizes him, turns out to be as cruel and ruthless as any monster she had imagined, and not half so remote. In the end she realizes that there was nothing absurd about her early conjunction of "Tilneys and trap-doors" except the notion she then had of traps. Otherwise, "in suspecting General Tilney of either murdering or shutting up his wife, she had scarcely sinned against his character or magnified his cruelty."

Yet this is not the last word of Catherine's story. While the sentimental Isabella and the chivalric General educate her liberally in the realities of life, it remains for the anti-heroic Henry to offer himself as a figure of romance—true-life romance as opposed to the make-believe finesse of love. For though money and prudence rule the world, they do not rule it to the total exclusion of more disinterested feelings. A Henry Tilney may prove himself a hero after all by standing up to his father, by refusing to accompany him to Herefordshire in pursuit of prudential matrimony, and by quietly presenting himself instead at the Morland parsonage. Certainly in the novel Henry's reality is as indubitable as that of the General, and on the whole so is the reality of the relationship that Jane Austen develops between him and Catherine. In this respect "the tell-tale compression" (according to Jane Austen herself) of the last pages, the "hastening together to perfect felicity," can create a false impression. The final chapter of *Northanger Abbey,* like the final chapter of *Mansfield Park,* is a quick winding-up. Its jauntiness is directed not so much at what is being wound up as at the custom and necessity of literary windings-up in general. It certainly should not be allowed to wipe out at one stroke all that has been shown as happening between Henry and Catherine. What has developed between them is not a great love—suspect as all great loves would be in the context—but a quiet and convincing affection appropriate to the general purpose of the novel.

The real weakness of the novel lies in this very general purpose. It is not an absolute but only a relative weakness. The novel would have sufficed to make the literary fortune of a lesser comic writer, if a lesser comic writer could possibly have written it. It is weak only as a Jane Austen comedy, being too directly and heavily involved with books, too closely and crudely dependent upon the presence of the source of its inspiration—sent into the world powerless, as it were, to dispense with its umbilical cord. Or, to change the metaphor, it may be regarded as the chrysalis of Jane Austen's comedy: an enormous step forward from burlesque-parody, but still a work whose full effect demands a visible correspondence to a literary formula and whose comic quality is therefore itself a little too formulaic.

The formulaic quality constitutes likewise the chief weakness of *Sense and Sensibility*. Unlike *Northanger Abbey*, this novel does not parody a specific book; nevertheless it defines its central issue, on the surface, in terms of a literary debate—that is to say, in terms which are oversimplified. Since beneath the surface the novel rejects the oversimplification of the question as formulated even in its own title, the result is an internal confusion or contradiction—an excessive complication in developing the action or an excessive simplicity in resolving it, depending on the direction from which the novel is viewed. Thus, as several critics have observed, while a sort of contrast of opposites is suggested between Elinor Dashwood (Sense) and Marianne Dashwood (Sensibility), the contrast does not in fact hold in the novel. The two sisters are more alike than one would suppose, not merely from the title but from a good deal that happens and is said in the novel itself. The novel, indeed, both supports and at the same time plays ironically against the simple antithesis implied in its title. Our impression of Elinor is predominantly that of a somewhat stodgy representative of Sense, yet she is also said and shown to have "an excellent heart; her disposition was affectionate, and her feelings were strong." On the other hand, Marianne, who has much of her sister's sense, is not only taken to task for lacking the rest of it but almost burlesqued as a figure of false sensibility and romance. There are moments, in fact, when she might be the Laura of "Love and Freindship." For instance, she seems as incapable as her mother of entertaining any "sentiment of approbation inferior to love," and both daughter and mother are said to luxuriate in sorrow, "seeking increase of wretchedness in every reflection that could afford it." Like Laura, Marianne disdains money—"Beyond a competence, it can afford no real satisfaction, as far as mere self is concerned"—which is very well, except that her idea of competence turns out to be about "eighteen hundred or two thousand a year; not more than *that.*"

For the most part, however, Marianne, as she is presented dramatically, has little to do with a character and conception such as Laura's. She is not a hypocrite; it is her judgment that is questioned, not the reality of her feelings. The Laura of this novel is discarded early in the third and youngest Dashwood sister, who, we are told, had already at thirteen "imbibed a good deal of Marianne's romance, without having much of her sense." But even this "good-humoured, well-disposed," and senseless girl is less like Laura than she is like Lydia Bennet of the later *Pride and Prejudice.*

The truth of the matter is that there is little room in this novel either for a conception like Laura's or for the burlesque that goes with such a conception, though Jane Austen in many ways suggests and insists on both. Essentially *Sense and Sensibility* is concerned, like the later novels, with an exploration of the modes and possibilities of love in the contemporary situation: libertine-prudential (as in Willoughby), sentimental-prudential (as in Lucy Steele), and what for want of a better term can only be called "real" love. Both Marianne and Elinor are seeking this last. Marianne quite rightly judges all purely prudential marriages as a kind of "commercial exchange." But so does Elinor, and even Mrs. Jenkins ("I have no notion of

people's making such a to-do about money and greatness");
and it is characteristic of Marianne that she misunderstands
both of them. The prudence that Elinor insists on is not the
prudence of Lucy Steele: it advocates not conformity to
worldly values but the proper management of one's own;
stands for emotion informed by true judgment; and opposes
that tendency to luxuriate in feeling which can only lead to
display and self-deception, one abetting the other. If this is
sense, it is sense that Marianne clearly needs. True, in most
ways she is as sensible as Elinor, but that is beside the point—
or, rather, that *is* the point. For Marianne's romantic theory of
love is her comic hamartia, the one vulnerable aspect of an
otherwise admirable character. Where "love" is concerned—her
own as well as other people's—she forsakes both her sense of
reality and her judgment of possibility. Whatever she or her
mother "conjectured one moment, they believed the next . . .
with them, to wish was to hope, and to hope was to expect."

Marianne's greatest mistake is, of course, Willoughby—the
man who causes her to suspend judgment exactly in proportion as he fits her theory. Despite all that has been written by
the critics in his favor, Willoughby is a picture-book lover—and
nowhere more so than in Colonel Brandon's rake's-progress
account of his early life and his own later rake's-remorse scene
with Elinor. It is curious that critics who have seen Colonel
Brandon's narrative as a crude and unconvincing device on the
part of Jane Austen should have taken the scene with Elinor
not as equally unmotivated and unconvincing, but at its face
value as revealing at last the true Willoughby and his real passion. Willoughby is nothing more nor less than a diminished
echo of the familiar Restoration rake, a figure we see to greater artistic advantage in Wickham in *Pride and Prejudice* and
again in Henry Crawford of *Mansfield Park,* where Jane Austen
finally succeeds in doing something truly original with it. To
speak of Willoughby as a living character, and a passionate one
at that, is ridiculous; he is an idea, and one can only speak of

his function. Just as we see in Lucy Steele the real prudential motives of the sentimental tradition, Willoughby's function is to reconcile, as did Restoration lovers, the claims of prudence and pleasure by combining profitable marriage with the pleasure of various random seductions. His confession of love for Marianne in the scene with Elinor carries as little conviction as does his direct or reported love-making in the novel generally. The question with regard to him is not the number of his previous seductions, which is supposed to be all that the strait-laced Jane Austen can possibly have against him; it is more the sort of question that Fielding's Sophia asks concerning Tom: Can such a man be capable at any time of real feelings? Tom can, but not Willoughby. "The world had made him extravagant and vain; extravagance and vanity had made him cold-hearted and selfish." Cold-hearted and selfish—precisely the phrase Jane Austen uses to characterize Mr. and Mrs. John Dashwood, Lady Middleton, Mrs. Ferrars, and all other characters in the novel with whom Willoughby shares the unscrupulousness of the prudential motive.

Marianne's case, then, is that while she can see through the selfishness and vulgarity of other characters, she is taken in when the same attributes appear in the form of the romantic and picturesque Willoughby. Basically she is a sound girl: a figure of comedy, not of burlesque. Yet Jane Austen treats her almost as the latter in more than just authorial comments. Instead of making her a comic example, she chooses to make an example of her. For her naïve expectations of picture-book romance she is punished with a marriage that has little to recommend it except her own notion—to the last digit—of pecuniary competence. The whole novel in fact concentrates at the end on a minor and silly theme, all the principal characters except Elinor becoming living proofs of the perfect validity of second attachments. The novel, however, reveals its weakness most clearly in its male lovers, all of whom are formula-types. If Willoughby is the continuing Restoration rake,

Colonel Brandon—his successor in Marianne's affections—is an equally lifeless echo from the other side of the same literary past, sentimental comedy being the ultimate source of this patient, solid, virtuous hero. As for Edward Ferrars, Elinor's shy and reticent young man, we really see him as little as we hear him. The male cast of no other Austen novel is so populated with shadows and dullness.

Returning, however, to the central question of Marianne, it is obvious that *Sense and Sensibility,* unlike other Jane Austen novels, has made no provision for a lively and admirable heroine who is eventually to be chastened out of her folly and who is shown as fully capable of being so chastened. In *Pride and Prejudice,* for instance, Elizabeth Bennet eventually sees through Wickham and can happily return to Darcy; her interest in Wickham is in fact a perverse corollary of her previously awakened interest in Darcy. For Marianne there is only Brandon, and accepting him is very much like an act of resignation. She is thus turned at the end into something less than the comic heroine she has been. Making her a proof against her disapproval of second attachments has nothing to do with her real question: the possibility of a marriage that is not a commercial exchange. The resolution of her story is a resolution according to the letter and not the spirit of her comedy. The answer to her question lies rather in Elinor's story. But then Elinor is not only the less interesting of the two heroines, she is less interesting because she is less of a comic heroine. While the treatment of Marianne only tends toward the burlesque, Elinor is much more firmly put farther beyond the center of comedy in the other direction, being from the first too much of a blameless and serene character. In her case there is no need to resolve—only to reward. The idea of the double heroine—clearly inspired by the formulaic character of the novel, its quality of a literary debate—has thus the effect of dislocating the answer from the question. Of the two stories, it is Marianne's that embodies the characteristic conflict of a comic action, but Elinor's that is crowned by an authentic comic resolution.

The question in *Pride and Prejudice* is the same as that in *Sense and Sensibility,* although it is now raised without interference from such debating points as the validity of second attachments or the respective merits of sense and sensibility. This, too, is a novel about possible "modes of attachment"—a phrase used by Jane Austen herself in Chapter 46. Perhaps more of these modes are exhibited here than were seen in *Sense and Sensibility,* for over and above the usual forms of prudential attachment we have the case of Lydia—a silly, high-spirited, and rather hoydenish girl who, we are told, is willing "to attach herself to anybody." Certainly her motivation is not prudential, but neither is it sexual in the way in which some recent critics seem to have read it. It is thoughtlessly social and competitive. From the world around her Lydia has imbibed the idea of marriage as a sort of race; without inquiring what the usual rewards of this race are, she is determined to win it in record time. Beyond that she is moved not by passionate love but by the desire for reputation—eventually, of course, the reputation of attaching no less a person than the much-attached Wickham. To see her as a picture of sexual vitality, a girl untouched by the values of her world, is to romanticize her out of recognition. She strikes us rather as childish, and that not because she is in any romantic sense above or beyond the reach of her world but because that world has done only half its business with her—it has given her the spirit of matrimonial competition but not the substance of matrimonial prudence.

In any event, Lydia's is a minor case and exists in the novel mainly to perform a plot function. The more important subsidiary cases are all varieties of the prudential mode; and more nakedly than in *Sense and Sensibility,* prudence is a matter of money. As Elizabeth Bennet puts it at a particularly revealing moment in the story: "what is the difference in matrimonial affairs, between the mercenary and the prudent motive? Where does discretion end, and avarice begin?" Elizabeth has, of course, never shared her sister Jane's confidence in the goodness of all mankind; nevertheless, when she makes this remark, in considerable bitterness of spirit, a gathering sequence of events in the world around her has put into doubt even her own limited and qualified opinion of its better possibilities. The first shock has come from Charlotte Lucas, her best friend: Elizabeth finds it incomprehensible that this "sensible, intelligent young woman" should so readily accept Mr. Collins. Charlotte herself has no high opinion of Mr. Collins or, indeed, of men and matrimony in general. But marriage, she realizes, is "the only honourable provision for well-educated young women of small fortune," their one "preservative from want." She has accepted the ridiculous clergyman "solely from the pure and disinterested desire of an establishment." To Elizabeth it is plain that her friend has "sacrificed every better feeling to worldly advantage" and that, much as she likes and sympathizes with her, "no real confidence could ever subsist between them again." The very quality of intelligence that prevents Charlotte from deluding herself with regard to her motives makes the nature of those motives more clear and painful. As Elizabeth puts it a little later, in answer to Jane's defense of their friend: "You shall not defend her, though it is Charlotte Lucas. You shall not, for the sake of one individual, change the meaning of principle and integrity, nor endeavour to persuade yourself or me, that selfishness is prudence."

Soon, of course, it becomes evident to Elizabeth that Charlotte's defection is no exceptional case, but rather an example of the general rule. The truth comes home when, with the sudden departure of the Netherfield party, she sees Jane's prospects virtually blotted out. Although Jane characteristically puts the most charitable construction on the event, Elizabeth sees right through it and has no difficulty imagining the reasons that have thus led to the separation of Jane and Bingley. It is naïve to argue, as Jane does, that Bingley's friends can have no wish except for his happiness; "they may wish his increase of wealth and consequence; they may wish him to marry a girl who has all the importance of money, great connections, and pride." Close on the heels of these two events comes a third in which Elizabeth is herself involved, mildly but nevertheless instructively, via George Wickham. When news comes that this young man, who had shown marked partiality to Elizabeth and in whom she herself had taken some interest, is engaged to Miss King, the same truth stares her in the face again. For it is obvious to her that the "sudden acquisition of ten thousand pounds was the most remarkable charm of the young lady to whom he was now rendering himself agreeable." It being Wickham, however, Elizabeth is "less clear-sighted perhaps in this case than in Charlotte's" and finds no immediate reason "to quarrel with him for his wish of independence." But the lapse from clear-sightedness is of short duration. With Darcy's disclosures about Wickham, she corrects herself and acknowledges the true character of his attentions to Miss King as "the consequence of views solely and hatefully mercenary." In the meantime Colonel Fitzwilliam, Darcy's friendly and likable cousin, has provided her with yet another example of views solely, though in this instance not hypocritically and therefore not hatefully, mercenary. She has felt some mild interest in him too, but, unlike Wickham, he quickly comes into the open and remarks to her in a general yet discreetly pointed way: "Our habits of expense make us too dependent, and there are not many in my rank of life who can afford to marry without some attention to money."

Here, then, is Elizabeth's problem together with all the mounting evidence. First Charlotte, then the Bingleys and Darcy with them, then Wickham, and finally even the thoroughly likable Fitzwilliam—where in their various matrimonial speculations and maneuvers did "discretion end, and avarice begin"?

Charlotte had pleaded in her own justification: "I am not romantic, you know; I never was." Did this mean that any idea of marriage on other than mercenary principles was a romantic delusion, and Elizabeth's insistence on integrity and principle simply quixotic?

Elizabeth's position, in other words, emphasizes with greater clarity Marianne's idea in *Sense and Sensibility* of a love that is not a commercial exchange. Yet to note the similarity of the issue is also to note immediately the wide divergence between its conception and development in the two novels. The comparable phrasing of their titles notwithstanding, the action in *Pride and Prejudice* has broken loose completely from the format of a false conflict of categories. In this novel, sense by itself gets dismissed with the sensible Charlotte; sensibility, with such an obviously romantic character as Wickham. Appearing by themselves, that is, sense and sensibility are now seen not as partial virtues, not indeed as virtues at all, but as modes of rationalized surrender and deception. Unlike *Sense and Sensibility,* whose form demands the opposition of sense and sensibility, *Pride and Prejudice* unites the two in the emotional intelligence of its single heroine, insisting at the same time on this indivisible quality as the one active defense against the corrupting and deadening pressures from within and without. And the clarity of thought that led to the creation of one heroine instead of the earlier two also marks the final dissipation of the confusion between burlesque and comedy. (As for the other character—Jane in this case—she is no longer an equal heroine but a foil, a sort of Hero to Elizabeth's Beatrice: "I am happier even than Jane; she only smiles. I laugh.")

The maturity of *Pride and Prejudice,* its status as a classic of comedy, can be discussed from the more crucial aspect of the role played by abstraction in it. Quite obviously books and literary theories do not have the function here that they were assigned in Jane Austen's earlier work. True, as several critics have pointed out, looming in the background of *Pride and Prejudice* one can still perceive the outlines of previous literary works—particularly Fanny Burney's *Cecilia,* to which Jane Austen alludes (as we shall see) through much more than just the title of her own novel. Or there is a character like Mary Bennet who, by reading "great books" and constantly applying the nuggets of wisdom drawn from them to concrete situations, reminds us of that pedantry which is the pole of comic intelligence. However, although these points reinforce the general design, they have no primary importance in the outlining of the main comic action.

The exact definition and role of abstraction in *Pride and Prejudice* can be best given through Schopenhauer again:

> Abstraction consists in thinking away the less general predicates; but it is precisely upon these that so much depends in practice. . . . Therefore in everything that excites laughter it must always be possible to show a conception and a particular, that is, a thing or event, which certainly can be subsumed under that conception, and therefore thought through it, yet in another and more predominating aspect does not belong to it at all, but is strikingly different from everything else that is thought through that conception.[10]

Narrowly interpreted, this passage can only point to an explanation of Mary Bennet's comedy—something that needs little explanation anyway. But there is no need to confine ourselves to the idea of an instantaneously perceived, laughter-producing incongruity. There is room here to proceed rather to that larger and more complicated irony upon which the entire action of *Pride and Prejudice* is built. For not only does this novel concern itself directly with real-life abstractions such as the one—"a truth universally acknowledged"—that it sets forth in the opening sentence; its relation to this proposition—the

10. Schopenhauer, *World as Will and Idea, 1,* 79; *2,* 271.

proposition namely "that a single man in possession of a good fortune must be in want of a wife"—is curiously ironic. In a sense the events of the novel only prove the truth of the proposition, for in the end the intended single men do in fact marry the girls intended for them. Yet the proposition is not true the way it is meant by the universe and especially by Mrs. Bennet. Jane Austen goes on:

> However little known the feelings or views of such a man may be on his first entering a neighbourhood, this truth is so well fixed in the minds of the surrounding families, that he is considered as the rightful property of someone or other of their daughters
>
> "My dear Mr. Bennet," said his lady to him one day, "have you heard that Netherfield Park is let at last?"

Here we have a conception and a particular, but we notice more than their mere copresence, as in the case of Mary Bennet's wise and weighty comments. What the passage describes rather is a deliberate movement from the one to the other—a movement that, in fact, launches the novel into action. Mrs. Bennet is making a highly favorable deduction; in subsuming the specific case of the new tenant of Netherfield Park and her own marriageable daughters under the universal truth declared in the first sentence, she is disregarding precisely those "less general predicates" upon which "so much depends in practice." Mrs. Bennet is, of course, banking on her daughter's good looks and the magic of love, yet she disregards the prior question of the other individual's as yet unascertained feelings or views on the whole subject. As the novel makes clear, and as is suggested even at this stage through references to fortune and property, so long as the individual remains unknown, the only reasonable guess one can make about his feelings or views would prove unfavorable to Mrs. Bennet's daughters. For the truth is that if a single man in possession of a good fortune be in want of a wife, it is usually a wife who is herself in possession of a good fortune. This is a rule proclaimed everywhere, and not the least at Netherfield, toward which Mrs. Bennet prods the action of the novel with such unsuspecting confidence. True, in point of fact the rule is breached by the cases of both Jane and Elizabeth, but this point of fact takes a whole novel to establish itself; it would be no exaggeration to say that if the point is established in the end, it is established in the teeth of Mrs. Bennet's easy and self-indulgent notions.

Mrs. Bennet's notions have their practical consequences, and it is worth noting that each step she takes on their strength, far from corroborating their truth, actually goes further to disprove them—separating rather than bringing together Jane and Bingley, not to mention Elizabeth and Darcy. And curiously enough, when at the very end of the novel matters have been arranged as she always desired but never deserved them to be, we find her exactly where she began: "And who knows what *may* happen? . . . As soon as ever Mr. Bingley comes, my dear, you will wait on him, of course. . . . I knew how it would be. I always said it must be so, at last." It is perfectly fair to say that she has no idea of what that "at last" means. Like all deductive characters or characters of abstraction in the novel, she has neither changed her position nor learned anything from experience. She has really had no experience; her proposition is still axiomatic to her, automatic in its proof. In starting all over again as she had in Chapter 1, asking her husband to wait on Bingley and so on, she is virtually inviting the whole comic action to begin a second time. Yet if the action is now resolved, if the proposition has been proved, it has been proved by Elizabeth—and proved, moreover, not as inevitable truth, but only as a possibility that depends for its fulfillment on those same less general predicates of which Mrs. Bennet is oblivious but which have meant everything in bringing about the novel's happy resolution.

This is to say that the action of the novel is directed toward testing the truth of abstraction by the truth of experience—

directed, that is, toward revealing what its being true, or its being made true, involves. Concretely it involves, of course, the views and feelings of the individuals concerned; and we can say quite simply that if the story of Elizabeth and Darcy, and through that the whole novel, ends happily, the reason is that it becomes a story in which views are overcome and gradually corrected by feelings—by an emotion which, once it is experienced, becomes more real and powerful than the earlier and opposing views. These views, as we have seen, are chiefly mercenary, but in the central case of Elizabeth and Darcy the question of money is overshadowed by the more interesting question of family importance and rank. This is a consideration that is finally revealed as indeed a shadow, a pure and meaningless abstraction. But for that very reason it plays the most important role in the action of the novel. It represents something that needs to be recognized and combated not so much in the social world outside, where it has no real power, but more crucially within the characters themselves, where it still remains a motive force. Through this recognition and the process necessary for it, Elizabeth and Darcy become characters of experience (as against the characters of abstraction). These two are primarily responsible for vanquishing the shadowy but not ineffective villains of comedy—for, as Elizabeth puts it, "without scheming to do wrong, or to make others unhappy, there may be error, and there may be misery." Once the error is recognized, however, the misery can be easily averted. Consider, for example, the famous scene toward the end of the novel in which Lady Catherine imperiously commands Elizabeth to give up Darcy in the name of duty and honor—meaning the family honor of the Darcys and the de Bourghs. The scene is, of course, Jane Austen's summary answer to the *Cecilia* situation. So far from being tormented like Fanny Burney's lovers by the conflict between love and family duty, Elizabeth has no hesitation in dismissing "this extraordinary application" as "frivolous" and "ill-judged," and Darcy himself later gives it no countenance at all. It actually has the ironic effect of hastening the union of the two lovers, for it only succeeds in removing from the mind of each all doubt concerning the feelings of the other.

It is easy enough to see that Jane Austen can dismiss the central situation of *Cecilia* as false and ridiculous because she recognizes the irrelevance of family honor as a material issue in the burgeoning bourgeois world of the day. As compared with *Cecilia, Pride and Prejudice* presents us with what may be called a "homogenized" social scene. Leaving aside Fanny Burney's glimpses of the lower reaches of contemporary society, the world that Cecilia confronts and has to make choices in is in a real sense a divided world. Contending in it for social supremacy are three mutually antagonistic classes or orders of men, represented signally by Cecilia's three appointed guardians: men of fashion and pleasure; men from families of ancient name and pride; and the miserly, uncouth, but moneyed businessmen. It is true that the contention, despite Fanny Burney's constant realism of social portrayal, has almost an allegorical quality, with Pleasure, Pedigree, and Parsimony each revealing its own species of pride for the moral instruction of the young and friendless heroine. Nevertheless, by exerting an objective and primarily external power on Cecilia's affairs, each is also a real force in her world—and none more so than the power of honor or family pride, which in fact turns out to be the kingpin of the entire plot.

The world of *Pride and Prejudice* is more homogenized in the sense that in it these three powers or attractions appear united, chiefly in the person of Darcy, and also because money has long since won the battle, leaving the other two very little real importance. Yet the question of family pride is not so easily settled—not, that is, when it survives as an error within the mind. In this respect Jane Austen's title is not a mistaken attempt at allegorical generalization of the novel's theme but rather a precise statement of the specific social and comic situation. "Pride" is "Prejudice"; it has become reduced, that is, to an idea that influences conduct but has no standing in reality. The purpose of the comedy is to bring home and eradicate this error.

The outcome has a sort of resounding social importance that we witness in the scene between Elizabeth and Lady Catherine referred to above. But this is quite literally the outcome, the final demonstration of a process that takes place throughout the novel. For, since it is the prejudice of family pride that has to be overcome—and that too through the experience of a personal emotion and the consequent discovery of a personal value—the theme is in fact developed by means of a series of concrete and low-keyed encounters, with only a few major scenes used to mark the climactic points. The pivotal figure is Darcy, but the theme of pride, of which he is the primary source, undergoes several ramifications before it is finally resolved. Not that Darcy's pride is in itself a simple or single thing; it includes, for instance, a sense of personal superiority which the novel concedes to him not only as his due but, more important, as an admirable quality almost necessary for dealing honestly with a world so largely composed of knaves and fools. No one blames him for his contemptuous dismissal of Mr. Collins, or his curtness toward Mrs. Bennet, or his haughty disdain for Wickham; nor does he himself ever repent of this sort of pride. The pride that is called in question is a pride which Darcy does not only abjure but of which he comes to see the root cause. Toward the end of the novel, when he and Elizabeth look back together over their story, he is led to acknowledge both the change and the discovery. He had always been taught, he says,

> to care for none beyond my own family circle, to think meanly of all the rest of the world, to *wish* at least to

think meanly of their sense and worth compared with my own. Such I was, from eight to eight-and-twenty; and such I might still have been but for you.

This gives us not only a clue to Darcy's character but quite precisely the first cause of the entire comic action. Darcy's error is simply the confusion between personal merit and family pride. For, while the values he respects are personal values, the judgments he makes in practice are class or group judgments. To him want of importance is want of sense. This is his presupposition, his prejudice—the practical consequence of his pride and the practical cause of his comedy.

Thus when he comes to Longbourn it is with a mind made up to stand aloof and detached from what, to his view, can only be an assemblage of unimportant and therefore vulgar and silly people. Accordingly, in his first meeting with Elizabeth he disdains to give her any consequence, even though at that same first meeting he is already impressed and attracted by her. The effect on Elizabeth is the creation of a proud prejudice of her own: "I could easily forgive *his* pride, if he had not mortified *mine*." As far as he is concerned, her judgment too will henceforth be increasingly deflected by prejudice until the time of her agonized reappraisal following his first proposal at Rosings.

But Elizabeth's awakening, which takes place halfway through the novel, does not settle the main issue. Her prejudice has been almost self-induced and has no deep roots. The main question is the older and more significant prejudice of Darcy's—"his pride, his abominable pride," as Elizabeth calls it in the first rush of emotion after the rejection scene. Earlier she had admitted the most preposterous of Wickham's accusations against Darcy because Wickham had intelligently enough attributed everything to one plausible failing: "Family pride, and *filial* pride." This is something that cannot be dismissed as easily as Wickham's other charges which Elizabeth does in fact dismiss immediately on perusal of Darcy's letter. She can even readily see the justice of Darcy's comments on the ignorance, vanity, and folly of her own family because her judgment has never been clouded by family and filial pride. But the question remains whether Darcy's can ever be freed of these same blind considerations. That is why, for all her shame and depression, Elizabeth does not "for a moment repent her refusal, or feel the slightest inclination to see him again."

Darcy's familial pride (or prejudice) is something that Caroline Bingley constantly exploits in her jealousy of Elizabeth. It is also the one regard in which the easygoing and uncomplicated Bingley is Darcy's superior from the outset. Early in the novel, when Caroline at one point observes derisively that one of the Bennet girls' uncles happens to be a small-town attorney and the other "lives somewhere near Cheapside," Bingley declares: "If they had uncles enough to fill *all* Cheapside, it would not make them one jot less agreeable." Darcy, of course, disagrees. In fact, as he becomes more and more aware of his feelings for Elizabeth, he constantly reassures himself that "the inferiority of her connections" is a secure safeguard against any real danger. He even says this to Elizabeth in the very act of surrendering to that danger. Needless to say, her scornful rejection comes as an inexplicable shock, upsetting the most cherished though least examined part of his sense of self-importance. It becomes in effect the first step of that new education for which he is to thank her in the end, involving not the abandonment of judgment and value but their disengagement from the chimera of hereditary rank and family importance. The process begins at Rosings but is seen as concluded only at Pemberley. At Rosings the crucial test is provided by the de Bourgh family. For the same Lady Catherine who evokes abject awe and reverence in Mr. Collins strikes Elizabeth as little other than a piece of "dignified impertinence." Underneath her titled wealth—"the mere stateliness of money and rank"—she is more vulgar, indecorous, self-impor-

tant, interfering, and obtuse than even Mrs. Bennet. Her establishment is as insipid as the conversation at her table is "super-
latively stupid." And the question is whether Darcy, looking
on through the lenses of family pride, will fail to perceive all
this and thereby prove himself a superior but for that very
reason an inexcusable Mr. Collins. However, the presence of
Elizabeth on the scene has already caused him to waver a little
and has made him see things somewhat as they are. He has
even begun to be "a little ashamed of his aunt's ill-breeding."

When Elizabeth and Darcy meet again much later at Pemberley, we see the full extent of the change that has in the
intervening months resulted from these beginnings. Elizabeth,
looking over the beautiful house and grounds, musing how she
could have been mistress of them, and rejoiced in her uncle
and aunt there as her visitors, suddenly checks herself: "But
no—that could never be; my uncle and aunt would have been
lost to me; I should not have been allowed to invite them."
These relatives, the Gardiners, her present companions, are of
course the uncle and aunt from Cheapside. They are sensible,
affectionate, and intelligent people. Mr. Gardiner, though an
active London merchant, belongs to an entirely different cultural species from Briggs, the sour and uncouth moneymaker
of *Cecilia.* But will Darcy perceive the difference? It is really
the reverse of the test at Rosings, though it is a test of the
same basic issue. Darcy surprises not only Elizabeth but everyone except himself by now. When he asks to be introduced to
the Gardiners, Elizabeth cannot help noticing the irony of his
"now seeking the acquaintance of some of those very people
against whom his pride had revolted in his offer to herself."
Her recollection goes even farther back, for as she identifies
the Gardiners, she fully expects him to take alarm and decamp
"as fast as he could from such disgraceful companions"—as,
indeed, he and his friends had done from her own family at
Longbourn. When this does not happen, when on the contrary
Darcy shows the Gardiners the courtesy they deserve—their

Cheapside inferiority notwithstanding—Elizabeth can only wonder: "Why is he so altered? From what can it proceed?"

She will learn the answer from Darcy himself in that later review scene: "Such I was from eight to eight-and-twenty; and such I might still have been but for you." Before that, however, their story passes through a final ironic twist, occasioned by the sudden elopement of Lydia. This event is regarded as a mere device of plotting insofar as the story of Elizabeth and Darcy is concerned: it gives rise to a series of external complications whose resolution helps materially to bring the two together. Yet there is more to it than that. As Elizabeth reflects on Lydia's elopement, she concludes that, among other things, it is sure to put an end to her relationship with Darcy—perversely, just at the time when she has found herself ardently wishing for its continuance. After this fresh and final evidence of family disgrace it is improbable, she reflects, that "they should ever see each other again on such terms of cordiality as had marked their several meetings in Derbyshire." But she is wrong for, as far as Darcy is concerned, this is not an unprecedented but a parallel occurrence, a more successful version of the same man's intrigue with his own sister. (Indeed, it is Darcy's earlier experience that makes his present intervention so expeditious and successful.) Thus if Lydia's elopement is a family disgrace, it is a disgrace that can occur in any family. What Elizabeth imagines a final blow to their relationship embodies in fact a final recognition. It is a blow to that pride and prejudice which has kept them apart so long, at the same time that it has ironically brought them closer together at each successive stage. After this struggle with themselves, Lady Catherine can hold no terrors for them. Quite unknown to her, the incubus of family pride has been exorcized; and her grand, onstage invocation of it only demonstrates publicly that it no longer has any power.

The next two novels, *Mansfield Park* and *Emma,* will have to be passed over with only brief comment. Something of what has been said so far applies to these novels, but there is much in them, especially in *Mansfield Park,* that cannot be profitably discussed under the present line of inquiry. Both works contain elements that strike us as disturbingly modern, or at least as anticipating certain modern developments whose consequences include a radical dislocation of older comic traditions. Something further will be said about this in the following chapter. Here one can only note the extent to which *Mansfield Park* marks a change of course. Jane Austen herself declared that she was attempting a complete change of subject and that *Mansfield Park* was to be about ordination. Yet this is not all that the novel is about. The one complete change is a change of mood; but, as far as the subject is concerned, while there are undoubtedly several new interests, some of the older ones remain important. What is more, the old interests—marriage and the possibility of love and earthly happiness—are not at all subordinated to the new ones, certainly not to the one supposedly central theme of ordination, but stand out very much in their own right. As far as these interests are concerned, one notices not a change but rather a reversal of previous attitudes. Love itself—not sex, which is never directly a subject in Jane Austen, but the emotion of love—now stands more or less ruled out as a possible value. So does intelligence. As a result Fanny Price becomes one of the weaker of Jane Austen's heroines, just as Edmund is among her weaker heroes, and their marriage one of the least plausible of her ideal marriages. When we are told in conclusion that Fanny and Edmund have found a happiness "as secure as earthly happiness can be," it is not the security of their happiness that we question, but its quality as happiness. On the other hand, the other two main characters—the Crawford brother and sister—who are given the vitality of emotion and intelligence are also banished ultimately and hurriedly to a limbo of shame and frustration.

Any reader who comes to *Mansfield Park* after *Pride and*

Prejudice cannot help fancying a different pairing—of Henry Crawford with Fanny Price and, to a more qualified extent, even Mary Crawford with Edmund—up to that late point in the story where the Crawfords suddenly stand revealed as finally irredeemable. That this is not altogether a fancy but rather a sign of uncertain connection in *Mansfield Park* between mood and execution is clear from Jane Austen's own uncertainty on precisely the same point. "Would he [Henry] have persevered, and uprightly, Fanny must have been his reward, and a reward very voluntarily bestowed, within a reasonable period from Edmund's marrying Mary" is the author's comment in the last summary chapter; and, whatever one says of Edmund and Mary, there is no doubt that the novel builds the Henry-Fanny relationship as both plausible and promising —as, indeed, the only relationship that promises something like the realization of total value. Edmund is not far wrong when he tells Fanny: "You have both warm hearts and benevolent feelings . . . there is a decided difference in your tempers, I allow. He is lively, you are serious; but so much the better; his spirits will support yours. It is your disposition to be easily dejected and to fancy difficulties greater than they are. His cheerfulness will counteract this." Nor can one fail to hear in these words an echo of Jane Austen's own comment on the marriage of Elizabeth and Darcy in *Pride and Prejudice*.

Furthermore, not only does the novel show Henry Crawford possessing these high comic values; in his developing emotion for Fanny we get a more characteristic and convincing portrayal of love than we do in the unchanging feeling that exists between Fanny and Edmund. Henry's first and wholly unexpected proposal leaves Fanny "feeling, thinking, trembling, about everything; agitated, happy, miserable, infinitely obliged, absolutely angry. It was all beyond belief!" This is something far truer and more vibrant than the set conversation pieces about goodness, contentment, the stars, and so on, between her and Edmund. By the time Henry visits Portsmouth,

Fanny's initial alarm has vanished, she has already begun to look upon him as "somebody of the nature of a friend." He himself seems freed from the frivolities of the fashionable world, and altogether it does not appear impossible—rather it appears highly probable at this stage—that the action will move in the direction we fancy. To have the action move in this direction, to have it realize its own most attractive possibility, would mean a reaffirmation of the values of vitality and intelligence in a more difficult and complicated situation than any Jane Austen had attempted hitherto. This, however, is exactly what she was not in a mood to do. Her point was not to show these values as triumphant, as capable of overcoming the dangers to which they are naturally liable; her point was to show them as untrustworthy, as helpless before a world whose influence can lead, as Edmund observes in dismissing Mary from his thoughts, to a permanently "blunted delicacy and a corrupted, vitiated mind." Thus Henry Crawford becomes less redeemable than Tom Jones or even Etherege's Dorimant. To make this point Jane Austen suddenly reduces him to a rakish actor in a piece of melodrama, his elopement with Maria being about as convincing as the reported villainies of Willoughby in *Sense and Sensibility,* a novel with which *Mansfield Park* shares a sense of strained good intentions or simple priggishness on the part of the author.

For the goodness—the goodness of duty—that Jane Austen offers in place of the rejected values can hardly be said to solve or even properly connect with the problems raised by the novel. As a word it sounds well enough, but the substance of Fanny Price's duty and indeed devotion to Mansfield Park is unclear. The ideal of Mansfield Park is, of course, defined at its best through the contrast with Fanny's home in Portsmouth. This picture of relatively low life is true as far as it goes, but it is also unfair in the sense that it leaves out those redeeming aspects which Jane Austen herself emphasizes when she turns to more or less the same area of life (and the same contrast)

again in *Persuasion.* Here, although Fanny has some sense of
the disadvantages against which the Prices have to struggle;
although she realizes that her mother would have "made just
as good a woman of consequence as Lady Bertram"; and although she even goes so far as to credit her sister, Susan, for at
least trying to cope with the situation "where *she* could only
have gone away and cried"—she nevertheless dismisses the
household as "the abode of noise, disorder and impropriety"
(as evil a place as any in Jane Austen's writings). In contrast
Mansfield Park, with "its beloved inmates, its happy ways,"
Fanny goes on to recall glowingly, was a house where "all
proceeded in a regular course of cheerful orderliness; everybody had their due importance; everybody's feelings were consulted." Now Fanny may be forgiven, but not the reader, if he
gets carried away by this contrast or exaggerates its importance. To say the least, it is overly flattering to a house whose
direction has been substantially in the hands of Mrs. Norris,
whose mistress lives for the most part the life of a contented
vegetable, and whose master is himself as obtuse on some occa-
sions as he is kind and worthy on others. What the contrast
leaves out mainly, however, is the evidence of Fanny's own
experience at Mansfield. As Henry Crawford reminds her: "I
know Mansfield, I know its way, I know its faults towards
you. I know the danger of your being so far forgotten, as to
have your comforts give way to the imaginary convenience of
any single being in the family." True, there is a sort of cere-
monious regulation of daily life at Mansfield, but this does not
make it in any sense the abode of order and propriety—moral
or domestic. No one who thinks of the Bertram children, all
except Edmund, can say that it does.

The truth is that Mansfield solves no problems; all it can do
is to shut them out. It is a refuge. For Fanny Price—the memo-
rably timid, nervous, delicate, and delicately persecuted heroine—its well-regulated existence and the authority of its master
are a therapeutic refuge against all those complicated emo-

tional and social challenges with which she is unable to cope.

In *Emma* Jane Austen is back on relatively familiar ground, but still with a radical difference. Here is no story of ordination or of any theme apparently more somber than marriage and matchmaking. Like the earlier heroines, the "imaginist" Emma is liable to errors of perception and judgment, from which, however, she rescues herself in time to see things as they are and unite herself with a sensible lover of long standing. But the difference, noted by several critics, may be seen briefly in two ways. First, Emma's errors are not what one would call honest errors, not even just willful in the ordinary sense, but rather disturbingly egotistical and manipulative. In this she is less like Jane Austen's earlier heroines than like a character such as Henry James's Isabel Archer. Second, there is the related fact that she makes not one but a series of errors, or rather the same error repeatedly, thus calling into question the whole process and efficacy of awakening and with it the possibility of achieving a stable rationality. Her honesty, as Mudrick has observed, "operates characteristically in the trough of failure and disaster, before the next rise of confidence and self-delusion."[11] Is imagination, then, only a source of subjectivism and delusion? Are there no external standards, of perception, judgment, and conduct, powerful enough to educate a mind like Emma's, put its illusions to flight, and so make it rational and intelligent as well as free and lively? Are her illusions in fact illusions or the deepest truth of her nature?

Emma, of course, is a comedy and answers these questions happily in various ways, but chiefly through the large fact of Knightley's existence in the novel and through Emma's final recognition and acceptance of him. Nevertheless, these are disturbing questions in that they are too powerfully raised throughout the novel to be laid aside at the end with complete

11. Mudrick, *Jane Austen,* p. 204.

conviction. Fanny Price, though virtually born into a state of subjection, welcomes submission to external authority as the only valid guarantee for right conduct. There are moments in *Emma* when the heroine—the most free of all Jane Austen's heroines, the least subject to any authority except her own— becomes so disastrously self-indulgent that Jane Austen may well be said to be proving the same point again from the opposite direction.

The imaginist self and its illusions, freedom and duty—in *The Portrait of a Lady* Henry James was to reconsider the question in a more modern and cosmopolitan context.

In her last completed novel Jane Austen reexamined the old comic issue of love against prudence; and she did not merely reexamine it but, like some of her predecessors in their last works, put it in the most final when-all-is-said-and-done terms. For when all is said and done, what matters for Jane Austen is not wealth and eminence, not social rank and style and elegance, and certainly not calculation and utilitarian prudence. What matters is love.

> Azrael's eyes upon her,
>   Raphael's wings above,
> Michael's sword against her heart,
>   Jane said: "Love."

"Jane's Marriage"—Kipling's poem from which these lines are taken—is a truthful little fantasy, and *Persuasion,* the text that inspired it, is itself in a way the most honest and truthful of Jane Austen's novels. The mistake is, of course, to interpret the truthfulness (as Kipling does) in too narrowly biographical terms: to see *Persuasion* as chiefly an intimate personal revelation combined with much wish-fulfilment—a retelling, in short, of Jane Austen's own unhappy love with a happy ending. Not that there is any doubt about this quality of personal emotion that lies at the core of *Persuasion* and gives the novel much of

its strange, haunting power. But the emotion is encased in
something still more striking: an artist's considered statement
of a lifetime's hard-earned wisdom. The wisdom is, in fact, as
personal as it is traditional. *Persuasion* not only sums up the
lesson of Jane Austen's own previous novels, but it includes
the wisdom of *Amelia* and of Shakespeare's last comedies as
well. That love which one learns to prize because it is threatened and almost lost is the love that all these works proclaim
as the supreme value of life; its recovery involves, in all of
them, a stepping down from high places and a recognition of
ordinary, even commonplace, humanity. Thus when one
speaks of the superior truthfulness of *Persuasion,* one speaks at
once of an extension as well as a deepening of Jane Austen's
theme of love. While the sense of personal urgency gives it a
new emotional authenticity, there also occurs a simultaneous
extension of its meaning into hitherto more or less unexplored
areas and problems of life. Love in *Persuasion* is still primarily
the lovers' love, but it is also something more. It is the necessary emotion of all relationships: not marriage alone but family, friendship, hospitality—all those big and small relationships
of day-to-day social life which, without it, stand exposed and
almost destroyed, their warm human substance corroded by
bourgeois reason and prudence.

What distinguishes Anne Elliot, the heroine of *Persuasion,* is
her quiet but deep and constant sense of loss, a sense in which
is contained very nearly her whole story. More largely than
any other novel of Jane Austen's, this one is concerned with
"experience" as James defined it later—with the process of
apprehending and measuring what has happened rather than
with that happening itself. Anne's story in the latter sense is
over long before the novel opens, and a short early chapter
suffices to recapitulate its essentials. At nineteen she had fallen
in love with Captain Wentworth, a young man at that time
with "nothing but himself to recommend him, and no hopes
of attaining affluence." A short period of "exquisite felicity"

had followed, but troubles had arisen and the engagement had been broken off. Sir Walter, Anne's father, had frowned upon the match as a degrading alliance, and Lady Russell, "though with more tempered and pardonable pride," had done everything to discourage the unfortunate attachment. She had succeeded; the young and gentle Anne could have resisted her father's ill-will, but not the persuasion of Lady Russell, her only friend and almost a mother to her. Lady Russell was motivated by a horror "of anything approaching to imprudence," and yet, despite her great influence on Anne, it was not her kind of prudence—"not a merely selfish caution"—that had finally persuaded the young girl. The final argument had come from Anne's own more generous idea of prudence. "Had she not imagined herself consulting his good, even more than her own, she could hardly have given him up. The belief of being prudent and self-denying, principally for *his* advantage" had guided and consoled her, even though she had found Captain Wentworth himself "totally unconvinced and unbending." In consequence her lover had left the country and all communication between them had ceased. It was "a final parting." Now, at the age of twenty-seven, Anne is deeply convinced that she had been wrong, that prudence was certainly not the good she had imagined it to be, not even when supported by what had seemed a generous spirit of self-denial. "She was persuaded that under every disadvantage of disapprobation at home, and every anxiety attending his profession, all their probable fears, delays, and disappointments, she should yet have been a happier woman in maintaining the engagement, than she had been in the sacrifice of it."

Thus, unlike other Austen heroines, Anne has made her mistake and learned the wisdom of the case before the action of the novel begins. And indeed this is her great strength, her only strength in what remains otherwise a painfully exposed and helpless situation. The action of the novel, however, does not only confirm the wisdom she has already arrived at but also enforces a recognition of its full implications. Like Fanny Price, with whom she is often compared, Anne is slighted and disregarded by her family. She is in fact more friendless than the heroine of *Mansfield Park*. Nor can duty in the sense in which Fanny had embraced it console or fortify her in her loneliness. In Lady Russell she has a living proof of how little one can depend for happiness or rectitude on even the most benign external authority. Moreover, unlike Fanny, she has not been altogether passive but is conscious of having made an active (and wrong) choice. Of this she is made constantly and acutely aware as Wentworth, now successful and affluent, returns to the neighborhood. The former lovers are inevitably thrown together, but only in what seems "a perpetual estrangement." She thus realizes that what she has lost is not only the joy of youthful love, but her place permanently in the living world. The only privilege she can claim for herself is the one she claims for all women in a later conversation with Captain Harville: "that of loving longest, when existence or when hope is gone."

The presence of this inner strength, of resilience in resignation, which is the hallmark of the heroine's consciousness is also externalized in the novel through its pervasive autumnal imagery, the season and its landscapes corresponding closely with the spiritual import of the story. But, then, there is a "poetical" autumn—scenes that recall a "tender sonnet, fraught with the apt analogy of the declining year with declining happiness, and the images of youth, and hope, and spring, all gone together." However, Anne can rouse herself from contemplation of such scenes to look at others, which are equally authentic but show the "ploughs at work" where "the fresh made path" reveals "the farmer counteracting the sweets of poetical dependence, and meaning to have spring again."

No skill in the novel deserves so much attention as the various strokes which make the heroine's sense of loss strong and real by preventing it from ever becoming an indulgence. The introduction of the farmer's autumn in the passage above is meant, of course, to foreshadow the happy ending of the story; but it also represents an effort on Anne's own part to escape the self-pity of false or sentimental sorrow. Of the latter Jane Austen in fact introduces two examples which serve as deliberate foils. One is the case of Mrs. Musgrove's fond regrets over the loss of a long-forgotten son, who while alive had never given cause to be remembered, and at death had been "scarcely at all regretted." Critics have accused Jane Austen of a lack of feeling in making gratuitous fun of Mrs. Musgrove on the occasion when she is shown as sorrowing over her son. Yet the fun is not at all gratuitous to the extent to which it is directed at the patent falsity of Mrs. Musgrove's exhibition. "An unhappiness that one can sit comfortably talking about," as Henry James has his heroine observe in *Madame De Mauves*, "is an unhappiness with distinct limitations." Mrs. Musgrove (on the whole a likable character) does not only sit comfortably talking about her sorrow, she offers it as a social amenity, specially got up in honor of Captain Wentworth's visit.

The other case is the later one of Captain Benwick, the young naval officer bereaved by the unexpected death of his fiancée. Although his loss is real enough, he is in the process of developing a self-conscious posture of poetical melancholy. He has read Scott and Byron and is "intimately acquainted with all the tenderest songs of the one poet, and all the impassioned descriptions of hopeless agony of the other; he repeated, with such tremulous feeling, the various lines which imagined a broken heart, or a mind destroyed by wretchedness." Anne, "feeling in herself the right of seniority of mind," offers Captain Benwick "suggestions as to the duty and benefit of struggling against affliction" and recommends "a larger allowance of prose in his daily study." This is another version of her attempt to correct the falsity and exaggeration of poetical autumn by reference to the truth of the farmer's autumn. And, indeed, in the present case the very affectation of total hopelessness is a sign that the young officer is already on the way to having "spring again." Anne, however, is again reflecting upon her own situation; her sorrow is neither imaginary nor exaggerated, and its cause has been not providential but willfully human. In fact, her case admits of very little real hope. Yet she can plead the duty of struggling against affliction because she has come to realize that, whether or not she herself has spring again, in the larger, natural or providential, scheme of things there is nothing like a permanent truce with winter.

This is a part of the heroine's final experience, of her moral discovery. But the novel's happy ending involves the recognition of a prior though related truth. The ending is made possible superficially by the fact that Wentworth now possesses the fortune he had lacked before. But this is an accidental good. The way Anne has come to see things—and in her seeing lies the novel's meaning—affluence is no longer a necessary condition, not even for reasons of unselfish prudence. At the very opening of the novel, Anne not only believes that breaking her engagement was a mistake, but she believes this "without reference to the actual results of their case, which, as it happened, would have bestowed earlier prosperity than could be reasonably calculated on." This, of course, involves us, as it does Anne, with the very different position of Lady Russell. Yet the question of Lady Russell's position and of Anne's relation to it, which seems the most difficult question in the novel, points in fact to its deepest meaning. It is a question that is specifically (and apparently confusingly) raised in both the early flashback and the late review chapters of the novel. In Chapter 4 we are told:

> Anne, at seven-and-twenty, thought very differently from what she had been made to think at nineteen. She did not blame Lady Russell, she did not blame herself for having been guided by her; but she felt that were any young

person in similar circumstances to apply to her for counsel, they would never receive any of such certain immediate wretchedness, such uncertain future good.

In the penultimate chapter, while going over the same ground with her lover, Anne is at once more halting and more charitable, but nevertheless she maintains her position:

> I have been thinking over the past, and trying impartially to judge of the right and wrong, I mean with regard to myself; and I must believe that I was right, much as I suffered from it, that I was perfectly right in being guided by the friend whom you will love better than you do now. To me, she was in the place of a parent. Do not mistake me, however. I am not saying that she did not err in her advice. It was, perhaps, one of those cases in which advice is good or bad only as the event decides; and for myself, I certainly never should, in any circumstance of tolerable similarity, give such advice. But I mean, that I was right in submitting to her.

How can this be? How can Anne have been both right and wrong? How can Lady Russell's advice be "good or bad as the event decides" and yet Anne believe it to be bad "without reference to the actual results" of the case?

There are several distinct questions here which should not be misunderstood or at any rate confused with each other. First of all, a distinction is made between the conduct of a nineteen-year-old girl, who has been made to think in a certain way, and the more independent and mature understanding she possesses at age twenty-seven. Furthermore, a particular context not only influenced Anne's conduct strongly, but in a sense made it right. And finally there is the question of Lady Russell's position as a general principle. Enveloping all, however, is what one can only call the spirit of the passages, a spirit that envelopes much of the novel. While this is undoubtedly the spirit of almost general forgiveness, such as characterizes the last works of many another comic writer, Jane Austen gives us the least reason to forget that this spirit cannot come into play unless there is something to forgive, and unless that something is first recognized for what it is.

We see, then, that Anne may well forgive all, but it is primarily her own conduct she is defending. "To me, she was in the place of a parent," she explains, and she herself was very young, very inexperienced. To be guided by Lady Russell was, as it then seemed to her, to obey the voice not only of filial piety but of wisdom. What other rule could she possibly apply at the age of nineteen? As for Lady Russell's conduct, there is no defense of principles; there is only an understanding of them. What Anne is saying is that Lady Russell had her best interests at heart and had given sincere advice according to *her* lights. But, while this sounds like a compromising concession, it actually points to the main conflict of values in the novel. For it is precisely these lights that Anne has come first to question and then to reject. Lady Russell, for all her distinction and good points, is after all a part of that same Kellynch milieu from which the novel progresses steadily into other and better modes of living and being. Sir Walter, the master of Kellynch, is an extreme case—a man in whom pride has degenerated into a grotesque vanity, into a worse than foppish, almost perverted obsession with physical appearance, dress, figure, face, hair. This is a kind of self that exists nowhere but in the self and therefore ceases to exist even there. When the Crofts move into Kellynch, the Admiral sends away the large mirrors from the Baronet's dressingroom. As he explains to Anne: "Such a number of looking-glasses! oh, Lord! there was no getting away from one's self."

This certainly does not state Lady Russell's case. By comparison with Sir Walter, she can even be called unselfish. Yet her prudence, like Sir Walter's pride, has to some extent the same effect of cutting off the self from all relationships, at least all new relationships. More important, she too judges the desirability of relationships on the basis of external criteria which, while not so grotesquely superficial as those of Sir Walter, still exclude everything that goes to make a human relationship human. It is not accidental that, for all her cleverness, she is taken in fully as much as Sir Walter by the elegant Mr. Elliot. In trying to persuade Anne to marry this gentleman she is motivated again by Anne's own good as she sees it—and yet this good is largely a matter of what Wentworth terms quite rightly "the horrible eligibilities and proprieties of the match." But by now Anne has a judgment and principles of her own. Prizing "the frank, the open-hearted, the eager character beyond all others," she has already judged and dismissed her attractive cousin as "rational, discreet, polished, but ... not open." And this before Mr. Elliot has given anyone reason to suspect him of being anything other than what he appears to be.

If Anne, so far from succumbing to this second attempt at persuasion, can turn it aside without trepidation, it is because she has come to realize that Lady Russell can only persuade as she is herself persuaded. The novel turns so fundamentally on the question of persuasion in this sense that one is tempted to interpret the title as meaning belief—a way of seeing and understanding life. The novel certainly sets up one belief against another: put simply, the belief in Providence against the belief in prudence. Schopenhauer says at one point in his discussion of comedy that while "many human actions can only be performed by the help of reason and deliberation ... there are some which are better performed without its assistance."[12] This is, of course, preeminently true of the actions of love, especially if by "reason and deliberation" we understand the sort of cold calculation that motivates the friends and advisers of Anne Elliot. What Anne has come to believe is that, without

12. Schopenhauer, *World as Will and Idea, 1,* 76.

love, life becomes sour and sterile, turning into a thing of coldness and confinement instead of the open, warm, not strictly foreseeable, but nevertheless trusting adventure that it should be, that—inescapably and happily—it is.

This idea is, of course, broached in the earlier novels, and in some places it is even stated in the form in which it becomes the theme of *Persuasion.* In *Northanger Abbey,* for instance, Henry Tilney, ordered to the parsonage to prepare in advance for the family's visit, declares with mock solemnity: "I am come, young ladies, in a very moralising strain, to observe that our pleasures in this world are always to be paid for, and that we often purchase them at a great disadvantage, giving ready-monied, actual happiness for a draft on the future that may not be honoured." (What gives the idea its weight is both the language of commercial calculation and the contrast between the calculated future pleasures and the present happiness.) In *Pride and Prejudice* Elizabeth Bennet is certainly not speaking altogether in a mocking vein when she tells her aunt: "I should be very sorry to be the means of making any of you unhappy; but since we see every day that where there is affection, young people are seldom withheld by immediate want of fortune from entering into engagements with each other, how can I promise to be wiser than so many of my fellow-creatures if I am tempted, or how am I even to know that it would be wisdom to resist?" In *Persuasion* the question—"how am I even to know that it would be wisdom to resist?"—has moved to the center of the story, and it is no longer a question.

> How eloquent could Anne Elliot have been! how elo-quent, at least, were her wishes on the side of early warm attachment, and a cheerful confidence in futurity, against that over-anxious caution which seems to insult exertion and distrust Providence!

This may be only a view or even just Anne's personal wish. But the action of the novel, by revealing its full implications, confirms it into belief, into a true persuasion, into a way of looking at all of life. As other critics have pointed out, Anne's movement from Kellynch through Uppercross to Lyme is carefully worked into the novel's meaning. It is a movement away from wealth and social importance and toward humanity. At Uppercross the Musgroves's crowded and noisy drawing room at Christmas becomes, in however qualified a way, a sign of that cheerful, warm, even vulgar life which throws into relief the heartless elegance of Kellynch. Of course, Lady Russell is distressed, as Fanny Price had been at Portsmouth, by the noise and the disorder, but now Jane Austen simply scores it off as false fastidiousness. Later, she writes, when Lady Russell drove through the noisy streets of Bath, "she made no complaint. No, these were noises which belonged to the winter pleasures; her spirits rose under their influence."

The full recognition, however, comes only at Lyme, where Anne is introduced to Captain Harville's home and to the naval officers who are Wentworth's friends. These people live in constrained circumstances and have to contend with difficulties unknown at Kellynch or Uppercross. There is even a touch of shabbiness, or what would be shabbiness in the lives of men other than these—the sort of reduced and shabby circumstance that Fielding introduces in *Amelia*—and indeed here, as in that novel, we have the sense that the art of love has yielded to has become one with the larger and more difficult art of life. Anne's heart warms at the officers' attachment to one another and at the "bewitching charm" of a "hospitality so uncommon, so unlike the usual style of give-and-take invitations, and dinners of formality and display." She is likewise astonished to see how Captain Harville has transformed the living quarters, using his labor and ingenuity "to turn the actual space to the best possible account, to supply the deficiencies of lodging-house furniture, and defend the windows and doors against the winter storms to be expected," so that his home now presents a perfect "picture of repose and domestic happiness." Nor is there the slightest touch of condescension here, either on the part of Anne or her author. The scene in fact makes Anne reflect poignantly on what real happiness—and real living—mean, and what it is she rejected in rejecting Captain Wentworth. " 'These would have been all my friends,' was her thought; and she had to struggle against a great tendency to lowness. . . . Anne thought she left great happiness behind her when they quitted the house." Later, thinking back of Lyme, she realizes "how much more interesting to her was the home and the friendship of the Harvilles and Captain Benwick, than her own father's house in Camden Place, or her own sister's intimacy with Mrs. Clay."

The representation of the navy is a new departure in Jane Austen, and not only because she is now more extensively engaged with a subject she had only touched upon in *Mansfield Park*. It is a new departure because she now makes extended use of it to stand for something more than itself—uses it as a ready means to represent a view of things not observable in the social world with which she deals customarily. The naval life, still being itself faithfully, becomes in this novel a metaphor for life itself, especially for the adventure of married life. In *Mansfield Park* Mary Crawford had urged the superiority of a naval career over Edmund's own choice of a secure parsonage, but she had thought mainly of fortune and glamor. She knew only of "Rears and Vices" and very little of the struggling inferior ranks or the profession itself as a profession. By comparison, Anne has always known that "sailors work hard enough for their comforts." Even Admiral Croft, who has achieved fortune and rank, still remains his ordinary uncorrupted self. It is, however, in the account of the Crofts's married life—their having journeyed together over rough and calm seas, braving difficulties rather than hesitating or turning back out of over-anxious caution—that Anne sees the living proof of that cheerful confidence in love, life, and futurity which she has come to identify as the rule of Providence. The only time

Mrs. Croft "ever really suffered in body or mind" was when she was separated from "the Admiral (*Captain* Croft then)." The other dangers she has known are not dangers but the common difficulties of life, any life—the "storms to be expected," as in the description of Captain Harville's house. To be frightened of them is to be frightened of life. "But I hate to hear you talking so like a fine gentleman," as Mrs. Croft rebukes her nephew, "and as if women were all fine ladies, instead of rational creatures. We none of us expect to be in smooth water all our days."

In reality, however, it is precisely this view of the world that Captain Wentworth, with his love, ardor, and confidence, had offered in offering himself to the daughter of Sir Walter and the ward of Lady Russell. Anne did not know it then, but it is clear to her transformed vision now that this is indeed a brave new world, brave if only because loving, living, and natural—unlike Kellynch, neither rarified above nor deformed beneath the level of ordinary humanity.

Chapter 7

The Portrait of a Lady:
Henry James and the
Avoidance of Comedy

The Portrait of a Lady is widely regarded as a lucid novel, a masterpiece of James's early and relatively uncomplicated period. This is undoubtedly true if all we mean by lucidity is a lucidity of style and presentation. Our thinking on the subject is heavily and perhaps unavoidably influenced by the contrast between, not to mention the controversy over, James's early and late manner. But if we think not of the manner, not of how but rather of what is being presented—if we think, that is, of the actions and developments as they are imagined and fitted together into a connected and comprehensible sequence —we certainly cannot entertain for long the sense of ease and clarity with which this novel is so often credited and which, indeed, its own verbal facility seems to convey on almost every individual page. *The Portrait* is in fact a novel bristling with many difficulties; above all its action, viewed as a whole, reveals a strange and central incoherence that derives basically from the very source upon which James relied, as he tells us in the preface, for the unity and logic of the whole story—the character and destiny of his heroine.

This is not to say that the heroine, Isabel Archer, is incoherent, confused, and lacking in self-knowledge. She is so quite obviously. But that is the deliberate starting point of her story. Nor is the objection altogether that she seems to us as willfully

and romantically ignorant at the end as she was at the beginning, for in itself there is no reason why this should not be so.
The real difficulty arises from the fact that James offers her
career as involving a critical development and that the whole
movement of the novel, as I shall point out, is directed toward
effecting in her a profound inner change. The question, then,
is one not only of Isabel's understanding or lack of it but also,
as James himself might put it, of his understanding of her
understanding; and the problem created is both moral and
structural.

F. R. Leavis is one of the very few critics who, despite a high
valuation of *The Portrait,* has pinpointed some of its puzzling
defects, its "inconsistencies" and "moral incoherences" which
"become apparent when we ponder the story" although they
"pass undetected at first because of the brilliant art with
which James, choosing his *scènes à faire,* works in terms of
dramatic presentation."[1] Indeed, anyone who scrutinizes the
story of *The Portrait* with half the care and seriousness usually
accorded the imagery or craftsmanship of a Jamesian work will
recognize more, and more kinds of, difficulty than even Leavis
has noted. Underneath the apparent control and clarity of the
surface such a reader will come up against not just the major
unresolved inconsistencies but any number of minor opacities,
weaknesses, and failures. He will notice obscurities of motive
and character development; discrepancies, on both the small
and large scale, between narrative ascription and dramatic
effect; more than occasional incongruities between the author's attitude and the realities of the character or situation
concerned; and, most persistently, small implausibilities or in-
felicities of the dramatized word and gesture—the many lapses
of imagination at that level of detail and moment-to-moment

1. Leavis, *The Great Tradition,* p. 139. See also the entire section
on *'Daniel Deronda' and 'The Portrait of a Lady,'* pp. 101-54, particularly pp. 136-40. In view of this criticism Leavis's overall evaluation of
the novel seems overly generous, to say the least.

action upon which depends so much of the life and cogency of a novel like *The Portrait*.

With all these considerations, however, I am not directly concerned. Although a detailed analysis of the novel along these lines would unquestionably prove a highly instructive exercise, my purpose here is to focus attention on one main problem with which the novel confronts us from beginning to end, but most pointedly at the end. The problem can be indicated simply by observing that *The Portrait* is a comic novel laboring under an imposed sense of tragedy. This is not to suggest that James's tragic sense is somehow imported from the outside, much less that it is a cheap artifice or pretense. It may well be the most authentic aspect of his vision, and certainly the evidence of any number of his novels goes to show how deep and ineradicable a part it played in his imaginative thought. One can even argue that it is the comic structure that is borrowed, from Jane Austen or George Eliot or the main body and direction of the English novel before him. But then, if James borrowed, there was something in his own imagination that made the borrowing happily and congenially possible. Such argument, however, is fruitless, for regardless of the direction from which we look at James we are forced to recognize within him the simultaneous and equal existence of two opposed visions. On the one hand he is the heir of Jane Austen, her "lawful issue," as Kipling's cockney character in "The Janeites" claims before his outraged superiors. But James's descent on the other side is from so vastly different a line that it is not surprising that the immediate challenge to the cockney—"By what sire? Prove it"—remains unanswered in Kipling's story.[2] Yet for us today the question virtually answers itself. Quite obviously James's literary ancestry goes back on the other side to Hawthorne and that dark aspect of the Puri-

2. Rudyard Kipling, *Debits and Credits* (New York, Doubleday, Page, 1926), p. 129.

tan imagination of which Hawthorne himself was a severely critical and, in literary terms, consistent and highly successful legatee.

Nor is this a matter of opposed literary traditions alone. A great deal of external evidence can be cited to show the uncertainty or unresolved inner division in James's response to the social world of his own day, his valuation of this world, and even his valuation of life in general. But at this stage only one illustration will have to serve. The illustration comes from two letters, one containing James's well-known declaration: "I have the imagination of disaster—and see life indeed as ferocious and sinister," and the other expressing with equal conviction what amounts to a diametrically opposed view. Writing in the latter case to a young novelist about her first novel, James criticizes her for "want of perspective and proportion," adding: "You are really too savage . . . *life* is less criminal, less obnoxious, less objectionable, less crude, more *bon enfant,* more mixed and casual, and even in its most offensive manifestations, more *pardonable,* than the unholy circle with which you have surrounded your heroine."[3] The perspective on life advocated here is essentially the perspective of all the works considered so far in this study. It is the perspective of comedy, and in a large measure James shares it with his predecessors. But he also entertains in its own right the other perspective— "the imagination of disaster"—and while the two may or may not be reconcilable, it seems to me that James does not reconcile them. In *The Portrait* at any rate the two come together not to comment on but virtually to contradict each other.

3. *Henry James: Letters to A. C. Benson and Auguste Monod,* ed. E. F. Benson (London, Elkin Mathews and Marrot, 1930), p. 35; *The Selected Letters of Henry James,* ed. Leon Edel (London, Rupert Hart Davis, 1956), p. 238. Both letters are cited by J. A. Ward, *The Imagination of Disaster: Evil in the Fiction of Henry James* (Lincoln, University of Nebraska Press, 1961), pp. 5, 172.

The step from Jane Austen's comedy to *The Portrait* is neither direct nor easily negotiable. Yet, looking only at the comic structure of James's novel, it seems a small and natural one. At the center of each stands an engaging and superior girl eminently qualified to fall into deep confusion. The confusions are not alike from one Jane Austen heroine to the next, much less if we compare all or any of them with James's heroine. Moreover, it must be admitted that unlike most Austen heroines, the superiority of Isabel Archer is more insisted upon by the author than revealed by the heroine herself. Nevertheless she, like Catherine Morland or Marianne or Elizabeth or Emma, is "booked to make a mistake"—to use a phrase from *Daisy Miller* which, together with some other early short novels, is clearly related in theme and method to the later and fuller *Portrait*. And the mistake is one that follows from the sort of blindness that we have already noted in Jane Austen and other previous writers. It is connected with a self-centered quality in the heroine which in its turn is related to her taking an abstract, theoretical, romantic view of herself and the world. Indeed in the very first glimpse we are given of her, via Mrs. Touchett, Isabel is discovered in an empty house "seated alone with a book . . . trudging over the sandy plains of a history of German Thought."

The comic theme of abstraction thus introduced is consistently emphasized throughout the early chapters of the novel and most pointedly in the flashback scenes, where we see Isabel as she is before her entry into the action proper or, for that matter, into the real world. Of the three Archer sisters she is the intellectual one: her "love of knowledge had a fertilizing quality and her imagination was strong." Her imagination, in fact, was not only strong but "by habit ridiculously active; when the door was not open it jumped out of the window. She was not accustomed to keep it behind bolts; and at important moments, when she would have been thankful to make use of her judgement alone, she paid the penalty of having given undue encouragement to the faculty of seeing without judging." Of practical affairs she is completely and proudly ignorant, disclaiming any knowledge of such matters as money, inheritance, and even the possible fate of her beloved paternal house in Albany, the house in which her favorite room and habitual retreat is the musty old library or office where Mrs. Touchett first discovers her. The fascination of this room is obvious, for it is the secluded castle of her romantic imagination. "The place owed much of its mysterious melancholy to the fact that it was properly entered from the second door of the house. . . . She knew that this silent, motionless portal opened into the street; if the sidelights had not been filled with green paper she might have looked out upon the little brown stoop and the well-worn brick pavement. But she had no wish to look out, for this would have interfered with her theory that there was a strange, unseen place on the other side." Indeed, as James concludes in Chapter 6:

> Isabel Archer was a young person of many theories; her imagination was remarkably active. It had been her fortune to possess a finer mind than most of the persons among whom her lot was cast. . . . It may be affirmed without delay that Isabel was probably very liable to the sin of self-esteem; she often surveyed with complacency the field of her own nature; she was in the habit of taking for granted, on scanty evidence, that she was right; she treated herself to occasions of homage. Meanwhile her errors and delusions were frequently such as a biographer interested in preserving the dignity of his subject must shrink from specifying. Her thoughts were a tangle of vague outlines which had never been corrected by the judgement of people speaking with authority. In matters of opinion she had had her own way, and it had led her into a thousand ridiculous zigzags. At moments she discovered she was grotesquely wrong, and then she treated herself to a week of

passionate humility. After this she held her head higher
than ever again; for it was of no use, she had an unquench-
able desire to think well of herself. She had a theory that it
was only under this provision life was worth living.

With the exception of a word or two this sounds remarkably
like the opening paragraph of a novel by Jane Austen, and the
question James poses squarely through this early description
of his heroine is the familiar comic question of book knowledge versus practical knowledge, theory versus reality, imagination versus judgment, and self-confidence versus the possibility, indeed the inevitability, of error under such circumstances.
The question carries its own dynamics. As James says in the
same chapter, his heroine "would be an easy victim of scientific criticism if she were not intended to awaken on the reader's part an impulse more tender and more purely expectant."
For the point of true interest as always in such a situation lies
not in the world of abstraction from which the hero starts but
in the world of experience that awaits him. How will he nego-
tiate his entry from one into the other? How will he change
and grow? What illusions will fall by the wayside, and what
new wisdom will have to be fought for and won? In a word,
what will such a person "do"? This is the question with which,
according to his preface, James started building the action of
his novel after first having conceived the character of his heroine, and it is a question echoed at several points within the
novel. Isabel herself, although she "had a great desire for
knowledge . . . really preferred almost any source of information to the printed page; she had an immense curiosity about
life." This curiosity is so strong that not merely the reader and
the author but even her fellow characters in the novel look
upon her with the expectant attitude recommended by James.
Thus at their first meeting Ralph wonders what this "brilliant
girl" was "going to do with herself," and after she has turned
down Lord Warburton he again speculates "what a young lady

does who won't marry Lord Warburton"; this kind of interest continues through the time he persuades his father to leave her a large legacy up to the end of the book. Likewise Henrietta's main business in life seems to be to wonder about Isabel and to warn her, often with good common sense. These two characters, it may be added in passing, also feel for Isabel that tender impulse which James demanded and expected on his heroine's behalf but which the reader, not being James's creature entirely, is not always able to share.

James's theme of experience, of the realities of the world as he saw them, is different from that of previous writers in two main respects, although if we think specifically of Jane Austen the difference would seem a natural development rather than a radical break. In the first place, and this is a subject that will be taken up again later, James understood experience itself in a deeper, more psychological and self-conscious sense. In fact, most of his formal and technical innovations can be attributed to the requirements of this deeper or different understanding. Secondly, the social world of comedy is enlarged immensely in James's writing, taking for its province not just Somersetshire or Highbury but the range and glitter of bourgeois civilization across the whole breadth of the Western world. This no doubt introduces thematic enrichments and complications of its own —but not at the cost of the basic traditional comic design, which remains remarkably evident and clear. The recourse to the international situation, was the only way in which James felt that he, an American writer, could best portray those established values and possibilities of a culture which alone can test the culture's abstractions properly. In *The Portrait,* in any event, Isabel's coming to Europe is seen as the handiest way to bring this romantic girl face to face with reality. The idea is not very different from that which takes Catherine Morland from a dreamy parsonage to Bath and then to Northanger Abbey. The two girls are not only equally theoretical but also equally curious about life. "What will she 'do'?" James asks

about his heroine in the preface, answering himself with the
almost automatic suggestion of an adventure that will be as
natural for him, his times, and his heroine as going to Bath was
for Miss Morland: "Why, the first thing she'll do will be to
come to Europe." And yet Isabel's adventure, though mild,
will eventually prove as portentous with respect to her cherished illusions as Catherine's experiences in Bath. To put this
romantic girl in touch with realities is in fact the reason why
Mrs. Touchett proposes the European trip. As she tells Ralph,
she had found Isabel "in an old house . . . reading a heavy
book" when it occurred to her "that it would be a kindness to
take her about and introduce her to the world. She thinks she
knows a great deal of it—like most American girls; but like
most American girls she's ridiculously mistaken."

Once in Europe Isabel continues for a while to be romantic
in the way she had been before crossing the Atlantic. This
includes, first of all, the habit of viewing life through the
medium of literature. She cannot, for instance, believe that the
English are "very nice to girls" for "they're not nice to them
in the novels." On first seeing Lord Warburton and being informed of his standing with the Gardencourt family, she exclaims: "Oh, I hoped there would be a lord; it's just like a
novel!" Isabel's imagination, unlike Catherine Morland's, runs
not to the gothic but the picturesque, with only a mild, playful, and distant touch of the macabre. She is delighted with
the idea of a revolution in England, for though she would start
out on the side of the revolutionaries, "after it was well begun
—I think I should be a high, proud loyalist. One sympathises
more with them, and they have a chance to behave so exqui-
sitely. I mean so picturesquely." As might be expected, however, in a novel that makes as much of houses as *The Portrait*
does, Isabel constantly lavishes her literary-romantic imagination on Gardencourt itself. In this respect she feels that she has
at last come home, even from her grandmother's house in
Albany. She demands that Ralph show her the "ghost," the

"castle-spectre," a thing she is convinced they ought to possess "in this romantic old house."

> "It's not a romantic old house," said Ralph. "You'll be disappointed if you count on that. It's a dismally prosaic one; there's no romance here but what you may have brought with you."
> "I've brought a great deal; but it seems to me I've brought it to the right place."

However lightly it is introduced here, all this will later play its part in another and a more somber light, not only the desire to see the "ghost" but equally the value placed on the exquisiteness or picturesqueness of attitude and behavior.

There is, however, a more radical aspect to Isabel's romanticism which has a far greater bearing upon her story and its deepest meanings. This has to do with her belief, variously reiterated through the novel, in a highly idealized personal freedom, a sense of absolute and inviolable independence vested in her inmost self. As several critics have observed, it is not for nothing that she is first discovered closeted with "a history of German Thought"; and while this Emersonian aspect of her romanticism makes her a representative heroine of her culture and her time, it also makes her finally the example of a comic heroine in extremis. If the heroes and heroines of earlier comedy had to fight and overcome their illusions, they did so, as we have seen, in order to ascertain and seize a measure of personal freedom which, however limited its nature, had a real existence in their world. But Isabel's idea of freedom, a logical though extreme development of theirs, is in itself her greatest illusion, a pure abstraction "It was one of her theories that Isabel Archer was very fortunate in being independent"—that cannot stand the test of reality and experience. As Arnold Kettle puts it in what is perhaps the most perceptive essay written on the novel, *"The Portrait of a Lady"* is one of the most profound expressions in literature of the illusion that freedom is an abstract quality inherent in the individual soul."[4]

James's overall attitude concerning this romanticism, however, is not as clear as suggested above but rather ambiguous, uncertain, and even self-contradictory; and herein lies the reason for the moral and structural confusion of the novel. On the one hand he sees Isabel's conviction clearly for the illusion it is and builds his comic structure upon that understanding. On the other hand, unable to see what worthy realities can possibly lie beyond such illusion, he surrounds it with a sense of high tragic vindication and thus makes a value of it, reestablishing precisely that which he discredits. In the end one is forced to admit that James shares with his heroine the confusions he reveals, and this explains his otherwise inexplicable tenderness for a girl whom he recognizes not only as wholly theoretical and ridiculously mistaken but also, at various times, as cold, hard, proud, entirely self-centered, and incorrigibly unyielding.

Isabel's confusions become apparent, of course, as soon as the comic action begins; that is, as soon as her theories are brought into contact with reality and she herself is called upon to make choices and to act. The question of what she will do leads, as in earlier comedy, into the immediate question of marriage. She no doubt handles her suitors with dispatch and firmness, yet her decisiveness is superficial—the dubious self-confidence of a person motivated by strongly held but unverified theories. Indeed the most striking and constant feature of Isabel's conduct throughout the novel is the incongruity between the firmness of her actions and the irresolute, shifting, unconvincing quality of the reasoning with which she attempts to support and justify them. Consider the case of Lord War-

4. Arnold Kettle, *An Introduction to the English Novel,* 2 vols. (London, Hutchinson's University Library, 1953), *2,* 28.

burton. It is not often brought out just how tangled the motivation behind Isabel's rejection of him is; each reader usually picks up the reason that seems most plausible to him. Yet the point surely lies in the implausible multiplicity of motives advanced. Speaking of Isabel's father early in the novel, James mentions the man's "incoherency of conduct," attributing it to his "large way of looking at life." Much the same can be said of Isabel's own conduct and motivation. There is, of course, an objective criticism of Lord Warburton, which is best expressed by Ralph when he dismisses Warburton's "radicalism" as the false position of an aristocrat "who can neither abolish himself as a nuisance nor maintain himself as an institution." The position involves a lack of true purpose and energy, the sort of built-in vocational and intellectual frivolity which had led one of James's earlier heroines—Bessie Alden of "An International Episode"—to reject a comparable offer, and which indeed constitutes a weakness that might weigh heavily with any serious-minded American girl. In fact, Ralph later wonders if his comments had influenced Isabel's decision, for, as he is anxious to explain, "they were not faults, the things I spoke of: they were simply peculiarities of his position. If I had known he wished to marry you I'd never have alluded to them."

But Isabel's decision had little relation to this criticism. As she tells Ralph, she does not even "understand the matter." On the other hand, the same aristocratic position in which Ralph sees such drawbacks appeals to her through its picturesque and romantic qualities. If she began by considering Lord Warburton's presence at Gardencourt "just like a novel," she soon sees the nobleman himself "as a hero of romance" and her own situation under his impending proposal as "deeply romantic." Even in a worldly sense she realizes, as she tells him, that it would be "impossible for me to do better in this wonderful world, I think, than commit myself, very gratefully, to your loyalty." This very proper and heroine-like speech is

followed up later when, deeply impressed by Lockleigh, Warburton's house, and its inhabitants, she reflects, like Elizabeth
Bennet at Pemberley, on all that "she had rejected in rejecting
Lord Warburton—the peace, the kindness, the honour, the possessions, a deep security and a great exclusion." What, then,
are the reasons for her decision that she gives to herself and
others? There is of course the obvious one that she is not in
love with him, but it is curious how Isabel fumbles her way to
it as a last resort—"I mean—I mean that I don't love Lord
Warburton enough to marry him"—showing how little she is in
reality concerned with love and how little she even understands what love means. Of the reasons she advances earlier,
the main ones are as follows: that she "was disposed to believe
that on the whole she could do better"; that she was not sure
she wished "to marry any one"; that "the idea failed to support any enlightened prejudice in favor of the free exploration
of life"; that she simply did not "know why"; that by marrying Warburton she would be attempting to "escape" her "fate"
(a subject that will be touched on later); and that "furthermore there was a young man lately come from America . . .
who had a character of which it was useless to persuade herself
that the impression on her mind had been light."

The "young man lately come from America," Caspar Goodwood, who thus figures as one possible reason in Isabel's rejection of Warburton, is nevertheless speedily rejected himself
with still more revealing apparent resolution. The motivation
here is rather easy to understand—at one level. Except for his
similar fate at the hands of Isabel, Caspar Goodwood is the
direct opposite of Lord Warburton. An American business ex-
ecutive, engineer, and inventor, he is a man of active purpose
and restless energy. But while Isabel admires him as a "mover
of men," she finds his jaw "too square" and "his figure too
straight and stiff," and he seems to her to suggest "a want of
easy consonance with the deeper rhythms of life"—the sort of
harmony, one may add, which she has just seen romantically

exemplified in the high civilization of the old world. Indeed, as we are told when Caspar Goodwood is first introduced in the Albany flashback, "He was not romantically, he was much rather obscurely, handsome." This obscure appeal of Goodwood's, however, introduces a sexual motif that creates considerable difficulty, complicating the whole question of marriage and of what Isabel will and ought to do—the more so since James, modern enough to introduce the motif, is also old-fashioned enough to give it neither the open recognition nor the sort of importance with which later writers have invested the subject. It remains as obscure for him as for his heroine, who can neither disregard nor quite confront it.

What all this adds up to is a portrait of immaturity, and the novel at this stage seems conscious of the fact. As James observes, commenting on the two rejections and on Isabel's own "sense of her incoherence": "where, ever, was any tangible link between her impression and her act? Caspar Goodwood had never corresponded to her idea of a delightful person, and she supposed that this was why he left her so harshly critical. When, however, Lord Warburton, who not only did correspond with it, but gave an extention to the term, appealed to her approval, she found herself still unsatisfied. It was certainly strange." The reason for this incoherence of conduct, for the lack of connection between "impression" and "act," lies, of course, as already suggested, in Isabel's romanticism—in the lack of connection between her theories and the realities of life—and above all in her illusory ideal of personal freedom. What Warburton on the one hand and Goodwood on the other seem to threaten is the sanctity of this egocentric abstraction, and it is in the interests of its preservation that she resists both. Warburton's threat is primarily that of social reality; no matter how eminent and free a position he offers her, she rejects it because it would still represent the definition in real terms of something she regards as undefinable and absolute. As James puts it: "At the risk of adding to the evidence of her

self-sufficiency it must be said that there had been moments
when this possibility . . . represented to her an aggression almost to the degree of an affront . . . What she felt was that a
territorial, a political, a social magnate had conceived the design of drawing her into the system in which he rather invidi-
ously lived and moved. A certain instinct, not imperious, but
persuasive, told her to resist—murmured to her that she had a
system and an orbit of her own." With Goodwood, "who had
no system at all," she is still threatened with "a diminished
liberty"; but this time because, unlike Warburton, whose passion "had sifted itself clear of the baser parts of emotion—the
heat, the violence, the unreason," the straight and bristling
young man from Boston expresses "for her an energy—and she
had already felt it as a power—that was of his very nature."
The consequence is that Goodwood, though easy to handle in
one way, proves in another regard the most difficult of her
suitors. Although the offer of any love, from Warburton or at
the last minute even Osmond, fills Isabel with panic and fear,
her reaction to Goodwood is such that each time she succeeds
in dismissing him, the outwardly calm performance leads immediately afterward to uncontrollable and convulsive fits of
hysterical relief. Once again, however, if this is to be understood at all clearly, it can only be seen in terms of Isabel's
high-minded, little girl's notion of sex and marriage, for, as
James puts it in the early analytical Chapter 6: "Of course,
among her theories, this young lady was not without a collection of views on the subject of marriage. The first on the list
was a conviction of the vulgarity of thinking too much of it.
From lapsing into eagerness on this point she earnestly prayed
she might be delivered; she held that a woman ought to be able
to live to herself . . . and that it was perfectly possible to be
happy without the society of a more or less coarse-minded
person of another sex."

The point here is that this early portrait is clearly designed with a view to, an expectation of, and a movement toward an eventual and salutary change in Isabel Archer—a change that will bring her true judgment, maturity, and wisdom. Obscurities and scattered portentous hints aside, Isabel is at this stage what one would expect a comic heroine to be before the awakening that will come with experience. She is quick and vital, with a great curiosity about life and a desire for happy participation in it. But she is also immature, lacking in knowledge of herself and of the world, and all her follies and confusions proceed from theories that are wholly abstracted from human reality, be it emotional, sexual, or social. Such a situation so presented virtually carries its own guarantee of impermanence and its own momentum toward a stable resolution. We have seen this in many previous works, and as we shall see the whole concept of experience in James only accentuates and enriches the promise of such resolution. As James puts it in one of his many anticipatory comments on Isabel's self-confident illusions, "if there was a great deal of folly in her wisdom those who judge her severely may have the satisfaction of finding that, later, she became consistently wise." Although this remark is made specifically in relation to Isabel's rejection of Warburton, or rather her inner debate as to "whether she should accept an English peer before he had offered himself," the same idea of awaiting maturity is hinted at in her attitude toward the more obscure but also more powerful and insistent reality that Caspar Goodwood represents. There are moments, we are told, when Isabel sees Caspar as "the stubbornest fact she knew; she said to herself at such moments that she might evade him for a time, but that she must make terms with him at last."

Of course, Isabel imagines that she has acquired the promised wisdom, overcome her confusions, and solved all her problems the minute she decides to marry Gilbert Osmond. In her opinion she has at last made what she considers a deliberate and happy choice. Gone are those salad days when in the raw freshness of her absolutism she had demanded nothing less than a "free exploration of life," an exploration so free that it could have no imaginable relation to life. She expresses this rationale of her decision most clearly in a discussion with Ralph in Chapter 34. When he, expostulating against her choice, objects that she "must have changed immensely. A year ago you valued your liberty beyond everything. You wanted only to see life," Isabel answers unhesitatingly: "I've seen it. It doesn't look to me now, I admit, such an inviting expanse. . . . I've seen that one can't do anything so general. One must choose a corner and cultivate that." And James reinforces this view in the following chapter:

> The desire for unlimited expansion had been succeeded in her soul by the sense that life was vacant without some private duty that might gather one's energies to a point. She had told Ralph she had "seen life" in a year or two and that she was already tired . . . What had become of all her ardours, her aspirations, her theories? . . . These things had been absorbed in a more primitive need—a need the answer to which brushed away numberless questions, yet gratified infinite desires. It simplified the situation at a stroke, it came down from above like the light of the stars.

Halcyon days seem to await the lovers as life stretches before them, in Osmond's phrase, like "a long summer afternoon."

But of course all this, so far from being what it seems, represents only a further and disastrous turn of the screw. James in fact has already changed his notes to tragic. By now his "imagination of disaster"—his view of life as "ferocious and sinister"—is definitely in command, having introduced through Gilbert Osmond a theme that comedy cannot survive and still remain comedy. In terms of the action of the novel this is the crossing of the Rubicon, a decisive change in course that alters not only what is to come but also our view of what has passed. As is usual in such cases, we begin to read disproportionate meanings into the slightest of previous hints, disregarding all contrary evidence and interpreting barely noticeable signs as careful preparation for the ultimate design. Examples of this are Isabel's early banter about the ghost which she will now live to see in earnest; her remark about "the cup of experience" containing "a poisoned drink"; her observation that while she will make no one a martyr, she can only hope that she will not become one herself; or her argument to Warburton that in marrying him she would be trying to escape her fate while she is convinced that she cannot escape it—that she cannot "escape unhappiness." It is not that these things are not in the novel; the point is that they become portents only after and because the novel has changed course. In themselves where they occur they can be explained in terms of Isabel's general incoherence and self-conscious posturing, and in any case they are not important enough to qualify the character of the action which, despite their presence, remains unmistakably comic through almost the first half of the novel.

No comparable statement can be made, however, about the second, "tragic" half. Not only does it have to contend with the full weight and contrary expectations of the first; what complicates matters further is the manner in which James perseveres with the structure of comedy, introducing elements into the Osmond affair which could conceivably make it the conclusion of his heroine's comic experience, proceeding firmly to the crisis of true awakening, and indeed leaving the comic possibility open, or at least toying with it, right up to the last paragraph of the novel. As some readers have complained, the development of Isabel's relationship with Osmond is somewhat shortcircuited—stated more than shown. Where there should have been a dramatic presentation, we get only a foreshortening. This, however, is a mistaken criticism, for the procedure is justifiable to the extent to which James continues to present Isabel's fantasy of love rather than love itself. There is, indeed, no development. Although we are told that Isabel, looking back over her year in Europe, "flattered herself she had harvested wisdom and learned a great deal more of life than this light-minded creature had even suspected," she is in reality acting out of the same illusions, the same romance that she had brought over from Albany. Her claim, in the conversation with Ralph cited above, of having learned the wisdom of not aspiring to generalities but choosing instead a specific corner of life, is a part of her characteristic and self-deluded rationalization. For, as Ralph argues, such a course is wise only if one takes care to "choose as good a corner as possible." Indeed, as we reflect on the dark and sterile corner she has chosen—the life which in terms of the novel's house imagery she herself will later recognize as "the house of darkness, the house of dumbness, the house of suffocation"—we see the connection between this act of hers and the temperament with which she had begun her adventure. As James puts it in an early remark about his heroine: "With all her love of knowledge she had a natural shrinking from raising curtains and looking into unlighted corners. The love of knowledge coexisted in her mind with the finest capacity for ignorance."

In fact James never shows Isabel indulging her sense of romance so consistently and insidiously as in the part of the novel which begins with her meeting with Osmond (or, even earlier, with Madame Merle), continues through her "little pilgrimage to the East," and concludes with her sudden announcement of her engagement. There is first of all that aspect of Osmond's situation which, as Madame Merle and Osmond realize, can be made appealing to Isabel because it can be made to appear picturesque—his melancholy but proud situation in the solitary hilltop house, disregarded by the common multitude, bereaved, but nobly devoted to the cultivation of sensibility and the care of a motherless daughter. And Isabel immediately and richly rewards their calculation:

> She had carried away an image from her visit to his hill-top which her subsequent knowledge of him did nothing to

efface . . . the image of a quiet, clever, sensitive, distinguished man, strolling on a moss-grown terrace above the sweet Val d'Arno and holding by the hand a little girl whose bell-like clearness gave a new grace to childhood . . . of a lonely, studious life in a lovely land; of an old sorrow that sometimes ached today; of a feeling of pride that was perhaps exaggerated, but that had an element of nobleness.

The imagination with which Isabel thus gilds Osmond's picture is such that were she a novelist and a contemporary of Jane Austen, she would surely provide material for a new and still more piquant "Love and Freindship." Nor, as James points out at the beginning of this passage, is this a matter of first impressions alone. On parting from Osmond in order to proceed on her Eastern voyage, "her adventure wore already the changed, the seaward face of some romantic island from which, after feasting on purple grapes, she was putting off while the breeze rose." On her return, when she is close to taking the plunge, she still tells no one—not even her inquisitive sister, Lily—of her state of mind regarding Osmond. "It was more romantic to say nothing, and, drinking deep, in secret, of romance, she was as little disposed to ask poor Lily's advice as she would have been to close that rare volume forever." Even during her travels—"even among the most classic sites, the scenes most calculated to suggest repose and reflexion," as her traveling companion, Madame Merle, observes —"a certain incoherence prevailed in her. Isabel travelled rapidly and recklessly; she was like a thirsty person drinking cup after cup." And as James says in conclusion, after Isabel has refused to yield to Ralph's arguments against the engagement, "it was characteristic of her that, having invented a fine theory about Gilbert Osmond, she loved him not for what he really possessed, but for his very poverties dressed out as honours."

As in her previous decisions, however, there is also a deeper and wholly uncomprehended motive at work here, a motive best indicated by Ralph's description of Osmond as "a sterile dilettante." Of course this is not how Osmond would describe himself, but it is nevertheless what all his claims and pretensions add up to. And thus as a man supposedly free and uninvolved, whose identity defies any social, professional, or even national definition, he can represent no threat to Isabel's ideal notion of independence. In choosing him freely (as she thinks she does), Isabel is still preserving her freedom, committing herself to no one recognizable and specific corner of life. And yet the greatest irony here lies precisely in her illusion of free choice, an irony that is underlined by what is not merely the plotting of the two blatant villains but virtually the plot of the novel itself: the effective point behind this otherwise melodramatic plot being to show how the highest promise of the modern age becomes, through an inner but perverse logic, its greatest spiritual trap. Isabel, imagining herself motivated by a fine and unfettered sense of personal freedom, wakes up to find herself delivered instead into the vilest worldly bondage— "ground," as Ralph puts it in their last scene together, "in the very mill of the conventional."

While there are warnings and hints before her marriage, it is only some years later that Isabel awakens to her true situation and learns the nature and extent of the mistake she has made. Rarely in James, however—more rarely than in any previous comic writer—is awakening a matter of disclosure alone, of coming to know external facts hitherto obscure or unknown. To become true discovery it must effect a recognition of and change in that inner landscape which has been the primary breeding place of the hero's confusions—his consciousness. Then alone can willful ignorance yield to knowledge, and illusions to wisdom. In this connection it is worth recalling for the final time in this study James's definition of exactly what constitutes experience in both life and literature: "Experience, as I see it, is our apprehension and our measure of what happens to us as social creatures—any intelligent report of which has to be based on that apprehension." The remark is worth pondering not only because of its relevance to James's fiction but also because much of the debate between the modern psychological novel on the one hand and the more traditional novel on the other has turned precisely on this question of what constitutes real experience. James's position, it seems to me, is halfway between the two extremes and, in theory at least, the farthest one can go in the direction of psychological truth and immediacy while retaining complete literary validity. He insists neither on social happenings by themselves nor on happenings within a locked consciousness but communication and balance between the two. The question is one of epistemology as well as of literary communication and form. It is true, for example, that the stone Dr. Johnson is said to have kicked in order to disprove Berkeley can in no sense be said to have experienced the kick. To qualify as experience it would have to be at the very least the kick that Sir Roger de Coverley received—that is to say, it would have to involve a human consciousness no matter how rudimentary. But while it is consciousness that thus *makes* experience, a novelist is still dependent on external happenings, and not merely as cheap raw material. He is dependent on an external objective drama both for articulating his central consciousness and, what is more important, for giving its history a public significance. On the formal side, James felt that a novel that dealt only with what happened followed by what happened next and so on, was doomed to formlessness, possessing no principle of selection but only an arbitrary beginning and an equally arbitrary end. Whether this criticism is justified or not, it is interesting to note how completely it applies to some of the more thoroughgoing psychological novels of the present century, novels which certainly have gained no greater internal logic of form by focusing exclusively on the happenings of a consciousness.

In James, typically, the inner story of a developing consciousness is surrounded by a full history of objective events, and if the former gives shape to the latter—providing a principle of selection and relevance—the latter in turn helps to dramatize and give meaning to the former. The crucial point in such a novel is the one where the two meet head-on, that moment of discovery when the central consciousness finally apprehends and measures what has happened to it "as a social creature." In *The Portrait* this happens in Chapter 42, which James cites in the preface as a prime example of the "rare chemistry" of his art, although the process begins somewhat before and continues beyond the famous chapter. This process, however, for all its theoretical emphasis, is not in practice as decisive as one might be led to expect. In fact the heroine and her story emerge from it as confused and incoherent as ever, but without any further artistic justification. Isabel is only made clearly aware of the objective facts of her situation. Even these disclosures are long drawn out, for by Chapter 42, though she suspects most of the facts, she has no positive knowledge of them. In Chapter 40, she is prepared to argue only that "Madame Merle might have made Gilbert Osmond's marriage, but she certainly had not made Isabel Archer's," that the "sole source" of her own mistake "had been within herself. There had been no plot, no snare; she had looked and considered and chosen." This is followed closely and pointedly by the famous impression she receives when she accidentally comes upon Madame Merle and Osmond with the lady standing and the gentleman still strangely seated. It is only much later (in Chapter 49), however, that Isabel realizes that the impression of intimacy conveyed was hardly an accident and is at last ready to concede that "Mrs. Touchett was right. Madame Merle had married her." She now seems "to wake from a long pernicious dream"; when Countess Gemini's full and blunt disclosure follows soon after, the awakening in this respect is complete.

The recognitions of Chapter 42, on the other hand, are remarkable in that they constantly move in the direction of *self*-recognition. They add up to the discovery that if Isabel found herself "strangely married," if "she had thrown away her life," then to a considerable extent the "source" of the mistake had indeed "been within herself." Had she not deceived Osmond as much as he had deceived her—"in fact" if not "in intention"? Had she understood her motives at all? Was she perhaps as much of a romantic egoist as he? Had she used money as a power to shape his life and become his "providence"? If he had wanted her money, could her own motives in wanting to give it to him bear any closer or more searching scrutiny than his? Of course she had fancied she loved him, but was it not at least partly because she had viewed him as a "charitable institution," as deserving as a needy hospital? "Isabel's cheek burned," as James adds, "when she asked herself if she had married on a factitious theory, in order to do something finely appreciable with her money."

If this inner discovery is not as conclusive as one would expect it to be structurally, its consequences are still less so. The question for the rest of the novel is, How, with this altered consciousness, will Isabel regard herself, her situation, and her own future role in it; how, in a word, will her awakening influence her conduct? Here the story itself becomes confusing, but it is possible to separate two main and sharply opposed trends or possibilities. On the one hand, Isabel is unable to acquiesce; she cannot help thinking of leaving Osmond and at one point even asks herself if he would "take her money and let her go." Simultaneously, however, she views her marriage as "the most serious act—the single sacred act—of her life," and when Henrietta wonders (like everyone else, though with characteristic bluntness) at her not leaving Osmond, she replies: "I can't change that way. . . . I married him before all the world; I was perfectly free; it was impossible to do anything more deliberate. One can't change that way."

Why not? Only Henrietta asks this question point-blank, but

it is useless to pretend that we are not all troubled by it. It is a question to which the novel itself gives no good answer, although an answer exists hidden somewhere in James's imagination and, beyond that, in the very condition of the life and times with which he was dealing. Of course, in terms of the chronology of the novel's action, Isabel makes this rejoinder before she has had the benefit of Countess Gemini's disclosure; therefore she can still regard her marriage as the result of a free and open choice. James even gives the impression that the disclosure is to prove the decisive turning point of Isabel's actions. For it is immediately afterward that Isabel finally decides to visit her dying cousin in England, and the decision is made to appear portentous and far-reaching in its consequences. Osmond has warned her that he would regard this first act of disobedience on her part as open defiance, and she herself concedes that it would be a rupture. And even earlier, in the same passage where her marriage is described as a sacred act, she has already concluded that to "break with Osmond once would be to break for ever."

Yet all this is a sort of trickery, a trifling with issues which are not only far too serious to be trifled with but which James has in reality already foreclosed. In the train journey that follows the rupture he shows us, with great approval, a reflective Isabel realizing that she had exercised no freedom or choice before and that she virtually possessed none now. There are moments when she imagines that "she should some day be happy again. It couldn't be she was to live only to suffer; she was still young, after all, and a great many things might happen to her yet," but the final vision is that of "the quick vague shadow of a long future. She should never escape."

Nevertheless James perseveres right up to the end in giving the impression of open options. In the last scene with Ralph the options seem to be squarely those of either love or death: "Dear Isabel, life is better; for in life there's love. Death is good—but there's no love." The idea of love naturally leads us back to the whole comic theme of the novel, as does Ralph's statement to her, almost the very last he makes in the novel: "I don't believe that such a generous mistake as yours can hurt you for more than a little." But, then, what love can she have? There is, of course, Caspar Goodwood, and there are readers who wish the novel would end with Isabel divorcing Osmond and marrying him instead—not to mention the critic who claimed that the novel does in fact end that way.[5] However mistaken such a desire for a happy ending might be, it can be somewhat exonerated by taking into account not merely James's own radical uncertainty and the expectations aroused by the comic structure of the novel but also the special claims that he himself makes in favor of Goodwood. Isabel's conviction that she must some day "make terms" with this young man has already been mentioned, and one should now add that she feels these would be "terms which would be certain to be favourable to himself." The idea of eventual maturity in this respect is likewise suggested when, after describing her childish theories of marriage, James goes on to observe: "Deep in her soul—it was the deepest thing there—lay a belief that if a certain light should dawn she could give herself completely." It is not possible to claim that all this necessarily points to Caspar Goodwood, but James does pick up the idea and the imagery in that last scene where Goodwood makes his final appeal. Not only do his words drop "deep into her soul," producing "a sort of stillness in all her being," but in his arms Isabel feels "that she had never been loved before."

Yet, if one remembers all the values of the novel and not just its few scattered and covert hints of sexuality, if one remembers that love in such a novel must involve emotional sensitivity and intelligence as well as sex, Goodwood clearly dis-

5. H. R. Hays, "Henry James, the Satirist," *Hound & Horn,* 7 (April-May 1934): 518: the situation "is resolved into a conventional happy ending with a divorce and a rescue by the American business man."

appears as a possible comic resolution. The truth of the matter
is that James has simply made no provision in this respect for
his heroine. If Isabel is a latter-day Emma, willful and
capricious to the end, *The Portrait* lacks a Mr. Knightley to
save her. James *saw* no such possibilities, and it is a tribute to
his honesty that he chose to write a confused novel rather than
to clear the confusion by seeking a superficial compromise.
The only Knightley he could see was the dying Ralph; indeed,
by the time Isabel arrives at a final understanding with her
cousin, not only is he already dead but she herself is half in
love with easeful death. Even before she reaches England, she
finds herself envying "Ralph his dying. . . . To cease utterly, to
give it all up and not know anything more." In their meeting
together, Ralph begins in this same strain (although he soon
corrects himself with the statement about love and life quoted
above): "With me it's all over," adding: "Isabel, I wish it were
over for you." To this she replies: "I would die if you could
live. But I don't wish you to live; I would die myself." This is
the choice she makes, her one real option, with the return to
Rome only a way of living it out. Death, death, death, death,
death—this is the final word, "the clew" that Isabel's story,
like the sea in Whitman's poem, seems to have whispered
deliciously into the ear of her creator.[6]

Hedge as he might about it, there was no other possible
ending to his "comic" novel that could satisfy James. The
sense of treachery and betrayal involved in such a destiny is

6. Late in his life James seems to have come to admire Whitman's
poems, especially "Out of the Cradle Endlessly Rocking." According to
Edith Wharton, James thought Whitman "the greatest of American
poets." One evening, as Mrs. Wharton goes on

> "Leaves of Grass" was put into his hands, and all that evening we
> sat rapt while he wandered from "The Song of Myself" to "When
> lilacs last in the door-yard bloomed" (when he read "Lovely and

not confined to *The Portrait*. In his introduction to the
World's Classics edition of the novel, Graham Greene maintains that this sense—the "Judas complex," as he calls it—is the
most common and powerful theme of James's work. While
several critics including Greene have speculated on possible
biographical connections—the early death of James's beautiful
and vivacious cousin, Minny Temple, in particular—what needs
to be pointed out is the extent to which this sense is also
connected with James's sense of the character and possible
destiny of a civilization for which he entertained the same
uncertain hopes and fears that he did for his favorite heroes
and heroines. The obvious place to look is, of course, *The
Princess Casamassima*, a "social" novel written only a few
years after *The Portrait*. "It's the old regime again, the rotten-
ness and extravagance, bristling with every iniquity and every
abuse, over which the French Revolution passed like a whirl-
wind; or perhaps even more a reproduction of the Roman
World in its decadence, gouty, apoplectic, depraved, gorged
and clogged with wealth and spoils, selfishness and scepticism,
and waiting for the onset of the barbarians." This is the Princess in Chapter 22 on the condition of England; and about a
year later James himself writes: "The possible *malheurs* reverses, dangers, embarrassments, the 'decline', in a word, of
old England, go to my heart, and I can imagine no spectacle
more touching, more thrilling and even dramatic, than to see
this great precarious, artificial empire, on behalf of which,
nevertheless, so much of the strongest and finest stuff of the

---

soothing Death" his voice filled the hushed room like an organ
adagio), and thence let himself be lured on to the mysterious music
of "Out of the Cradle," reading, or rather crooning it in a mood of
subdued ecstasy till the fivefold invocation to Death tolled out like
the knocks in the opening bars of the Fifth Symphony.

[Edith Wharton, *A Backward Glance* (New York and London, D.
Appleton-Century, 1934), p. 186.]

greatest race (for such they are) has been expended, struggling with forces which perhaps, in the long run, will prove too many for it."[7]

Nor is such a view surprising in a sensitive man who, for all his emotional and imaginative stake in Western civilization, witnessed the first two of its modern wars—whose adult career was in fact bounded by them, with the American Civil War coming at one end and World War I at the other. Commenting on the former in his study of Hawthorne, James thought that Hawthorne and his generation had been far too cheerful and optimistic until "that great convulsion" seized the country and

> their illusions were rudely dispelled, and they saw the best of all possible republics given over to fratricidal car- nage. This affair had no place in their scheme, and noth- ing was left for them but to hang their heads and close their eyes. The subsidence of that great convulsion has left a different tone from the tone it found, and one may say that the Civil War marks an era in the history of the American mind. It introduced into the national con- sciousness a certain sense of proportion and relation, of the world being a more complicated place than it had hitherto seemed, the future more treacherous, success more difficult.[8]

He strikes the same note in a discussion of World War I, talking again of a rude awakening from illusions which he seems to have shared and preserved almost to the very end: "The plunge of civilization into this abyss of blood and darkness . . . is a thing that so gives away the whole long age during which we have supposed the world to be, with whatever abatement, gradually bettering, that to have to take it all now for what the

7. Letter to Grace Norton dated 24 January 1885, in *The Letters of Henry James,* ed. Percy Lubbock, 2 vols. (New York, Charles Scrib- ner's, 1920), *1,* 114.

8. Henry James, *Hawthorne* (New York, Harper, 1879), p. 139.

treacherous years were all the while really making for and *meaning* is too tragic for any words."[9]

I have made these lengthy citations not only because of their obvious relevance to the ending of Isabel's story, but also because in a way they suggest the ending of the whole long story that I have attempted to sketch in this study. For although happy stories continue to be written, although all the stories James himself wrote do not end in comparable disaster, it is clear that no serious comedy is possible with such a sense as this, with such an *ultimate* view of the culture in which it is to take place. We have seen the shifts and confusions created through much of *The Portrait* by the exigencies of this dilemma; a final word about the novel's ending will indicate some of its larger literary and moral implications.

Although the morality of Isabel's final action is a question much confused through repeated argumentation, the objection is not to the absence of a happy ending—a "rescue" followed by marriage to Goodwood—but to her precipitate return to Osmond. For if marriage to Goodwood is impossible, there is no reason why the novel cannot remain open-ended, a possibility the author himself seems to have weighed quite seriously though with little sincerity. And what makes the return morally unbearable is the fact that to James the act seems to convey intimations of high moral achievement and even heroism. It is often argued, for instance, that Isabel is motivated by her sense of duty toward Pansy and her promise to the girl that she would return. But this is a red herring; on Isabel's part it is both a characteristic attempt at rationalization and an alibi aforethought. Not only does she admit this on more than one occasion to Henrietta—which can be dismissed as the humoring of a childish friend and her insistent but stupid cross-examinations—but as early as Chapter 40 we find Isabel ad-

9. Letter to Howard Sturgis dated 4 August 1914, in Lubbock, *Letters*, 2, 384.

mitting it to herself: "On her own side her sense of the girl's [Pansy's] dependence was more than a pleasure; it operated as a definite reason when motives threatened to fail her."

Yet there is no doubt that duty is the value James considers at the end as evidence that his heroine has changed at last and acquired that maturity which had previously eluded her. What, however, is the content of this duty, and what the nature of Isabel's change? The Isabel who returns to Rome is motivated by the same absolutist theories and the same romanticism that has characterized her conduct throughout. She is still fascinated not by the rightness but by the picturesqueness of attitudes and actions. The girl who began with the belief that marriage could only be a gross vulgarity has progressed to the conclusion that all life is such and that only death or suffering can ensure a fine nobility. On her train journey to England, for instance, she dismisses all visions of possible happiness because any such aspiration would constitute "an admission that one had a certain grossness." For "Wasn't all history full of the destruction of precious things? Wasn't it much more probable that if one were fine one would suffer?" This is likewise true of what might seem a more important change: her abandonment of personal freedom in favor of a recognition of necessity. But not only is her notion of necessity as ironclad and absolutist as her ideal of independence had been; it is not even her real motivation. Instead, she is still acting out of a sense of perverse pride, a sense that she can and must do absolutely what she will. She is thinking little of other people and even less about the objective facts of her situation; she is concerned only with herself, or rather with her conception of herself which, needless to add, is as immature now as ever before. "Better death," as Arnold Kettle sums it up, "than a surrender of the illusion" that lies at the base of her story.[10]

Now to recognize the logic of this is one thing, but to see it

10. Kettle, *The English Novel*, 2, 34.

as the acquisition of maturity and wisdom, as James does, is another. Showing the other side of a coin does not alter the coin, and Isabel's standing her illusions on their head at the end is an inversion of her romanticism but not a movement forward from it. The change, if any, is such as separates an early Emerson essay from the later "Experience," an essay that can be read next to *The Portrait* in far closer detail than I propose to do here. For if Isabel sets out in the happy and self-confident posture of the early Emerson, she certainly progresses no farther than the mood of an essay that begins: "Where do we find ourselves?" and goes on to observe: "Dream delivers us to dream, and there is no end to illusion." Of course, neither Isabel nor James would say this of her; quite to the contrary, as we have seen. Nevertheless, Emerson's seven "lords of life" do govern her story, and in his order and succession: "Illusion, Temperament, Succession, Surface, Surprise, Reality, Subjectiveness these are threads on the loom of time, these are the lords of life." Of course, neither James nor any other writer considered in this study would mean what Emerson meant by "Reality," but if we make this necessary substitution, Emerson's sequence up to and including this lord could very well stand for the governing sequence of a comic action. Unlike his predecessors, however, James goes on to include "Subjectiveness," and this seventh and final lord is, in Isabel's case, indistinguishable from the first. In other words, *The Portrait* which began by making comedy out of romance ends by romanticizing comedy. In a reversal of the comic artist's traditional function, illusion is overthrown—but only in favor of further illusion.

The installation of duty as a value represents a comparable reversal. It is, indeed, a curious value; its egocentric and illusory character is obvious. It can be argued that there is nothing illusory about it if only because, regardless of the false premises on which it is assumed, it can still provide an inner stay against confusion. In the case of Fanny Price in *Mansfield*

Park, for example, it is the only possible refuge and source of
serenity for a heroine unable to cope with the difficult world
outside or fight its battles. But then Mansfield Park is not
Isabel's hate-filled Roman house, nor is Isabel's existence there
comparable to Fanny's future life with Edmund. Fanny may
have chosen timid security, but Isabel chooses spiritual death.
Her concept of duty has no real ethical content; it is an abstraction, ultimately a matter of mere form. Indeed, some of
the same concepts and words with which modern comedy had
first started reappear, but routed out of existence then, they
now seem triumphant again. Honor is the most obvious of
these concepts. While arguing against Isabel's going to England
and thus breaking with him, the most telling reason that Osmond can find in favor of the sanctity of marriage is that what
he values "most in life is the honour of a thing." And Isabel
finds these words compelling: "they represented something
transcendent and absolute, like the sign of the cross or the flag
of one's country. He spoke in the name of something sacred
and precious—the observance of a magnificent form." If we
recall here, as we can hardly help doing, the statement from
Chapter 6 about the danger inherent in a "high spirit" such as
Isabel's—"the danger of keeping up the flag after the place has
surrendered; a sort of behaviour so crooked as to be almost a
dishonour to the flag"—the point becomes clear. While Isabel's
behavior has remained subject to the same danger, its dishonor
has somehow become honor, something not only transcendent
and absolute but now also sacred "like the sign of the cross."

Indeed, if we add this rather casual infusion of religious
sanction to the pride, the absolutism, the insistence on the
picturesque, and the other motivations of Isabel's conduct, her
concept of honor and duty will seem surprisingly like the late
medieval concept of chivalry described by Huizinga in *The
Waning of the Middle Ages:*

The conception of chivalry as a sublime form of secular

life might be defined as an aesthetic ideal assuming the appearance of an ethical ideal. Heroic fancy and romantic sentiment form its basis. But medieval thought did not permit ideal forms of noble life, independent of religion. For this reason piety and virtue have to be the essence of a knight's life. Chivalry, however, will always fall short of this ethical function. Its earthly origin draws it down. For the source of the chivalrous idea is pride aspiring to beauty, and formalized pride gives rise to a conception of honour which is the pole of noble life.[11]

Thus in a sense we have come full circle. It is conceivable that James's ideal of a noble form without any real content is itself something that calls out for a new comedy. But any such comedy can be truly conceived and undertaken only by a new age; to the present age it must remain a tragedy or perhaps a tragicomedy. For this reason James's heroes—not only the serenely dying and magnanimously indifferent Ralph, but Isabel herself, triumphant in that passively as she may yield to her destiny, it is as "a victim rather than a dupe"—can tell us something about those trapped winning-losers who are their proper descendants in contemporary literature.

11. Huizinga, *Waning of the Middle Ages,* p. 58.

Chapter 8

George Bernard Shaw:
From Anti-Romance to Pure Fantasy

Unlike Henry James, whose very inclusion in a book on comedy may seem questionable to some, George Bernard Shaw is
quite obviously and consistently a comic writer. Yet as clearly
as James, though in a different way, Shaw exemplifies the
impasse at which traditional comedy had arrived in England by
the end of the nineteenth century and the beginning of the
twentieth. To talk of an impasse in connection with a man of
Shaw's driving energy and decisiveness no doubt sounds odd.
The familiar image of Shaw as a writer who knew everything,
could explain anything on demand, and had solutions worked
out in advance for all possible problems of life as well as art is
still quite popular and not altogether unjust. It is indeed
Shaw's own conscious image of himself, an image which he
steadfastly promoted throughout his life and which can be
corroborated by almost everything he wrote. Yet neither this
untroubled sense of philosophical and artistic confidence nor
the related sense of everlasting cheerfulness or (as some would
prefer) naïve optimism represents the whole truth about Shaw.
While both are obvious, it is precisely the peculiar and forceful
character of Shaw's obviousness which, more than any ideo-
logical bias against him, has tended to obscure the subtler
qualities and deeper implications of his plays.

Some years ago Jacques Barzun, commenting on the difficulty of separating Shaw from his reputation, aptly described

him as "a man in a fog"[1]—a figure appearing larger than life perhaps, but indistinctly seen and, under the circumstances, eluding both our grasp and measure. Since then, of course, some of the fog has been dispelled, partly through the mere passage of time but mainly through the efforts of a handful of perceptive critics, sympathetic or otherwise. If this has resulted in Shaw's being cut down somewhat closer to his natural size, it has also repeatedly confirmed our sense that there is more to his work than at first meets the eye. While a full understanding and a fair estimate of his achievement still await their day, it is already evident that he is not the simple, one-sided author of popular supposition but an artist of varied effects and considerable richness and complexity. To confine ourselves to what concerns us directly here, it is no longer possible to think of Shaw's cheerfulness or optimism as either philosophically confident or even artistically self-assured. The very strenuousness with which he seeks to maintain it, the increasingly absurd leaps of thought and acrobatics of the imagination to which he resorts—in a word, the overtaking of comedy by fantasy in his work—all are signs of desperate uncertainty rather than easy or uniform confidence. Add to this the fact that the solution offered by a late play like *Back to Methusaleh* is less a resolution of the problems posed in it than an underlining of their fundamental hopelessness, and the problematic character of Shaw's comedy as comedy becomes evident. There is, indeed, much force in Joseph Wood Krutch's conclusion that in the last major plays "Shaw's 'optimism' turns out to be more a matter of temperament than of philosophical conviction. The chief difference between him and the more usual despairing moderns is simply this: Shaw takes his

1. Jacques Barzun, "Bernard Shaw in Twilight," *George Bernard Shaw: A Critical Survey,* ed. Louis Kronenberger (Cleveland and New York, World Publishing, 1953), p. 159.

despair more cheerfully. He wears his rue with a difference."[2]

It is my contention, however, that the seed of this despair or rue can be discovered in some of the earliest and happiest of Shaw's plays—in fact, as I have suggested, in the very act of undertaking serious comedy at this particular juncture in modern culture—and my purpose in this essay is to focus on a few selected plays in order to trace this development. In this connection the background of the traditional comedy outlined in this book is of the utmost importance, for Shaw began in his "Pleasant" plays with a fairly straightforward attempt to revive that comedy on the English stage after a lapse of over a hundred years. But the relationship to tradition, however straightforward in the beginning, becomes in the end highly problematic. Indeed, if one were to hazard a generalization at the very outset, it would have to be somewhat to the following effect. Where Shaw's older contemporary, Henry James, used in *The Portrait of a Lady* a comic structure to express a sense of life which in the end turned out to be anything but comic—with results that we have seen—Shaw persevered to the last with the sense, the mood, the hopefulness of comedy but only at the cost of its traditional form and its true substance. Thus in his case, even more than in the case of James's novel, one can say that what begins as comedy ends as something very much like its polar opposite.

Arms and the Man (1894) is the first of the "Pleasant Plays," as Shaw called them, or simply comedies of a more or less traditional character. The general title was meant, of course, to distinguish the group from the preceding "Unpleasant Plays"—plays of the sort that came to be known as "problem" plays, dealing with some special social problem

2. Joseph Wood Krutch, *"Modernism" in Modern Drama* (Ithaca, N.Y., Cornell University Press, 1966), p. 64.

such as slum-landlordism in *Widowers' Houses* or prostitution in *Mrs. Warren's Profession.* This does not mean, however, that *Arms and the Man* is a play without a problem—only that its problem is the general problem of comedy. It is, first and foremost, an anti-romance. With its historical setting in the Balkan wars of the 1880s, it might also be said to be a play about politics or at least about heroic patriotism and military glory. But this in itself is only incidental. Shaw himself explained his wider underlying subject in the Pleasant plays when he answered the attacks on Bluntschli, the Swiss officer in *Arms and the Man* who carries chocolate in his revolver holster instead of cartridges. The cool cynicism of this "hero," so the critics of the day objected, makes him not only wildly improbable but also politically neutral and martially inglorious. But the real issue between the critics and himself, Shaw said in the preface to *Pleasant Plays,* was

> whether the political and religious idealism which had inspired the rescue of these Balkan principalities from the despotism of the Turk, and converted miserably enslaved provinces into hopeful and gallant little states, will survive the general onslaught on idealism which is implicit, and indeed explicit, in *Arms and the Man* and the realistic plays of the modern school. For my part I hope not; for idealism, which is only a flattering name for romance in politics and morals, is as obnoxious to me as romance in ethics or religion.

A general onslaught on romantic idealism! Like other comedies, *Arms and the Man* has nothing to say about the substantive issues involved because it has taken their happy outcome for granted and is concerned only with the survival or otherwise of outmoded ideals beyond the event. Raina Petkoff and Sergius Saranoff, the two main comic characters of the play, are not even honest dupes in this respect. They are not the victims of romance so much as its willful and highly

self-conscious votaries, and they have assumed in that spirit
the burden of their notions of honor, heroism, and the higher love. The higher love, in particular, they see as their most
painful but necessary duty. Neither of them is deluded
enough not to see the absurdity, or at least the patent falseness, of the role they are playing, and neither really stands
in much need of any external assistance or illumination in
order to discard it. The "cynical" Bluntschli and Louka,
Raina's servant girl, are necessary only to make them acknowledge their disillusionment and be ready, once they
have done so, to provide each with the typically less high-
minded but more real love of the final comic resolution.

The very opening scene of the play, with its picture post-
card setting of "a peak of the Balkans, wonderfully white
and beautiful in the starlit snow," makes this clear. For although, as the stage direction goes on, Raina is "intensely
conscious of the romantic beauty of the night, and of the
fact that her own youth and beauty are part of it," the
scene that follows begins by showing her doubting the romance in the very act of dedicating herself to it. News has
just arrived of a great battle and a great victory, and as
Raina learns that her fiancé, Sergius, has defied orders to
make the charge and heroically carried the day, she exclaims: "I am so happy! so proud!" but goes on:

> It proves that all our ideas were real after all. . . . Our
> ideas of what Sergius would do. Our patriotism. Our
> heroic ideals. I sometimes used to doubt whether they
> were anything but dreams. Oh, what faithless little crea-
> tures girls are! When I buckled on Sergius's sword he
> looked so noble: it was treason to think of disillusion or
> humiliation or failure. And yet—and yet—*(She sits down
> again suddenly)* Promise me you'll never tell him. . . .
> Well, it came into my head just as he was holding me in
> his arms and looking into my eyes that perhaps we only

had our heroic ideas because we are so fond of reading
Byron and Pushkin, and because we were so delighted
with the opera that season at Bucharest. Real life is so
seldom like that! . . . Yes: I was only a prosaic little cow-
ard. Oh, to think that it was all true! that Sergius is just
as splendid and noble as he looks! that the world is
really a glorious world for women who can see its glory
and men who can act its romance!

This romantic mood is interrupted by the entrance of
Bluntschli. Unlike the "tall romantically handsome" Sergius,
he is a man "of middling stature and undistinguished appearance" with a "hopelessly prosaic nose." The contrast is in
fact as sharp and simple as elsewhere in this sort of comic
drama, and it makes for what is called "good theater."
Bluntschli is on the run from the same battle where Sergius
has proved himself a hero; he has not only taken refuge in a
lady's bedchamber, but quite unchivalrously threatened her
with a revolver to make sure she does not betray him to his
pursuers. The revolver, however, is as empty as the holster
from which the last chocolate-cream went so long ago that
he happily devours the ones that Raina scornfully offers
him. Not only is Bluntschli himself unromantic and un
heroic, what is more important—or should have been to
Raina—he openly ridicules the romantic heroism of Sergius.
The charge was folly, not bravery; it succeeded only because
through a logistical blunder the other side had been supplied
with wrong ammunition. There was this "regular handsome
fellow, with flashing eyes and lovely moustache," as he puts
it, "shouting his war-cry and charging like Don Quixote at the
windmills. . . . thinking he'd done the cleverest thing ever
known, whereas he ought to be court-martialled for it. Of all
the fools ever let loose on a field of battle, that man must be
the very maddest."

Of course, Bluntschli says this in complete ignorance of

Sergius's identity; when Raina defiantly informs him of it,
he even tries to take it back. But the curious thing is that
this one overt contribution of his toward Raina's disillusionment leaves her neither more nor less disillusioned than
when she first heard the news of the charge. Indeed, it is in
the following act that Raina and Sergius play their roles to
the hilt, overdoing their own expectations, as it were.

> *Sergius.* Dearest: all my deeds have been yours. You
> inspired me. I have gone through the war like a knight in
> a tournament with his lady looking down at him!
> *Raina.* And you have never been absent from my
> thoughts for a moment. *(Very solemnly)* Sergius: I think
> we two have found the higher love. . . .
> *Sergius.* My lady and my saint! *(He clasps her rever-
> ently)*.
> *Raina. (returning his embrace)* My lord and my—

The parody of medieval or chivalric love here is quite revealing, in terms of what has gone before in this study and still
more in terms of Shaw's own work. Here it will suffice to
say that in turning to traditional comedy, it would seem as
though Shaw felt it necessary to turn also to the time in
which that tradition originated and to take up, in whatever
small measure, some of those same abstractions which had
provided modern comedy with its first subjects.

How little the lovers are deluding even themselves, however, becomes clear again when immediately after the above
exchange Sergius takes advantage of Raina's momentary absence to turn to Raina's attractive serving maid: "Louka: do
you know what the higher love is? . . . Very fatiguing thing
to keep up for any length of time, Louka. One feels the
need of some relief after it." Whereupon he proceeds to
seize and kiss her. On her side Raina too feels this same
need for relief: "I always feel a longing to do or say something dreadful to him—to shock his propriety—to scandalize

the five senses out of him." Everything comes into the open, of course, in the last and final act. Sergius changes his epithets for Raina from "lady" and "saint" to "viper" and "tiger cat," but otherwise no one's five senses are overly scandalized by the public acknowledgement of romance as romance. Raina puts it simply. "How did you find me out?" she asks Bluntschli. "I mean the noble attitude and the thrilling voice. *(They laugh together).* I did it when I was a tiny child to my nurse. *She* believed in it. I do it before my parents. *They* believe in it. I do it before Sergius. *He* believes in it." It is doubtful, as we have seen, that Sergius, or anyone else, ever really believed it. At any rate he no longer does, though he is still somewhat Byronic in acknowledging the fact: "Oh, war! war! the dream of patriots and heroes! A fraud, Bluntschli. A hollow sham, like love. . . . Raina: our romance is shattered. Life's a farce."

However, life without romance is not a farce; it is, as Bluntschli soon after reminds Sergius, "something quite sensible and serious." Earlier he has made much the same point to Raina in a different way:

> *Raina.* Do you know, you are the first man I ever met who did not take me seriously?
>
> *Bluntschli.* You mean, dont you, that I am the first man that has ever taken you quite seriously?
>
> *Raina.* Yes: I suppose I *do* mean that.

Seriousness, good sense—herein we may find the answer to the question of what values this comedy substitutes in place of the romantic ones which it has shattered. As against the noble-minded abstractions of Sergius and Raina, Bluntschli and Louka are meant to represent the real thing—in love mainly but in war as well. As Louka says to Sergius about Bluntschli, whom she had briefly observed during his refuge in the Petkoff household: "And I tell you that if that gentleman ever comes here again, Miss Raina will marry him, whether he likes it or not. I know the difference between the sort of manner you and she put on before one another and the real manner." This is an insight worthy of Shaw himself—and of the Shaw of *Man and Superman* more than the Shaw of *Arms and the Man.* Louka herself stands for sexual or passionate love, clearly neither as fatiguing nor as false as the higher love. On the question of Arms, too, what Bluntschli's cynicism amounts to is a recognition that in modern warfare organization and logistics count for much more than personal bravery and heroism—that, indeed, the latter is often merely an exhibition of Quixotry. He is personally a more expert man of arms than Sergius and can prove it in the duel. "He has beaten you in love," Louka tells Sergius. "He may beat you in war." But Bluntschli has no taste for such heroics and prefers rather to conduct the business of war by continuing to work on the logistical problem over which Major Petkoff and Sergius have been hopelessly muddled before his arrival and which they have now happily referred to him. So quickly and efficiently does he solve the problem for his erstwhile enemies, at the same time winning the battle of love without resorting to any of the lies and worse-than-empty rhetoric of the higher love, that Sergius can do little but bring the curtain down with: "What a man! Is he a man?"

The note of puzzlement is in a way easy to explain. Bluntschli is a "modern" man—a bourgeois man or bourgeois hero. Sergius may be baffled by his success and call him "a machine" or "a commercial traveller in uniform. Bourgeois to his boots!" but Shaw clearly admires his qualities: skill, intelligence, efficiency, expertise, freedom from humbug, the desire to get on with the job in hand, and an energy to match. These were Shaw's own values of conduct as we see in play after play. Here they are even more admirable because they are opposed to the aspiring but ludicrous feudalism of the Petkoffs and the Saranoffs. It is, indeed, curious that these people should see what Shaw calls "the arrival of western civilization in the Balkans" as the historical occasion for constituting themselves a feudal aristocracy. Even as a modish attitude, Sergius's Byronism is at least two generations behind the rest of the Western world, being something that "fascinated the grandmothers of his English contemporaries." In other ways they imagine the clock to have been set back a millennium just when in fact it has been made to strike the present hour. Much light comedy is made out of the situation at the beginning through Raina's self-conscious enumeration of the aristocratical qualities and features of the Petkoff family and the Petkoff house and at the end where Mrs. Petkoff objects not only to Louka but to Bluntschli as well, as commoners aspiring to marriage with nobility: "Our position is almost historical: we can go back for twenty years." The parody of chivalric or courtly love we have, of course, already seen. And just as the claims of that love are quickly set aside, so Bluntschli answers Mrs. Petkoff's objection by saying: "My rank is the highest known in Switzerland: I am a free citizen." In the same spirit he also blesses Louka's union with Sergius: "Gracious young lady: the best wishes of a good Republican!"

Yet all this does not quite dispose of the question "Is he a man?"—not in Shaw's mind, it would seem, for at the last minute he invests his hero with one further and rather surprising attribute. "And I," says Bluntschli, comparing himself humbly and unfavorably with the beautiful and romantically inclined Raina, "a commonplace Swiss soldier who hardly knows what a decent life is after fifteen years of barracks and battles: a vagabond, a man who has spoiled all his chances in life through an incurably romantic disposition, a man—" Of course, he is not allowed to complete the sentence, and it is fair to say that the disclosure surprises the audience as much as it does the other characters who exclaim at it in amazement. The abrupt shift in the middle of the sentence is good theater presumably but, but, if we take it seriously, it would not so much add to as it would reverse what we know of Bluntschli. Romance, not good sense, is after all the key to Bluntschli's character too; indeed, he himself proceeds to reinterpret the play's main events for us in this light. It is his "incurably romantic disposition" which sent him into the army instead of his father's business, which made him climb the Petkoff balcony "when a man of sense would have dived into the nearest cellar." As Sergius comments: "Bluntschli: my one last belief is gone. Your sagacity is a fraud, like everything else. You have less sense than even I!"

It is perhaps wrong to take the matter too seriously—to see in it anything except an example of Shaw's inability to leave well enough alone. There would, at any rate, be little point in pursuing it were it not for the fact that Bluntschli's last-minute romanticism happens to be one of those problems which, however minor in any given work, are highly revealing for an author's work as a whole. As such, it can best be approached from outside of *Arms and the Man.*

Before starting on the *Pleasant Plays,* Shaw had not only written *Widowers' Houses, Mrs. Warren's Profession,* and the novel *An Unsocial Socialist;* but he had heard Henry George, read *Progress and Poverty* and Marx's *Das Kapital,* and been converted to socialism. He had also read and written on Ibsen. From these various events two main conclusions of interest to us here may be drawn. In a recent essay, Reed Whittemore has observed that one can "set up two small armies of words that are constantly at war with each other in Shaw's work. One army would consist of, among others: illusion, romance, chivalry, convention, fiction, sentiment, unreason, morality. The other army would consist of, among others: facts, hard facts, actuality, reason, realism."[3] Now this idea of a war of words

3. Reed Whittemore, "Shaw's Abstract Clarity," Corrigan, *Comedy,* p. 418.

may seem to support the familiar charge that Shaw's plays are all talk, that his characters talk but do nothing—meaning, as Shaw once put it, "that they do not commit felonies."[4] But Whittemore, I think, has no such intention, and his statement is on the whole a fair description. It can also, quite obviously, be allowed to stand for not just Shaw's comedy but that of all the authors discussed in this study. In this connection it is worth pointing out to what extent Shaw's point of departure, like that of other comic writers before him, was provided by the literary conventions of the day—the conventions, in his case, of such popular exponents of the well-made play as Scribe and Sardou. As Eric Bentley concludes, after a fine analysis of Shaw's relation to the "School of Scribe" or what Shaw himself was to call "Sardoodledom": "It is certain that Shavian comedy is parodistic in a way, or to an extent, that Plautus, Jonson, and Molière were not. These others, one would judge, took a convention they respected and brought it to the realization of its best possibilities. Shaw took conventions in which he saw no possibilities—except insofar as he would expose their bankruptcy."[5]

Now if Whittemore's statement allows us to see once again the traditional affiliations of Shaw's comedy, it can as well be made to stand for a more or less pertinent summary of Shaw's view of Ibsenism in particular and the "New Drama" in general. Indeed, as we can learn from *The Quintessence of Ibsenism* itself—to go no farther afield—Shaw regarded Ibsen and the drama he pioneered as part of a wider and radical shift in Western thought which began at this time to go up in arms everywhere against the long-standing philosophies, ideals, and conventions of modern Western society. In this he was not far wrong, and his crusade on Ibsen's behalf was a well-timed part

4. Shaw, *Quintessence of Ibsenism*, p. 180.
5. Eric Bentley, "The Making of a Dramatist (1892-1903)," *G. B. Shaw: A Collection of Critical Essays*, ed. R. J. Kaufmann, Twentieth Century Views (Englewood Cliffs, N.J., Prentice-Hall, 1965), p. 62.

of his and other people's larger crusade on behalf of life itself. If he still misinterpreted Ibsen, as he did to some extent no doubt, it is because he saw at once too much and too little in the Norwegian dramatist—on the one hand, saw him as more of a social and moral revolutionary than he was; and on the other, tended to account for him as though his theme were hardly to be distinguished from the theme of the sort of comedy that we have been considering, including Shaw's own theme in *Arms and the Man* or *The Devil's Disciple*. For, on this last point, even accepting Shaw's description of Ibsen as essentially a realist at war with ideals and idealists, the fact remains that the ideals Ibsen deals with are not as a rule ideals that are historically obsolete and therefore false—as they are in the plays of Shaw named above. Hence in Ibsen they cannot be put away as easily, and the resulting drama is not always comic in its central conflict, its outcome, or its tone.

If it can be said nevertheless that Ibsen confirmed Shaw in the habit of looking beneath ideals to concealed social and moral realities, his experience with Henry George and Marx's *Capital* had taught him to look still deeper to the economic base of all these. It was a speech of Henry George's, as is well known, that first "kindled the fire" in Shaw's soul and forced him to recognize much of the intellectual debate of the time as "a mere middle-class business." "The importance of the economic basis dawned on me." Soon afterwards he became one of the first Englishmen actually to read *Capital,* which he described as "a jeremiad against the *bourgeoisie,* supported by such a mass of evidence and such a relentless genius for denunciation as had never been brought to bear before." "From that hour," he said, "I became a man with some business in the world."[6]

The impact of Marx was even greater because of Shaw's own

6. Archibald Henderson, *Bernard Shaw: Playboy and Prophet* (New York and London, D. Appleton, 1932), pp. 151-52, 154, 155.

experience with the English social conditions of the 1880s—the same conditions that had prompted James to write the letters and descriptions cited in the last chapter. James never attempted to gain the sort of understanding that Shaw acquired; outwardly he took the economic basis of bourgeois culture almost as much for granted as did Jane Austen. Yet somewhere in this culture James sensed obliquity enough to make his treatment of money and material possessions so portentous that in the end the author of *Pride and Prejudice* would surely have found him more alien than Shaw on these subjects. Indeed, in Shaw's case there would be no difficulty except Shaw's socialism, and that too only occasionally. At bottom Shaw had a straightforward and healthy respect for money, based on the fact that without it, or without the will to pursue it, there simply would not exist in the world that he knew those values of intelligence and thought, of purpose, energy, and efficiency which he admired. The only trouble with the poor, he thought, was poverty. In this, as in so much besides, he was himself the best type of bourgeois man—a "Puritan," as Chesterton described him.

For all this, however, he still had to contend with Marx, not to mention his own firsthand witness. Talking only of what concerns us here, it is not too much to say that the "business in the world" that Shaw conceived for himself upon reading *Capital* and the business of writing bourgeois comedy are not easily reconcilable; in fact, in the end they do prove incompatible. Consider just the question of the economic basis and its literary implications for Shaw. "Indeed," he wrote to Henderson in 1904, "in all the plays my economic studies have played as important a part as a knowledge of anatomy does in the works of Michael Angelo."[7] This by itself, of course, means nothing except that an understanding of the economic structure of society can be for an artist, any artist, the source

7. Ibid., p. 7.

of added strength and self-assurance. Jane Austen was not innocent of such understanding, and yet it did not in any way
prove incompatible with the superb comedy of her novels. The
matter can, however, be argued as follows: If Jane Austen had
not only mentioned her heroes' handsome incomes but inves-
tigated their source and included the findings in her novels, she
would have created problems for herself which her comedy
now avoids. If she had also doubted the soundness and permanence of the system that generated these incomes, she
would have been a troubled and divided artist, to say the least.
And if finally she had come under the appeal of Marx's jeremiad—his "appeal to an unnamed, unrecognized passion—a
new passion—the passion of hatred in the more generous souls
among the respectable and educated sections for the accursed
middle-class institutions that had starved, thwarted, misled and
corrupted them from their cradles"[8]—she would not have been
able to attempt comedy at all.

This no doubt puts the argument far too strongly, for Shaw
did attempt comedy after all. Nevertheless, it is equally true
that he began his dramatic career with plays that centered
precisely on this question of investigating the source of un-
earned incomes. In *Widowers' Houses* the climax comes when
the youthful and romantic hero discovers that his hands are no
cleaner than those of the slum-landlord whose wealth and position he has highmindedly disdained even at the risk of losing
the girl he loves; when he finds out that his own income,
which he has always called just "interest," is in fact interest on
a mortgage on that same slum-property. In *Mrs. Warren's Profession* Vivie Warren breaks with her mother not because Mrs.
Warren had been led to prostitution—this she understands and
even sympathizes with—but because Mrs. Warren has gone on
to become the manager and joint-proprietress of a string of
high-class "private hotels," a fact she has carefully concealed

8. Ibid., p. 154.

from the daughter. As Vivie puts it in their final interview: "You explained how it came about. You did not tell me that it is still going on." While, however, the hero of *Widowers' Houses* recovers from his shock and accepts the situation as it is, Vivie runs away from it all to seek refuge in actuarial work at an office desk. The two subjects she declares she never wants to hear about again are "love's young dream in any shape or form" and "the romance and beauty of life."

Shaw did not only investigate the system; his economic studies led him to doubt both its justice and its permanence. This is not merely because he was a generous soul and therefore came to believe in socialism. More important, bourgeois society itself had come to a stage where Marx's appeal to "a new passion"—the revolutionary passion of hatred—had become in one form or another widely plausible and effective. Accordingly, the knowledge of the economic structure did not help Shaw in the same way as the knowledge of anatomy helped Michael Angelo—or knowledge of social anatomy helped Jane Austen. The structure became, for Shaw, something in the nature of a skeleton in the cupboard; at least in all but the historical plays he dealt with it consistently as such. This does not mean that he treated it in any one uniform way. On the contrary, his successive strategies in this respect can prove a good index to the successive broad stages of his development as a playwright. When he first decided to drag the skeleton into the open, as it were, and make an edifying exhibition of it, he wrote his early socialist plays. When he turned to comedy of more or less the traditional sort, he still thought it necessary to exhibit a few bare bones at least, though he now at the same time tended to stow them away as far out of view as possible (as in "The Revolutionist's Handbook" in *Man and Superman*) or to wrap them up in one sort of tissue or another (as in *Arms and the Man*)—neither procedure succeeding, of course, without some dramatic and other embarrassment. But when Shaw finally decided to jettison the economic facts entirely, together with other facts, hard facts, actuality, and the rest of that army—when indeed he decided that these painful facts were not even facts—he virtually abandoned the field to the opposing army of Whittemore's description which, unopposed and unchallenged, could hardly produce anything for Shaw except either pure farce or pure fantasy.

Returning briefly to *Arms and the Man,* we can see more clearly the unexpected disclosure at the end for what it is—a piece of bright but dramatically thin and transparent tissue to cover an embarrassment. Eric Bentley sees it differently, as a matter of considerable momentousness for the play. What gives the play its true significance, he says, is not "the disenchantment of Raina and Sergius but the discovery that Bluntschli the realist is actually an enchanted soul whom nothing will disenchant. He has destroyed their romanticism but is himself 'incurably romantic.' . . . In this scene, plot and theme reach completion together, and the play of thesis and antithesis ends in synthesis."[9] The interpretation is attractive but surely overgenerous if nothing else. Bentley himself cites the common feeling that Bluntschli's romanticism seems only a matter of "mere words" or "mere words stuck on at the end." He does not presumably share this feeling, but a man who does need not for that reason subscribe to the more general charge that Shaw's plays are all talk. He may well realize that much of drama is inevitably all talk and still be dissatisfied with this particular instance of it. Indeed, the real problem with the disclosure of Bluntschli's incurably romantic disposition seems to have completely escaped Bentley. The disclosure is found to be mere words not only because it contradicts our picture of Bluntschli as he is dramatically presented up to this last minute, but, more important, because it is impossible to see any recognizable content in the assertion,

9. Bentley, "Making of a Dramatist," p. 63.

let alone the sort of content one would associate with the idea
of thesis and antithesis ending in higher synthesis.

Yet if this is an empty gesture—and that is what I consider
it: an empty gesture stuck on at the end—why did Shaw give it
to his hero to make? The answer, I think, lies in the question
that Shaw gave Sergius to ask as the last thing in the play: Is
he a man? Sergius, we remember, had also thought of Bluntschli as a "machine" and "a commercial traveller in uniform.
Bourgeois to his boots!" It is only in this last scene, however,
that we are presented with the "facts, hard facts" of the situation, as we learn of the Bluntschli hotels and the whole inventory of seventy carriages, two hundred horses, nine thousand
six hundred pairs of sheets and blankets, and so on, is rolled
out. This is good comedy, especially since, given the added
historical alignments in the play, the commercial splendor of
the display enables the free citizen Bluntschli to squash the
pretentious airs of the aristocratic Petkoffs. Nor can Bluntschli's hotels be classed with the "hotels" of Mrs. Warren or
the slum-property of *Widowers' Houses* as something that
needs either exposure or apology and concealment. All this is
well enough. Nevertheless to Shaw Bluntschli's wealth remains
a piece of that economic skeleton which needs to be exposed
and yet, once exposed, needs to be covered up again somehow.
Furthermore, to the extent to which Bluntschli's character is
related to the hard facts of the situation, even that character,
no matter how admirable as already presented, must be raised
to a still more distinctive level.

To see this clearly we should turn briefly to Nicola, the
Petkoff manservant and Louka's betrothed, about whom the
question, Is he a man? can only be answered in one way. As
Louka says to him at one point: "Yes: sell your manhood for
30 levas, and buy me for 10!" He is, indeed, a calculating
machine: a servile fellow prepared to put up with insult and
hardship, to rise above all considerations of honor and passion
alike—capable, in short, of any conduct that will further his

commercial ambitions. He is not merely willing to let Louka go but personally instructs her carefully in the arts to use on Sergius, simply because as Sergius's wife Louka will become "one of my grandest customers, instead of only being my wife and costing me money." Now there is little danger offhand of our confusing this degraded Malvolio and Uriah Heep in one with Captain Bluntschli (a hero as admirable to Shaw as any of Jane Austen's heroes to Jane Austen). And yet it is curious how, in a way, Shaw also sees similarities between his two characters. For instance, Nicola, like Bluntschli, is described as among other things a man "of cool temperament" and "keen intelligence . . . who has no illusions." Both the servant and the hero are given the same capacity for remaining unflustered in trying situations, and especially for accepting intended insults as compliments or at least exact descriptions with which they have no quarrel:

> *Louka. (with searching scorn)* You have the soul of a servant, Nicola.
> *Nicola. (complacently)* Yes: thats the secret of success in service.

> *Raina. (furious: throwing the words right into his face)* You have a low shopkeeping mind. You think of things that would never come into a gentleman's head.
> *Bluntschli. (phlegmatically)* Thats the Swiss national character, dear lady.

The remarkable similarity between the two men here is, of course, in keeping with their common freedom from illusions and with that bourgeois realism which sees the value of personal qualities as strictly dependent on their practical effects and consequences. Bluntschli makes this clear in his one and only comment on his fellow realist. When in the last scene Nicola, in order to smooth the final step of Louka's path to Sergius, denies having ever been engaged to her himself, Sergius declares that Nicola must be credited with "either the finest heroism or the most crawling baseness. Which is it, Bluntschli?" But Bluntschli's answer cuts right through the Gordian knot. "Never mind whether it's heroism or baseness. Nicola's the ablest man I've met in Bulgaria. I'll make him manager of a hotel if he can speak French and German."

This is where the effect of Shaw's economic studies on the anatomy of his plays can be seen. The effect is less obvious than in the socialist plays, but it is there nonetheless. The difference between Nicola—the man on the make—and Blunt-schli—the made man of long standing who has had the time, the means, and the freedom to cultivate himself, to become a hero in fact—is the sort of difference that meant everything to Jane Austen. (Witness, for example, the shopkeeping Gardiners in *Pride and Prejudice*.) So in truth was it important to Shaw —emotionally. But in his case there remained an intellectual uncertainty stemming from his understanding that Nicola was as much a representative figure of bourgeois culture as Blunt-schli. Bluntschli's romanticism—the gesture at the end that would make a romance out of an anti-romance if it were not a mere gesture—is an acknowledgement of that uncertainty. It represents an attempt to distinguish the hero from the servant, not within their common culture but in some definitive way beyond it. Needless to add, the attempt is as intellectually hollow as it is dramatically unmotivated, unsuccessful, and unnecessary.

The play we must now turn to is *Man and Superman* (1901-03). For the present line of inquiry it is indeed a pivotal play. "No: I sing, not arms and the hero, but the philosophic man: he who seeks in contemplation to discover the inner will of the world, in invention to discover the means of fulfilling that will, and in action to do that will by the so-discovered means. Of all other sorts of men I declare myself tired." This is not Shaw but his Don Juan in the famous "philosophical" Act

III of the play. Shaw himself was by no means tired, at least not yet, of all other sorts of men except the philosophic; nor, we may add, of other sorts of writing—such as comedy. All this is clear from the three other acts of *Man and Superman* itself—the acts which constitute not only a self-contained unit, but perhaps Shaw's most sustained and brilliant piece of comic writing in the traditional mode. Nor, so far as Shaw's work before *Man and Superman* is concerned, is there anything particularly new or startling about Juan's description of the true hero as the man who is engaged in doing "the inner will of the world." This can be the description of a hero in history and as such can be applied even to a character like Bluntschli, who contributes, although only in a domestic (or comic) way, to the introduction of Western civilization into the feudal Balkans. More appropriately, however, it would describe the heroes of two of the *Three Plays for Puritans,* which intervene chronologically between the last of the *Pleasant Plays* and the new phase that opens with *Man and Superman.* For both Dick Dudgeon of *The Devil's Disciple* and Caesar of *Caesar and Cleopatra* are men who resist or rise above the appeal of love and romance (in Caesar's case somewhat unhistorically) because of historical missions involving the inner will of the world.

Thus if we review the plays of the first decade of Shaw's career, we notice that in almost every case the idea of love as a value in itself is held somehow to be inadequate. This is least true of a play like *Arms and the Man,* but even there, as we have seen, Shaw feels compelled to give his hero some quality beyond that of a sensible and successful bourgeois man and lover. In other plays the counterweight might be social action or the dawning of a consciousness of social or economic problems at the base of bourgeois society. And in a play like *The Devil's Disciple* the heroism consists entirely in sacrificing all personal considerations to the needs of such a historical situation as the American war of independence. The new element in *Man and Superman* thus lies not in its introduction of a theme over and above that of love but in the character of that theme: not now social problems or historical necessity, not anything readily recognizable as a force in and of this world, but philosophy understood as contemplation, and the human will understood as working in entirely speculative terms. To the extent to which this is the superadded theme of *Man and Superman*, the play looks forward to *Back to Methusaleh;* to the extent to which this theme can be disregarded, it looks back to the previous comedies and, in fact, can be seen as their crowning consummation. It is only Don Juan who, in the operatic and detachable Act III, sings "not arms and the hero, but the philosophic man." Shaw himself describes the whole play and its pivotal character better when he announces it in the subtitle as "a comedy *and* a philosophy" (my italics).

The comedy, like comedy generally, is a comedy of love that depends for its effect and even its purpose on the overturning of romantic convention—in this case the large-scale convention that regards and requires women to be the reluctant quarry and men the relentless pursuers in the chase or game of love. To John Tanner, the hero of *Man and Superman*, love is not a game at all, nor even the chase of a weak and helpless female by a strong and imperious male, but rather a deadly combat in which all the purpose, strength, and ferocity lie on the side of the woman. As early as in *Widowers' Houses* Shaw, in a stage direction, had described the encounter of lovers as follows: "For a moment they stand face to face, quite close to one another, she provocative, taunting, half defying, half inviting him to advance, in a flush of undisguised animal excitement. It suddenly flashes on him that all this ferocity is erotic: that she is making love to him." Charteris, the hero of *The Philanderer*, declares likewise that "at no time have I taken the initiative and persecuted women with my advances as women have persecuted me." Nor, as he points out, can he lay claim to the customary attractions of a romantic hero: "Have I a romantic

mysterious charm about me? do I look as if a secret sorrow
preyed on me? am I gallant to women?" Even in a pleasant
play like *Arms and the Man,* where Sergius imagines himself
just such a romantic hero, we have already seen not only his
final and quite unromantic description of Raina as "viper" and
"tiger cat," but also Louka's observation that Raina is sure to
marry Bluntschli "whether he likes it or not."

What all this adds up to is not so much the portrait of a new
woman as the exposure of the age-old romantic convention of
the womanly woman and the manly man. Of the resulting
comedy *Man and Superman,* with its sustained reversal of roles
between hero and heroine, becomes the fullest expression in
Shaw. Part of the fun lies, of course, in the fact that the
heroine, Ann Whitefield, assumes precisely this role of a
womanly woman and plays it for all it is worth. Unlike
Blanche in *Widowers' Houses,* though with a character as
strong and a purpose more determined, she pleads the helplessness of her situation and her own gentle weakness and uncertainty. Left an orphan, she claims that she has nowhere to turn
except to her two appointed guardians and the wishes of her
father—which to her are "sacred," she herself being "too
young, too inexperienced" to decide any question whatsoever.
In reality, however, she can and does wrap everyone around
her little finger; the only reason her dead father's wishes are
sacred to her is that these wishes happen to include the ap-
pointment as her joint guardian of John Tanner, the man she
has disposed of before he has proposed. So far, in fact, is
Tanner from proposing to her that, while everyone else is
taken in by Ann, he not only sees through what he at one
point calls "her confounded hypocrisy" but sees through to
the deadliness underneath. To him she is "an ironclad" pre-
tending to be "at the mercy of the wind and the waves," a
"boa constrictor," and a "Bengal tiger." The only possible
heroism under the threat of her embrace is to run for his

, Dona Ana's part-
father! a father for
II itself, however,
on the relation be-
hy of "The Revo-
f the other three
y to settle if only
eing something not
manticism in *Arms*
ext of the play. Yet
er play inasmuch as
the hero as a man
ass and the obvious
play. However, as
ism—which is only
atic presentation—
lf vague or without
nd deliberately de-
ntradicted by true
ate" pregnancy, or
andage of Mendoza
r such treatment is
ls after the name of
Member of the Idle
dently of the theo
er Shaw may think
nd Superman treat
all books and theo
l philosophy in hi
medy in his socie
le) his dilemma as

as a different stan
lay's resolution ar
different plane son

life—which is what Tanner does, putting the whole breadth of Europe between her and himself.

The two subplots, or the two subplots and the hint of a third, support the play's character as an anti-romance. On the one hand, we have the marriage of Violet and Hector, which is at first presented not as a marriage at all but as a passionate escapade involving what seems like a romantic but illegitimate pregnancy threatening disaster for Violet. Later, when Hector's identity as the legal husband becomes clear, there still remains the possibility of disinheritance by Hector's father, the American millionaire. Yet Violet has proceeded all along not only legally but with the coolest of heads: "You can be as romantic as you please about love, Hector; but you mustnt be romantic about money." On the other hand, though to the same purpose, we have Octavius's poetic and eternal devotion to Ann, his worshiping the ground she treads on and so forth. As Ann tells him in what does not sound like but is a final rebuke: "I wouldnt for worlds destroy your illusions. . . . I can see exactly what will suit you. You must be a sentimental old bachelor for my sake." Octavius's love for Ann has a ludicrous parallel in Mendoza's equally undying devotion to Louisa Straker, the unsuccess of which has turned the ex-waiter into a sentimental brigand and rebel against the world. While Octavius is only contemplating a great play with Ann as heroine, Mendoza can already pull at will from his stuffed pockets old hotel bills covered with such tributes to his love as "I saw thee first on Whitsun week / Louisa, Louisa—" or "Louisa, I love thee / I love thee, Louisa"—all of which only drives in with a sledge hammer the rebuke to the literary aspect of the convention.

Against these various romantic, sentimental, or cool-headed loves, Ann Whitefield's pursuit of Tanner becomes what we might call the real thing. While, however, the subplots thus clarify and support the simple central comedy, what compli-

cates it is Tanner's idea that of ;
none so treacherous and remorse
the artist man and the mother \
deadlier," as he goes on, "becau
they love one another." The stat
cifically to the artist Octavius, h;
only does the word *artist* mean
purpose in the world, the phr
woman suggest that all men ar
eventual and inevitable roles. (
women are conscious of these tr
tist Octavius is not. But Tanner ;
at first, but quite clearly at last.
are heroes on account of this re
cause of their anti-romantic ro
prelude to the other.

Here we see the full reach of t
shocking comedy (which deligh
to its connection with philosop
stage productions). One shoul
out how well the play, and e
without any of Shaw's special
Whitefield must indeed be cour
heroines of English comedy. S
find in Jane Austen or after
before Jane Austen, combinir
sourcefulness, and the artfuln
ines and the fine womanly st
Western. In Tanner, too, w
Jones's irrepressibility, expres
lectual wild oats. Even Shaw
the play, is licentious only
ther Tanner nor Ann share an
acters of Restoration drama—
invoke in view of Shaw's ap

cloud of love and romance"; and, above al
ing cry: "I believe in the Life to Come! A
the Superman!" Before turning to Act
some further observations must be made
tween its philosophy—as also the philoso;
lutionist's Handbook"—and the comedy
acts. The case of the "Handbook" is ea;
because it clearly falls beyond the pale, b
even stuck on at the end like Bluntschli's r
and the Man but merely appended to the t
in a sense it is like that gesture in the earli
it too represents an attempt to distinguish
well above or beyond the ideology of his cl
concerns of its life as established in the
compared with Bluntschli's vague romantic
irreconcilable with the preceding dram
Tanner's social philosophy, while not in its
intellectual and moral content, is plainly
flated within the play's action: either c
facts as in the case of Violet's "illegitim
simply parodied as by the high-minded bri;
and his fellow revolutionaries. The clue f
in fact given at the very outset in the initi
the author of the treatise: M.I.R.C., or
Rich Class. Whatever we may think indepe
ries expressed in the "Handbook"—whate
of them—we have to conclude that *Man a*
them exactly as comedy in general treats
ries. There is no place for Tanner's socia
comedy, just as there is no place for c
philosophy. And this is as much (or as lit
is his author's.

The philosophy of "Don Juan in Hell"
ing, what with the weight it exerts on the
the fact that its characters duplicate on a

of the main characters of the play. Yet if we think only of that last scene, with its combination of sense and nonsense in Tanner's speeches, we might indeed look upon the philosophy of Life Force exactly as it is looked upon by the characters present on the stage: as yet another of the comic hero's many talking points, yet another outrageous notion to be tolerated and deflated. (To Ann, Life Force sounds like "Life Guards.") This suggests the extent to which it is possible to see here again Shaw's comedy playing havoc with philosophical theory, making Nietzsche's idea of the Superman and Bergson's elan vital ridiculous simply by having them offered as justification for such everyday facts as love, marriage, and the prospect of offspring. Even with Act III thrown in, however, the play still remains a comedy *and* a philosophy, with the philosophy offered very much on a take-it-or-leave-it basis. And if I propose to take it up briefly rather than leave it, the reason is not that Shaw's creative evolution is any more impressive intellectually than Shaw's socialism. Nor is it that "Don Juan in Hell" is placed inside the play and only quarantined, as it were, within its own stylization, while "The Revolutionist's Handbook" is no more than an unfunctional tailpiece. My reason for turning to "Don Juan in Hell" is simply that at this point in Shaw's development it points forward, unlike the "Handbook" which is an obsolescence, a residual legacy of Shaw's Marxism and the early socialist plays.

About Shaw's biological and impossibly futuristic philosophy of creative evolution little need be said by way of explication or interpretation. My purpose is rather to examine the dramatic implications that such a philosophy holds. That "Don Juan in Hell" can be read as a disquisition on the possibilities of comic drama as much as the possibilities of life will not seem strange to anyone who remembers not only its placing in an out-and-out comedy and its discussion of precisely the same comic themes, but also the dramatic terms and metaphors in which that discussion abounds. Indeed, for all its

cosmic dimensions, Don Juan's argument is cast in terms familiar to us—illusion or romance on the one hand and facts or
reality on the other—and his cosmology itself assumes the
form of a vast three-tiered stage, or rather a stage with two
visible platforms and a third master platform hidden invisibly
behind. For, as he himself puts it: "If the play still goes on
here [in hell] and on earth, and all the world is a stage, heaven
is at least behind the scenes." The two visible shows of life, in
hell and on earth, are not so much alike as they are the reverse
versions of each other. Hell is "the home of the unreal"; it is a
theater that calls us, in the words of its manager The Devil, "to
sympathize with joy, with love, with happiness, with
beauty—." But such a claim, Juan argues, can only be a cheat
under the existing circumstances. If in hell people "talk of
nothing else but love" and "think they have achieved the perfection of love," it is only "because they have no bodies." This
is sheer "imaginative debauchery," like, as he later adds, "sit-
ting for all eternity at the first act of a fashionable play, before
the complications begin." The invitation is thus not to the
comedy of The Devil's claim but to a cheap and endless romantic indulgence: "Here you call your appearance beauty,
your emotions love, your sentiments heroism, your aspirations
virtue, just as you did on earth; but here there are no hard
facts to contradict you, no ironic contrast of your needs with
your pretensions, no human comedy, nothing but a perpetual
romance, a universal melodrama."

If true comedy is impossible in hell, so is it on earth, though
for the opposite reason. The hellish theater is in fact meant
only to serve as an admonition to the earthly play as it is
imagined by its characters. For The Devil has enough influence
on earth to deceive living men and women into thinking of life
in terms of the same high ideals of love, heroism, and human
progress. But these aspirations are pure illusion on earth too,
not because there is no reality on earth but because there is
too much, and it is too overwhelming to be ever remedied. It is

The Devil who best puts the case against the pretensions of the earthly show in that magnificent long speech which begins, "And is man any the less destroying himself . . ." The speech is far too long to quote, but The Devil himself sums it up when he says later: "Where you now see reform, progress, fulfilment of upward tendency, continual ascent by Man on the stepping stones of his dead selves to higher things, you will see nothing but an infinite comedy of illusion." No stronger case against the comic vision of life can be conceived than that made by The Devil on the basis of the world's political and social realities. But to this Don Juan adds a further argument, by its very nature the most hopeless of all—the argument of man's biological constitution itself. Human beings, he says, must inevitably be "dragged down from their fool's paradise by their bodies: hunger and cold and thirst, age and decay and disease, death above all, makes them slaves of reality"—just as the bodiless inhabitants of hell are the slaves of illusion.

The biological argument is at once Shaw's ultimate confession of disillusionment and his ultimate solution to man's future. It is the argument of Don Juan's heaven against The Devil's hell. Life, Juan argues, is not hopeless and purposeless just because there seems neither hope nor purpose among the living. If earth is "the home of the slaves of reality," and hell "the home of the unreal," there is still the invisible heaven which is "the home of the masters of reality." This reality has a function to perform and is at the same time an end in itself. It is the transcendent force that has willed and worked the evolution, embodying itself in successive species up to man, and being now engaged in evolving first the superman and finally god. Once this stage is reached, the force becomes wholly self-contemplative, and this contemplation becomes the highest good attainable—the supreme reality of heaven. "But even as you enjoy the contemplation of such romantic mirages as beauty and pleasures," says Don Juan, "so would I enjoy the contemplation of that which interests me above all things: namely Life: the force that ever strives to attain greater power of contemplating itself."

This, of course, leaves even John Tanner of the last act behind; it goes as far forward as the last speech in the last act of the last part of the five-part *Back to Methusaleh*. This is the meaning of the final stage of Don Juan's own progress, which he describes in detail, from the romantic man to the man of experience to the philosophic man. The reason why one takes this philosophy as a confession of disillusionment or a satirical fantasy rather than a solution is that bodiless self-contemplation seems as much of an imaginative debauch as the illusions of hell: both are equally devoid of moral content and equally repulsive. The Devil's warning against Juan's doctrine is quite to the point: "Beware of the pursuit of the Superhuman: it leads to an indiscriminate contempt for the Human. To a man, horses and dogs and cats are mere species, outside the moral world. Well, to the Superman, men and women are a mere species too, also outside the moral world." At any rate, whatever one thinks of this philosophy as a possibility of and for life, it is obvious that such a vision of "Life to Come" can hold no future for drama. To this extent at least, heaven does well in remaining "behind the scenes." For, as Juan adds, his heaven "cannot be described by metaphor"—and certainly not by the metaphor that we call drama.

The above discussion leads us directly to *Back to Methusaleh* (1921). To turn to that work, as I propose doing now, is not to suggest that Shaw wrote no worthwhile plays between the date of *Man and Superman* and 1921. On the contrary, at least two of Shaw's most highly regarded plays—*John Bull's Other Island* and *Major Barbara*—succeed *Man and Superman* immediately, and one other—*Heartbreak House*—precedes *Back to Methusaleh* by five years. *Back to Methusaleh* itself is no longer considered, and I think rightly, the major work that Shaw supposed it to be. For all its enormous length and pretended scope, it does not even develop but rather simplifies the thesis of "Don Juan in Hell." There is little point, accordingly, in examining its philosophy in detail, much less in studying it as a work of the dramatic imagination. My purpose, then, in turning to this extended version of Shaw's philosophy or vision of "Life to Come" is mainly to note its solemn and elaborate insistence on a point that Don Juan had already suggested more incisively and wittily—namely, the incompatibility of drama or any art with the ultimate concerns and possibilities of life. The idea of course owes something to Plato, reading whom had further disabused Shaw of the notion of inevitable progress—this time the progress of human intellect and art which he had assumed must necesssarily accompany the march of history from ancient to modern times, or from the writers of classical antiquity through Shakespeare to Ibsen and himself.

Indeed, as the philosophy of "Don Juan in Hell" blossoms into the full-blown Utopia of *Back to Methusaleh,* the reason becomes greater for viewing this philosophy less as a solution and more as a desperate recognition of the hopelessness of human affairs, of man himself as constitutionally created. The Utopia itself then becomes wholly satire-determined. Its content might come from Lamarck or Bergson or Plato, but its purpose remains that of the fellow-Irishman Swift or of a work like *Erewhon* by Samuel Butler—one of the few English writers whom (and especially whose pioneering critique of Darwin) Shaw admired without qualification. Seen in this light, Shaw's argument against the inherent and ineradicable limitations of man as he is created—the argument that man was not created but had evolved into his present state, and that therefore further biological progress was not only possible but was the only possible progress—becomes a trick of satire, a way of affirming the very premise that is overtly denied. And yet the significance of the philosophy of creative evolution for Shaw cannot be dismissed entirely in these terms. For the very elaboration

that makes the satirical purpose evident also makes us doubt
that the Utopia based on this philosophy is as completely a
device of satire as some of Shaw's recent apologists would like
to think. The Utopia of *Back to Methusaleh* is, indeed, less like
the Utopia of *Erewhon* than it is like that of William Morris's
News from Nowhere—that is, if it is meant to some extent as
satire against the existing state of affairs, it is also meant to
some extent as a vision of a future state that Shaw regarded as
desirable if not easily realizable. Despite all disillusionment,
despite the experience of the war, Shaw was not the man to
admit defeat and abandon all hope. He would rather abandon
all reason and common sense—which is exactly what he seems
bent upon doing in *Back to Methusaleh*.

At any rate, unlike *Man and Superman, Back to Methusaleh*
is not a comedy *and* a philosophy. It does not offer its philosophy on a take-it-or-leave-it basis. The philosophy is all there is
of comedy—not in the sense that it is a philosophy of comedy,
but in the sense that without it Shaw cannot support even the
elementary mood of hopefulness. Of "Don Juan in Hell" Shaw
had remarked in 1911: "I think it well to affirm that the third
act, however fantastic its legendary framework may be, is a
careful attempt to write a new Book of Genesis for the Bible
of the Evolutionists."[10] In *Back to Methusaleh* he wrote the
whole hopeful gospel—"A Metabiological Pentateuch," as he
subtitled it on the program. Beginning with Adam and Eve in
the Garden of Eden in Part I, the work concludes in Part V
with the year 31,920, by which time Don Juan's heaven is
already almost here. Not only has man willed and finally
achieved the power to live forever, barring physical accidents,
but the aged inhabitants of the earth, the Ancients, have become masters of reality to the extent to which they are, in
Juan's words, "omniscient, infallible, and withal completely,

10. Quoted in Henderson, *Bernard Shaw,* p. 516 n., from the fore-
word to the Constable Sixpenny Series edition of *Man and Superman*
(London, 1911).

unilludedly self-conscious." If they are not gods yet, it is only because they still have bodies; this further evolution will also come to pass, and then men will have freed themselves from their own biology as they have already freed themselves from all realities (or illusions as Shaw and his Ancients would have it) except the one supreme reality of thought. This is the prophecy with which Lilith's last speech both closes the play and refers its gospel to a still more hopeful future: "after passing a million goals they press on to the goal of redemption from the flesh, to the vortex freed from matter, to the whirlpool in pure intelligence that, when the world began, was a whirlpool in pure force."

The "redemption from the flesh" has in fact been already achieved insofar as the fact of birth is concerned. In *Man and Superman* Dona Ana had advanced in support of the human comedy of love and marriage the final argument that marriage is absolutely necessary if only because it "peoples the world." But the farsighted Don Juan had countered: "How if a time came when this shall cease to be true? Do you not know that where there is a will there is a way? that whatever Man really wishes to do he will finally discover a means of doing?" This time to come is none other than the year 31,920 of the last part of *Back to Methusaleh,* when human babies are not born but hatched out of huge eggs at what would seem to us the age of about seventeen. With such means of circumventing marriage goes also presumably the circumventing of all sexuality. For although the newborn feel impelled to make love to each other for the first two years of their life, their love has all the appearance of Platonic sentiment or the harmless dalliance of pastoral romance—the boys and girls bearing such characteristically romantic names as Chloe, Strephon, and Amaryllis. Not merely love but also science and art are relegated to the status of childish toys, all almost equally beneath the concern of four-year-olds. *Dolls* is in fact the word used by the Ancients alike for the products of science, the products of art, and the human body which, as the She-Ancient puts it, remains "the last doll to be discarded. . . . The day will come when there will be no people, only thought." And even Martellus, though an artist himself and barely out of his infancy, begins to agree: "The body always ends by being a bore. Nothing remains beautiful and interesting except thought, because the thought is the life."

The equation of pure thought with life is the final gospel—not longevity, which is only "the gospel of the brothers Barnabas" (as early as in Part II), a sort of machinery, together with much else, for the gradual exposition of the ultimate theme. The two Barnabas brothers are not masters of reality but relatively rudimentary instruments of the Life Force in the early twentieth century, seeking to push mankind over the first inch of the long way ahead to the final reality. Of this final reality as we meet it in the last part, and of its rejection of all art and what seems to us all life, there is little we can say in objection that Shaw has not himself thought of beforehand and actually said in the play. What should be noted is that he has also ruled out all objections by the very simple device of putting them into the mouths of two-year-olds who, living in the world of childish diversions and illusions, can form no idea of the reality of pure contemplation, its superior "ecstasy," and the "direct sense of life" which it gives the Ancients. We can also note that if this is reality and all the rest of life an illusion, it is again a reality that can be communicated neither through metaphor nor through art. The Ancients themselves come no nearer than the above phrases; the only character who even attempts to define the content of this reality is Chloe, the child-maiden, at the beginning of Part V. Like Martellus turning away from the illusions of his body and his sculpture, she is shown as turning away from love. But what will she contemplate? "Have you ever thought about the properties of numbers?" she asks her disconsolate lover. "They are fascinating, just fascinating. I want to get away from our eternal dancing and music, and just sit down by myself and think about numbers." The supposition is, of course, that Chloe's thought is still thought about something, but that as she grows older her thought will become purer and purer until it becomes the wholly indefinable contemplation of the Ancients.

Back to Methusaleh is a double fantasy, or a fantasy about fantasy. Facts, by which Shaw once set his store, dwindle constantly as we move from social and political realities to bureaucratic machinery to just biological details such as the exact number of years to which men and women live or can live. Finally all that remains of hard facts is the exact date of each part—3000 A.D. or 31,920 A.D. The work becomes a monstrous construction in which abstractions walk the stage more audibly than the characters who are supposed to represent them. In this, however, *Back to Methusaleh* does not differ materially from other Utopian fantasies. The difference lies rather in the character of Shaw's Utopia. For instance, in a work already mentioned—*News from Nowhere,* by Shaw's socialist friend, William Morris—the vision of future life, although vastly simplified, is still recognizably human. Men and women have wholesome bodies and art, so far from being dismissed as an illusion or childish diversion, is almost the condition of the good life, entering into all its aspects and indeed being its final perfection. By comparison with this "Nowhere," Shaw's "Life to Come" is not only not human, but it is not life.

Turning finally again to the satirical side of *Back to Methusaleh* and thinking now not of art in general but only of the possibilities for comedy as Shaw saw them, it is curious to note the extent to which the verdict of this work is in agreement with the verdict of those earliest plays that dealt with slums and prostitution in the late nineteenth century. In neither case is comedy as traditionally understood allowed anything more than a precarious relevance. Given the overwhelming problems of life—whether seen through satirical fantasy or through realistic drama—music and dance and love can only seem childish diversions, and the comic vision, which is based on these, can exert itself only at the risk of mocking reality and being in return mocked out of existence by it. There is a passage of dialogue between Adam and The Serpent in Part I of *Back to Methusaleh* which sums up the situation:

> *Adam.* *(Angrily)* How can I help brooding when the future has become uncertain? Anything is better than uncertainty. Life has become uncertain. Love is uncertain. Have you a word for this new misery?
> *The Serpent.* Fear. Fear. Fear.
> *Adam.* Have you a remedy for it?
> *The Serpent.* Yes. Hope. Hope. Hope.

And, of course, Shaw stuck to the remedy, even to the point where it meant divesting Adam's children not only of their misery and uncertainty but of love and life and everything else that makes them Adam's children.

After *Back to Methusaleh,* Shaw wrote mostly farces interlarded here and there with all kinds of fantasy. Only some of these kinds recall earlier plays. In *Mrs. Warren's Profession* we remember Vivie moving straight from a Cambridge tripos in Mathematics to an actuary's desk in London. But while her rejection of love and marriage was a gesture of social protest, Chloe's turning to "the properties of numbers" is presented as a normal biological impulse. The idea reappears in a residual and farcical shape in *Buoyant Billions,* Shaw's last play, as a search for the "mathematical hormone." The idea of selective breeding, treated to much comic effect in *Man and Superman,* develops in *The Simpleton of the Unexpected Isles* into the full-fledged farce of a eugenic group-marriage leading to the establishment of a "Superfamily." In *The Millionairess,* an Egyptian doctor agrees to marry the heroine only because her pulse is "irresistible: it is a pulse in a hundred thousand." In

Part III of *Back to Methusaleh* Shaw had shown England run by a bureaucracy of brainy Negroes and Chinese. Now, as in play after play the scene wanders to remote corners of the earth, the detail is expanded into a search for some transcendent vitality and wisdom among vague and shadowy foreign races of usually unspecified time, place, and culture.

On the whole it would not be unfair to say that after *Back to Methusaleh* Shaw wrote hardly any significant plays—except one, and that perhaps his best. *Saint Joan* (1923) is Shaw's best play if only in the sense that it is his one completely serious play, with all his characteristic wit and humor and freedom from humbug, but without any of that equally characteristic humbug of Shaw's own manufacture which he so often substituted in place of the humbug he exploded—without, that is, any of those intellectual sleights of hand, twists of argument, and promotion of novel theories which have the brave air of revelations that no one will believe, not even their author. *Saint Joan* is a serious play because in it the bourgeois artist and the Marxian student of political and social history can unite without difficulty, and Shaw is at one with himself. Or we can say, using Chesterton's two main terms for Shaw, that the Puritan and the Progressive can unite without one tugging at the sympathies in one direction and the other constantly nudging the intellect in another.

Saint Joan can be read as a tragedy, although Shaw himself called it not a tragedy (as he did *The Doctor's Dilemma*) but only a "chronicle" play. But if it is a tragedy, it is the tragedy of a historical hero rather than a saint. Louis Martz discusses it as the latter in an essay entitled "The Saint as Tragic Hero: *Saint Joan* and *Murder in the Cathedral.*"[11] But this rather brilliant tour de force succeeds only at the cost of sacrificing altogether that historical dimension which is of no particular

11. *Tragic Themes in Western Literature,* ed. Cleanth Brooks, New Haven, Yale University Press, 1955. Reprinted in R. J. Kaufmann anthology cited above.

interest in Eliot's play but constitutes, it is worth insisting, the very life and substance of Shaw's. Shaw's Saint Joan is, indeed, less "The Saint as Hero" than "The Hero as Saint"—comparable, if a comparison must be made, to Shaw's own other historical heroes rather than to Eliot's Becket. The importance of a play's or a novel's historical theme should not be confused with the far less interesting question of its historicity, meaning the adequacy of historical research and the authenticity of each character, event, or statement that has gone into the work. Nor can Shaw's own observation which Martz cites—"I deal with all periods; but I never study any period but the present, which I have not yet mastered and never shall"—be construed as a denial of that importance.[12] It is not only that Shaw made this remark years before he wrote *Saint Joan,* but that there is no contradiction involved in recognizing the centrality of the play's historical theme and at the same time granting Shaw the claim that he never studied "any period but the present." For though there are many ways of studying a period, the historical or genetic is basic to them all. At least that was Shaw's own persuasion. And while none of his historical plays is an antiquarian piece, and all bear the burden, however large or slight, of contemporary issues, in *Saint Joan* he was doing nothing less than dramatizing the historical origin of the present period. Of course, he made Joan a nationalist, a Protestant, a champion of the individual conscience and the inner light, before either Protestantism or nationalism was formally inaugurated, and he knew exactly what he was doing. Without these things Joan's tale, to use his own words from the note in the program, "would be only a sensational tale of a girl who was burnt" while the "true tale of Saint Joan is a tale with a glorious ending."[13] For Shaw she stands for an early and divinely inspired heroine of the long crisis out of which

12. Kaufmann, *G. B. Shaw,* p. 150. For Shaw's remark, see Preface to *The Sanity of Art* (New York, B. R. Tucker, 1908), p. 5.

13. Henderson, *Bernard Shaw,* p. 546.

was born a new culture—his own. He sees her as a historical hero all the more because she is the instrument of forces which she does not herself fully understand, except as her voices, but whose emergence she nevertheless both manifests and advances—for this is precisely what being a historical hero means.

Even that pride which is in a way the immediate cause of her personal defeat—as against her historical triumph—is not so much a personal failing of hers as again the manifestation of a general tendency. It is not the same thing as vanity, of which Joan has some ("the cloth of gold surcoat"), nor is it in the last analysis the traditional sin of pride. Of course, the Archbishop tells Joan that "you have stained yourself with the sin of pride. The old Greek tragedy is rising among us. It is the chastisement of hubris." But if Joan's pride can bear this traditional analogy, the play also defines it elsewhere as a new phenomenon, part of a larger force breaking out at several spots to challenge all traditional authority. It is that "pride and self-sufficiency" (as Brother Martin calls it at the trial) which makes the individual a threat as much to the power of the Catholic Church as to the interests of the feudal aristocracy, to Warwick as much as to Cauchon, as each of them realizes from his own side. The Archbishop himself, for all his traditional habits of thought, recognizes the far-reaching importance of what is being witnessed: "There is a new spirit rising in men: we are at the dawning of a wider epoch."

Thus Shaw is able not only to admire the bourgeois hero in Joan but to endorse her triumph without reservation. She is his perfect hero, representing as much the values he admired as the cause of historical progress which he championed—engaging, in short, all his serious but none of his frivolous interests. Indeed, of all his heroes her case calls least for Shaw's habitual hedging and dodging and special pleading, although it cannot be said that the habit has disappeared even here as completely as its cause. For instance, it is unfortunate that Shaw thought it necessary to underline the triumphant quality of Joan's tale, its glorious ending, by writing an Epilogue, which he not only wrote but defended against all objections. With its fantasy tableaux, its flip jokes, its common soldier (on a day's parole from Hell) railing against "kings and captains and bishops" and telling Joan that she has "as good a right to your notions as they have to theirs"—even with Joan's famous last cry: "How long, O Lord, how long?"—the Epilogue mostly brings back the Shaw so admirably absent from the play itself. It is Shaw's theme bereft of the historical sanction of its own time, and one is struck though not surprised by the uncertainties of tone and intellectual argument alike that accompany the shifting of the mental perspective to the present period. Of course, the Epilogue, being only an epilogue, does no damage; but it is worth insisting how much more effectively this same idea of future vindication is expressed within the play, especially at the very end when Warwick says: "I am informed that it is all over, Brother Martin," and Ladvenu, just back from the execution, replies: "We do not know, my lord. It may have only just begun." Warwick himself, thinking of what Ladvenu has said, answers the Executioner's "You have heard the last of her" with "The last of her? Hm! I wonder!"

Within the play itself, likewise, Shaw is neither unfair to those who sent Joan to her death nor contemptuous of their position and beliefs. It is in view of the historical construction he put on the case that he took to task previous writers on the subject, Mark Twain among them, for seeing Joan's judges as corrupt men who tricked and trapped her into false submissions. So far from this being the case, said Shaw, "Joan's judges were as straightforward as Joan herself," and "it cannot be too clearly understood that there were no villains in the tragedy of Joan's death. She was entirely innocent; but her excommunication was a genuine act of faith and piety; and her execution followed inevitably."[14]

14. In the note referred to above, p. 322, quoted in Henderson, *Bernard Shaw,* pp. 546-47.

What this means—and it is a point with which I should like to conclude the whole essay—is that Shaw understood perfectly that in a period of historical crisis there are no easy solutions, and it is erroneous to assume that the entrenched beliefs and institutions of a culture are mere chimera or foolish aberrations that a simple show of reason and ridicule can put to flight. Yet when it came to his own time, it would not be inaccurate to say that he both recognized it as a period of crisis and approached its problems somewhat in the easy spirit of the above assumption. Some such assumption was inevitably the basis of his comedy, and it had something to do likewise with all those fantasies by means of which he persevered in The Serpent's "Hope. Hope. Hope" against the misery and the uncertainties of Adam's "Fear. Fear. Fear." The same Shaw who realized that death and tragedy were the inevitable price Saint Joan had to pay for her adhering to the "inner light" and even just so much as "wearing male attire"[15] makes it all sound rather easy when he has Undershaft ("Saint Andrew") declare in *Major Barbara:*

> Well, you have made for yourself something that you call a morality or a religion or what not. It doesnt fit the facts. Well, scrap it. Scrap it and get one that does fit. That is what is wrong with the world at present. It scraps its obsolete steam engines and dynamos; but it wont scrap its old prejudices and its old moralities and its old religions and its old political constitutions.

And here we see again the reason behind Shaw's interpretation, or rather his misinterpretation, of Ibsen. For what Shaw failed to see in his account of Ibsen as a realist at war with idealists is what Ibsen himself saw only too clearly: that certain ideals are so inseparably a part of the present-day culture that it is not easy to "scrap" them, and that scrapping them would involve nothing short of scrapping that culture's foun-

15. Ibid.

dations. He thus wrote not Shavian comedy but what is increasingly called today tragicomedy. Shaw himself in his 1921 essay on Tolstoy described Ibsen as "the dramatic poet who firmly established tragi-comedy as a much deeper and grimmer entertainment than tragedy."[16] In this respect most significant recent drama is with Ibsen rather than Shaw. True, it is not realistic drama but, at least in its outward trappings, more farce and fantasy in the Shavian mode. Likewise, it can be called Shavian in its desperate recognition of the constitutional absurdity of man and the utter hopelessness of his state on this earth—that is, if we see only this aspect of a play like *Back to Methusaleh*, as is indeed done by most of Shaw's modern admirers. But this is not the only aspect; there are others more visible and persistent: the easy escapes, the many solutions, the constant hopefulness, in short, the insistence on comedy at all costs. Of all this recent drama has completely and quite self-consciously purged itself. It has in fact redefined the very content of the comic vision. "As the 'comic' is an intuitive perception of the absurd," as Ionesco puts it, "it seems to me more hopeless than the 'tragic.' The 'comic' offers no escape."[17]

Tragicomedy, or comedy of the absurd, insists that man's illusions are not only illusions, but that they are all he has; that his gestures are empty in themselves and meaningful only because he still makes them; that, for instance, waiting for Godot is waiting for nothing, only waiting; that Endgame is not Life but a game; that our acts are without significance except to our heroically deluded selves. There is undoubtedly heroism of sorts here for the characters concerned. But there is also the possibility that on this view, if it is taken too seriously or carried too far, there will one day be not only no tragedy

16. Bernard Shaw, "Tolstoy: Tragedian or Comedian," *The London Mercury, 4* (1921), p. 32.
17. Eugene Ionesco, *Notes and Counter Notes: Writings on the Theatre* (New York, Grove Press, 1964), p. 27.

and no comedy but no drama—only the absurd extreme of acts without words. Nevertheless, there is also here a heroism of sorts for the authors concerned. It lies in their realization that traditional forms of literature cannot truly represent a culture beyond the point of crisis in its development, and in their attempt to meet the situation as best and as sincerely as they can.

Index

Abstraction: in Aristophanes, 29-32; characters of, 225; defined as obsolete cultural ideas, 2, 38; in *Don Quixote,* 27-28; of honor, 66-71; of love, 78; as obstacle to practical living, 2, 38, 47, 49, 69; role of in *Pride and Prejudice,* 221-25; Schopenhauer's analysis of, 39-40, 222. *See also* Comedy; names of individual authors

Anti-romance. *See* Comedy; names of individual authors

Aristophanes, 23-32, 35-37; *The Acharnians,* 29; *The Birds,* 29; *The Clouds,* 29-31; *The Ecclesiazusae,* 23 f., 31-32, 36 f.; *The Frogs,* 29; *Lysistrata,* 13, 29; *Plutus,* 23

Austen, Jane, 3, 5, 8 ff., 35, 41 ff., 47, 54, 85 f., 105, 143, 152, 159, 162 n., 193-249, 252, 254, 256 f., 269, 297, 299, 302, 308; and anti-romance, 209-10, 211-12; attack of on false conventions, 195 ff., 204; on the battle of the books, 194 f., 206-13; and burlesque, 193-200; and Fanny Burney, 201, 222, 225-26, 230; divergence of from other burlesque writers, 203; and "the economic basis," 297; *Emma,* 43, 231, 236-37; and Fielding, 54-55, 152, 192 f., 203 f., 216, 234, 238, 247; formulaic quality of early novels of, 213; and James, 193, 236 ff., 254-58, 262, 269, 276, 281-82, 297; juvenilia of, 193-200; love in, 202-06, 232, 237-38; "Love and Freindship," 54, 195, 196-200, 204-14 passim; love vs. prudence in, 85, 199-203, 214-15, 219, 237-39, 244-47; *Mansfield Park,* 212, 215, 231-36, 240, 248, 281-82; modes of love in, 214, 218; *Northanger Abbey,* 194 f., 206-13, 246, 257-58; *Persuasion,* 10, 193, 201, 235, 237-49; position of vis à vis her culture, 193-95, 201-02, 204-06; *Pride and Prejudice,* 37, 43, 86, 159, 214 f., 217, 218-31 ff., 246, 297, 303; and the Restoration tradition, 193, 215-17, 234; role of abstraction and experience in *Pride and Prejudice,* 221-27; role of experience in *Persuasion,* 238; role of intelligence in, 205-